A NATIVE WOMAN SEIZED BY A CAYMAN.—*Page* 214.

TWENTY YEARS

IN

THE PHILIPPINES.

TRANSLATED FROM THE FRENCH OF

PAUL P. DE LA GIRONIERE,

CHEVALIER OF THE ORDER OF THE LEGION OF HONOR.

Revised and Extended by the Author, expressly for this Edition.

Portrait of the Author.

NEW YORK:

HARPER & BROTHERS, PUBLISHERS,

329 & 331 PEARL STREET,

FRANKLIN SQUARE.

1854.

CONTENTS.

Page

List of Illustrations 11

Preface 13

CHAPTER I.

A Family Sketch—My Youthful Days—I Study for the Medical Profession—Obtain a Naval Surgeon's Diploma—Early Voyages—Sail for Manilla in the *Cultivateur*—Adventurous Habits—Cholera and Massacre at Manilla and Cavite—Captain Drouant's Rescue—Personal Dangers and Timely Escapes—How Business may make Friends of one's Enemies—An Unprincipled Captain—Tranquillity restored at Manilla—Pleasures of the Chase—The *Cultivateur* sails without me—First Embarrassments . 17

CHAPTER II.

Description of Manilla—The two Towns—Gaiety of Binondoo—Dances—Gaming—Beauty of the Women—Their Fascinating Costume—Male Costume—The Military Town—Personal Adventures—My First Patient—His Generous Confidence—Commencement of my Practice—The Artificial Eye—Brilliant Success—The Charming Widow—Auspicious Introduction—My Marriage—Treachery and Fate of Iturbide—Our Loss of Fortune—Return to France postponed 32

Page

CHAPTER III.

Continued Prosperity in Practice—Attempted Political Revolution—Desperate Street Engagement—Subjugation of the Insurgents—The Emperor of a Day—Dreadful Executions—Illness and Insanity of my Wife—Her Recovery and Relapse—Removal to the Country—Beneficial Results—Dangerous Neighbours—Repentant Banditti—Fortunate Escape—The Anonymous Friend—A Confiding Wife—Her Final Recovery, and our Domestic Happiness restored 47

CHAPTER IV.

Hunting the Stag—Indian Mode of Chasing the Wild Buffalo: its Ferocity—Dangerous Sport—Capture of a Buffalo—Narrow Escape of an Indian Hunter—Return to Manilla—Injustice of the Governor—My Resignation of Office—I Purchase Property at Jala-Jala—Retire from Manilla to take Possession of my Domains—Chinese Legend—Festival of St. Nicholas—Quinaboutasan—Description of Jala-Jala—Interview with a Bandit Chief—Formation of Guard—Preparations for Building—Visit to Manilla, and Return to Jala-Jala—Completion of my House—Reception of my Wife by the Natives—The Government of the Philippines—Character of the Tagaloc Indians—Unmerited Chastisement—A Curate Appointed—Our Labours at Civilisation—My Hall of Justice—Buffalo Hunting Expedition 62

CHAPTER V.

Description of my House at Jala-Jala—Storms, Gales, and Earthquakes—Reforming the Banditti—Card-playing—Tagal Cockfighting—Skirmishes with Robbers—Courage of my Wife—

Page

Our Domestic Happiness — Visits from Europeans—Their Astonishment at our Civilisation—Visit to a Sick Friend at Manilla—Tour through the Provinces of the Ilocos and Pangasinan Indians—My Reception by the Tinguians—Their Appearance and Habits—Manners and Customs—Indian Fête at Laganguilan y Madalag—Horrible Ceremonies to Celebrate a Victory—Songs and Dances—Our Night-watch—We Explore our Cabin—Discovery of a Secret Well—A Tomb of the Tinguian Indians 95

CHAPTER VI.

Visit to Manabo—Conversation with my Guide—Religion of the Tinguians — Their Marriage Ceremony — Funereal Rites—Mode of Warfare—I take leave of the Tinguians—Journey to the Igorrots — Description of them — Their Dwellings — A Fortunate Escape—Alila and the Bandits—Recollections of Home—A Majestic Fig-tree—Superstition of Alila—Interview with an Igorrot—The Human Hand—Nocturnal Adventure—Consternation of Alila—Probable Origin of the Tinguians and Igorrots 117

CHAPTER VII.

I return to Jala-Jala—An Excursion on the Lake—Relempago's Narrative—Re-organisation of my Government—A Letter from my Brother Henry—His Arrival—He joins me in the Management of my Plantations—Cajoui, the Bandit: Anten-Anten—Indian Superstition—A Combat with the Bandit—His Death—A Piratical Descent—My Lieutenant is Wounded—I extract the Ball, and cure him 139

Page

CHAPTER VIII.

Death of my Brother Robert—Our Party at Jala-Jala—Illness and Last Moments of my Friend Bermigan—Recovery and Departure for France of Lafond—Joachim Balthazard: his Eccentricity—Tremendous Gale of Wind—Narrow Escape in Crossing the Lake—Safe Return to Jala-Jala—Destruction of my House and the Village by a Typhoon—Rendezvous with a Bandit—Ineffectual Attempts to Reform Him—His Death—Journey to Tapuzi—Its Inaccessibility—Government of the Tapuzians—Morality and Religious Character of their Chief—Their Curiosity at beholding a White Man—Former Wickedness and Divine Punishment—We bid adieu to the Tapuzians, and return to Jala-Jala 162

CHAPTER IX.

Suppression of War between two Indian Towns—Flourishing Condition of Jala-Jala—Hospitality to Strangers—Field Sports—Bat and Lizard Shooting—Visit to, and Description of, the Isle of Socolme—Adventure with a Cayman—Cormorants—We visit Los Banos—Monkey Shooting—Expedition to, and Description of, the Grotto of San-Mateo—Magnificent aspect of the Interior 181

CHAPTER X.

Dumont d'Urville—Rear-Admiral Laplace: Desertion of Sailors from his Ship—I recover them for him—Origin of the Inhabitants of the Philippine Islands—Their General Disposition—Hospitality and Respect for Old Age—Tagal Marriage Ceremony—Indian Legal Eloquence—Explanation of the Matrimonial Speeches—The Caymans, or Alligators—Instances of

Page

their Ferocity—Imprudence and Death of my Shepherd—Method of Entrapping the Monster which had devoured him—We Attack and eventually Capture it—Its Dimensions—We Dissect and Examine the Contents of its Stomach—Boa-Constrictors—Their large size—Attack of a Boa-Constrictor on a Wild Boar—We Kill and Skin it—Unsuccessful Attempt to Capture a Boa-Constrictor alive—A Man Devoured—Dangerous Venomous Reptiles 204

CHAPTER XI.

The Prosperity and Happiness of my Life at Jala-Jala—Destructiveness of the Locusts—Agriculture in the Philippines—My Herds of Oxen, Buffaloes, and Horses—My Wife presents me with a Daughter, who dies—The Admiration of the Indian Women for my Wife—Birth of my Son—Continued Prosperity—Death of my Brother Henry—My Friendship with Malvilain—His Marriage with my eldest Sister—His Premature Death—I take my Wife to Manilla—Melancholy Adieus—We Return to Jala-Jala—Death of my Wife—My friend Vidie—I determine to Return to France 228

CHAPTER XII.

My friend Adolphe Barrot visits me at Jala-Jala—The Bamboo Cane—The Cocoa-Nut Tree—The Banana—Majestic Forests of Gigantic Trees—The Leeches—A Tropical Storm in a Forest—An Indian Bridge—"Bernard the Hermit"—We arrive at Binangonan-de-Lampon—The Ajetas—Veneration of the Ajetas for their Dead—Poison used by the Ajetas—I carry away a Skeleton—We Embark on the Pacific in an old Canoe, reach Maoban, and ultimately arrive at Jala-Jala 245

Page

CHAPTER XIII.

I Determine not again to Separate from my Son--I take him to Manilla—The Effects of the Wound I received among the Ajetas—My Recovery—Kindness of the Spanish and other Inhabitants of Manilla—Illness of my Son—I return with him to Jala-Jala—Sorrowful Remembrances—The Death of my poor Boy—His Interment—My frantic Grief and Despair—I Determine to Quit the Philippines—I am Called to Manilla by Madame Dolorès Sencris—My Final Departure from Jala-Jala—I Arrive at Manilla, where I resume Practice as a Surgeon—I Embark for France—Discontent—My Travels through Europe—I Marry again—Death of my Mother and my Second Wife—Conclusion 283

STATISTICS OF THE PHILIPPINE ISLANDS.—Mechanical and Agricultural Products—I. The Soil of the Island of Luzon, and the Sources of its Fertility—II. Rice—III. Indigo—IV. Tobacco—V. Abaca, or Vegetable Silk—VI. Coffee—VII. Cacao—VIII. Cotton—IX. Pepper—X. Wheat—XI. Sugar Cane—XII. Bamboo—XIII. The Buffalo 305

AGRICULTURAL IMPLEMENTS.—I. The Indian Plough—II. Yoke for the Buffaloes—III. Lilit, or the Indian Sickle—IV. The Comb Harrow—V. Guiligen, or Hand-Mill—VI. The Mortar. 334

APPENDIX.—I. Testimony of M. Gabriel Lafond 337

II. Testimony of H. Hamilton Lindsay, Esq. . . . 340

Account of a Visit to the Cave of San Matteo, in the neighbourhood of Manilla 342

III. Testimony of M. Dumont d'Urville 356

IV. Testimony of Admiral Laplace 362

V. Testimony of M. Mallat 372

LIST OF ILLUSTRATIONS.

Page

FRONTISPIECE, A NATIVE WOMAN CARRIED OFF BY A CAYMAN.

TITLE PAGE, PORTRAIT OF THE AUTHOR.

NANTES 17

SAVING THE LIFE OF CAPTAIN DROUANT 22

MOUTH OF THE BAY OF MANILLA 32

SPANISH METIS, OR HALF-BREEDS 36

CHINESE METIS, OR HALF-BREEDS 37

SPANISH METIS OF THE SUPERIOR CLASS 47

BRIDGE OF MANILLA 50

STAG HUNTING IN THE MARIGONDON MOUNTAINS . . 62

PASSAGE-BOAT ON THE RIVER PASIG 70

TAGAL INDIANS POUNDING RICE 82

FATHER MIGUEL 86

SHOOTING A BUFFALO 93

HORNS OF THE BUFFALO 93

THE HOUSE AT JALA-JALA 95

HERD OF WILD BUFFALOES 98

TAGAL COCK-FIGHTING 101

TAGAL INDIANS 103

ILOCOS INDIANS 106

THE BRAIN FEAST 112

GUINAN INDIANS 117

Page

WEAPONS OF THE TINGUIAN INDIANS 123
BIRANGAS INDIANS—INHABITANTS OF BOULACAN . . 138
FISHING RAFT 139
THE HOUSE OF LA PLANCHE 162
CHURCH OF PANDACAN, IN THE ENVIRONS OF MANILLA . 178
HUNTING PARTY AT JALA-JALA 181
CASCADE NEAR JALA-JALA 185
VIEW AT SAN-MATEO 195
PORTRAIT OF DUMONT D'URVILLE 204
A TAGAL INDIAN DWELLING 208
YOUNG TAGAL INDIAN AND HIS BETROTHED . . . 209
ATTACKING A CAYMAN 219
BOA-CONSTRICTOR AND WILD BOAR 222
ATTACKING A BOA-CONSTRICTOR 224
RICE STACKING IN THE PHILIPPINES 228
THE LOCUST 230
VIEW ON THE RIVER PASIG 239
AJETAS INDIANS 245
LA GIRONIERE IN HUNTING DRESS 247
THE COCOA-NUT 250
THE BANANA 251
TRAVERSING AN INDIAN FOREST 254
FRUIT OF THE PALM TREE 256
INHABITANTS OF BINANGONAN DE LAMPON 265
VIEW OF MANILLA FROM THE ENVIRONS 283
THE INDIAN PLOUGH 334
YOKE FOR THE BUFFALOES 335
LILIT, OR THE INDIAN SICKLE 335
THE COMB HARROW 335
A GUILIGEN, OR HAND-MILL 336
THE MORTAR 336

PREFACE.

On hearing a recital of some adventures which had occurred to me during my long voyages, many of my friends have frequently begged of me to publish a narrative of them, which might perhaps be interesting.

"Nothing can be more easy for you," they said, "as you have always kept a journal since your departure from France.

I hesitated, however, to follow their advice, or to yield to their wishes, when I was one day surprised to see my name in one of the *feuilletons* of the "*Constitutionnel.*"

M. Alexandre Dumas was publishing, under the title of "*The Thousand-and-One Phantoms,*" a *romance,* one of the principal personages of which, in a voyage to the Philippine Islands, must have known me when I was residing at Jala-Jala, in the colony that I founded there.

It must be evident that the lively romancist has ranked me in the category of his *Thousand-and-One Phantoms;* but, to prove to the public that I am really in existence, I have resolved to take up the pen, under an impression that facts of the most scrupulous veracity, and which can be attested by some hundreds of persons, might possess some interest, and be read without *ennui*, by those especially who are desirous of learning the customs of the savage tribes amongst whom I have resided.

TWENTY YEARS

IN

THE PHILIPPINES.

CHAPTER I.

A Family Sketch—My Youthful Days—I Study for the Medical Profession—Obtain a Naval Surgeon's Diploma—Early Voyages—Sail for Manilla in the *Cultivateur*—Adventurous Habits—Cholera and Massacre at Manilla and Cavite—Captain Drouant's Rescue—Personal Dangers and Timely Escapes—How Business may make Friends of one's Enemies—An Unprincipled Captain—Tranquillity restored at Manilla—Pleasures of the Chase—The *Cultivateur* sails without me—First Embarrassments.

MY father was born at Nantes, and held the rank of captain in the regiment of Auvergne. The Revolution caused him the loss of his commission and his fortune, and left him, as sole remaining resource, a little property called *La Planche*, belonging to my mother, and situate about two leagues from Nantes, in the parish of Vertoux.

At the commencement of the Empire he wished to enter the service again; but at that period his name was an obstacle, and he failed in every attempt to obtain even the rank of lieutenant. With scarcely the means of existence, he retired to *La Planche* with his family. There he lived for some years, suffering the grief and the many annoyances caused by the sudden change from opulence to want, and by the impossibility of supplying all the requirements of his numerous family. A short illness terminated his distressed existence, and his mortal remains were deposited in the cemetery of Vertoux. My mother, a pattern of courage and devotedness, remained a widow, with six children, two girls and four boys; she continued to reside in the country, imparting to us the first elements of instruction.

The free life of the fields, and the athletic exercises to which my elder brothers and I accustomed ourselves, tended to make me hardy, and rendered me capable of enduring every kind of fatigue and privation. This country life, with its liberty, and I may well say its happiness, passed too quickly away; and the period soon came when my education compelled me to pursue my daily studies in a school at Nantes. I had four leagues to walk, but I trudged the distance light-heartedly, and at night, when I returned home, I ever found awaiting me the kind solicitude of our dear mother, and the attentive cares of two sisters whom I tenderly loved.

It was decided that I should enter the medical profession. I studied several years at the Hôtel-Dieu of Nantes, and I passed my examination for naval surgeon at an age when many a young man is shut up within the four walls of a college, still prosecuting his studies.

It would be difficult to form any idea of my joy when I saw myself in possession of my surgeon's diploma. Thenceforward I regarded myself as an important being, about to take my place among reasonable and industrious men; and what perhaps rendered me still more joyous was, that I could earn my own livelihood, and contribute to the comfort of my mother and my sisters.

I was also seized with a strong desire to travel abroad, and make myself acquainted with foreign countries.

Twenty-four hours after my nomination as surgeon I went and offered my services to a ship-owner who was about freighting a vessel to the East Indies. We were not long in arranging terms, and, at forty francs per month, I engaged myself for the voyage.

Within twelve months afterwards I returned home. Who can depict the sweet emotions which, as a young man, I felt on again beholding my native land? I stayed a month on shore, surrounded by the affectionate attentions of my mother and sisters. Despite their assiduities I was seized with *ennui*. I made a second and a third voyage; then, after having rounded the Cape of Good Hope half-a-dozen times, I undertook one which separated me from my country during twenty years.

On the 9th October, 1819, I embarked on board the *Cultivateur*, an old half-rotten three-masted vessel, commanded by an equally old captain, who, long ashore, had given up navigating for many years. An old captain with an old ship! Such were the conditions in which I undertook this voyage. I ought, however, to add, that I obtained an increase of pay.

We touched at Bourbon; we ran along the entire coast of Sumatra, a part of Java, the isles of Sonde, and that of Banca; and at last, towards the end of May, eight months after our departure from Nantes, we arrived in the magnificent bay of Manilla.

The *Cultivateur* anchored near the little town of Cavite. I obtained leave to reside on shore, and took lodgings in Cavite, which is situate about five or six leagues from Manilla.

To make up for my long inactivity on board ship, I eagerly engaged in my favorite exercises, exploring the country in all directions with my gun upon my shoulder. Taking for a guide the first Indian whom I met, I made long excursions, less occupied in shooting than in admiring the magnificent scenery. I knew a little Spanish, and soon acquired a few *Tagaloc* words. Whether it was for excitement's sake, or from a vague desire of braving danger, I know not, but I was particularly fond of wandering in remote places, said to be frequented by robbers. With these I occasionally fell in, but the sight of my gun kept them in check. I may say, with truth, that at that period of my life I had so little sense of danger, that I was always ready to put myself forward when there was an enemy to fight or a peril to be encountered.

I had only resided a short time at Cavite when that terrible scourge, the cholera, broke out at Manilla, in September, 1820, and quickly ravaged the whole island. Within a few days of its first appearance the epidemic spread rapidly; the Indians succumbed by thousands; at all hours of the day and of the night the streets were crowded with the dead-carts. Next to the fright occasioned by the epidemic, quickly succeeded rage and despair. The Indians said, one to another, that the strangers poisoned the rivers and the fountains, in order to destroy the native population and possess themselves of the Philippines.

On the 9th October, 1820, the anniversary of my departure

from France, a dreadful massacre commenced at Manilla and at Cavite. Poor Dibard, the captain of the *Cultivateur*, was one of the first victims. Almost all the French who resided at Manilla were slain, and their houses pillaged and destroyed. The carnage only ceased when there were no longer any victims. One eye-witness escaped this butchery, namely, M. Gautrin, a captain of the merchant service, who, at the moment I am writing, happens to be residing in Paris. He saved his life by his courage and his muscular strength. After seeing one of his friends mercilessly cut to pieces, he precipitated himself into the midst of the assassins, with no other means of defence than his fists. He succeeded in fighting his way through the crowd, but shortly afterwards fell exhausted, having received three sabre-cuts upon his head, and a lance-thrust in his body. Fortunately, some soldiers happened to pass by at the time, who picked him up and carried him to a guard-house, where his wounds were quickly attended to.

I myself was dodged about Cavite, but I contrived to escape, and to reach a pirogue, into which I jumped, and took refuge on board the *Cultivateur*. I had scarcely been there ten minutes when I was requested to attend the mate of an American vessel, who had just been stabbed on board his ship by some custom-house guards. When I had finished dressing the wound, several officers, belonging to the different French vessels lying in the bay, acquainted me that one of their brethren, Captain Drouant, of Marseilles, was still ashore, and that there might yet be time to save him. There was not a moment to lose; night was approaching, and it was necessary to profit by the last half-hour of daylight. I set off in a cutter, and, on nearing the land, I directed my men to keep the boat afloat, in order to prevent a surprise on the part of the

Indians, but yet to hug the shore sufficiently close to land promptly, in case the captain or myself signaled them. I then quickly set about searching for Drouant.

On reaching a small square, called *Puerta Baga*, I observed a group of three or four hundred Indians. I had a presentiment that it was in that direction I ought to prosecute my search. I approached, and beheld the unfortunate Drouant, pale as a corpse. A furious Indian was on the point of plunging his kreese into his breast. I threw myself between the captain and the poignard, violently pushing on either side the murderer and his victim, so as to separate them. "Run!" I cried in French; "a boat awaits you." So great was the stupefaction of the Indians that the captain escaped unpursued.

It was now time for me to get out of the dangerous situation in which I was involved. Four hundred Indians surrounded me; the only way of dealing with them was by audacity. I said in Tagaloc to the Indian who had attempted to stab the captain: "You are a scoundrel." The Indian sprang toward me; he raised his arm: I struck him on the head with a cane which I held in my hand; he waited in astonishment for a moment, and then returned towards his companions to excite them. Daggers were drawn on every side; the crowd formed a circle around me, which gradually concentrated. Mysterious influence of the white man over his coloured brother! Of all these four hundred Indians, not one dared attack me the first; they all wished to strike together. Suddenly a native soldier, armed with a musket, broke through the crowd; he struck down my adversary, took away his dagger, and holding his musket by the bayonet end, he swung it round and round his head, thus enlarging the circle at first, and then dispersing a portion of my enemies. "Fly, sir!" said my liberator; "now

LA GIRONIERE SAVES THE LIFE OF CAPTAIN DROUANT.—*Page* 22.

that I am here, no one will touch a hair of your head." In fact the crowd divided, and left me a free passage. I was saved, without knowing by whom, or for what reason, until the native soldier called after me: "You attended my wife who was sick, and you never asked payment of me. I now settle my debt."

As Captain Drouant had doubtless gone off in the cutter, it was impossible for me to return on board the *Cultivateur*. I directed my steps towards my lodgings, creeping along the walls, and taking advantage of the obscurity, when, on turning the corner of a street, I fell into the midst of a band of dock-yard workmen, armed with axes, and about to proceed to the attack of the French vessels then in harbor. Here again I owed my preservation to an acquaintance, to whom I had rendered some service in the practice of my profession. A *Métis*, or half-breed, who had quickly pushed me into the entry of a house, and covered me with his body, said: "Stir not, Doctor Pablo!"* When the crowd had dispersed, my protector advised me to conceal myself, and above all, not to go on board; he then started off to rejoin his comrades. But all was not yet over. I had scarcely entered my lodgings when I heard a knocking at the door.

"Doctor Pablo," said a voice, which was not unknown to me.

I opened, and I saw, as pale as death, a Chinese, who kept a tea-store on the ground-floor of the same house.

"What's the matter, Yang-Po?"

"Save yourself, Doctor!"

"And wherefore?"

"Because the Indians will attack you this very night; they have decided upon it!"

* Pablo signifies Paul, my Christian name. I was always called thus at Manilla and at Cavite.

"Is it not your apprehension on account of your shop, Yang-Po?"

"Oh, no! do not treat this matter lightly. If you remain here you are doomed; you have struck an Indian, and his friends cry aloud for vengeance."

The fears of Yang-Po were, I saw, too well-founded; but what could I do? To shut my door and await was the safest plan.

"Thank you," said I to the Chinese; "thank you for your kind advice, but I shall remain here."

"Remain here, Signor Doctor! Can you think of so doing?"

"Now, Yang-Po, a service: go and say to these Indians that I have, at their service, a brace of pistols and a double-barreled gun, which I know how to use."

The Chinese departed sighing deeply, from a notion that the attack upon the Doctor might end in the pillage of his wares. I barricaded my door with the furniture of the room; I then loaded my weapons, and put out the lights.

It was now eight o'clock in the evening. The least noise made me think that the moment had arrived when Providence alone could save me. I was so fatigued that, despite the anxiety natural to my position, I had frequently to struggle against an inclination to sleep. Toward eleven o'clock some one knocked at my door. I seized my pistols, and listened attentively. At a second summons, I approached the door on tip-toe.

"Who's there?" I demanded.

A voice replied to me; "We come to save you. Lose not an instant. Get out on the roof, and climb over to the other side, where we will await you, in the street of the *Campanario*." Then two or three persons descended the stairs rapidly. I had recognised the voice of a Métis, whose good feelings on my behalf were beyond doubt. There was now no time to be lost, for at the moment I got out of a window which served to light the staircase, and led on to the roof, the Indians had arrived in front of the house, and in a few minutes were breaking and plundering the little I possessed. I quickly traversed the roof, and descended into the street of the *Cam panario*, where my new preservers awaited me. They conducted me to their dwelling: there, a profound sleep caused me quickly to forget the dangers I had passed through.

The following day my friends prepared a small pirogue to convey me on board the *Cultivateur*, where, apparently, I should be in greater security than on shore. I was about to embark when one of my preservers handed me a letter which he had just received. It was addressed to me, and bore the signatures of all the captains whose vessels were lying in the harbour, and it informed me that, seeing themselves exposed every moment to an attack by the Indians, they were decided to raise anchor and seek a wider offing; but that two among them, Drouant and Perroux, had been compelled to leave on shore a portion of their possessions, and all their sails and fresh water. They entreated me to lend them my assistance, and had arranged that a skiff should be placed at my command. I communicated this letter to my friends, and declared that I would not return on board without endeavouring to satisfy the wishes of my countrymen; it was a question of saving the lives of the crews of two vessels, and hesitation was impossible. They used every effort to shake my resolution. "If you show yourself in any part of the town," said they, "you are lost; even supposing the Indians were not to kill you, they would not fail to steal every object intrusted to them." I remained immovable, and pointed out to them that it was a question of honour and humanity. "Go alone, then!" exclaimed that Métis who had contributed the most to my escape; "not one of us will follow you; we would not have it said that we assisted in your destruction."

I thanked my friends, and, after shaking hands with them, passed on through the streets of Cavite, my pistols in my belt, and my thoughts occupied as to the best means of extricating myself from my perilous position. However, I already knew sufficient of the Indian character to be aware that boldness would conciliate, rather than enrage them. I went towards the same landing-pace where once before I had escaped a great danger. The shore was covered with Indians, watching the ships at anchor. As I advanced, all turned their looks upon me; but, as I had foreseen, the countenances of these men, whose feelings had become calmed during the night that had intervened, expressed more astonishment than anger.

"Will you earn money?" I cried. "To those who work with me I will give a dollar at the end of the day."

A moment's silence followed this proposition; then one of them said: "You do not fear us!"

"Judge if I am alarmed," I replied, showing him my pistols; "with these I could take two lives for one—the advantage is on my side."

My words had a magical effect, and my questioner replied:

"Put up your weapons; you have a brave heart, and deserve to be safe amongst us. Speak! what do you require? We will follow you." I saw these men, who but yesterday would have killed me, now willing to bear me in triumph. I then explained to them that I wished to take some articles which had been left on shore to my comrades, and to those who assisted me in this object I would give the promised recompense. I told the one who had addressed me to select two hundred men, nearly double the number necessary; during the time he made up his party I signaled a skiff to approach the shore, and wrote a few words in pencil, in order that the boats from the French vessels might be in readiness to receive the stores as soon as they were brought to the water's edge. I then marched at the head of my Indian troop of two hundred men, and by their aid the sails, provisions, biscuits, and wines, were soon on board the boats. That which most embarrassed me was the transport of a large sum of money belonging to Captain Drouant. If the Indians had conceived the least suspicion of this wealth, they would no longer have kept faith with me. I therefore determined to fill my own pockets with the gold, and to traverse the distance between the house and the boats as many times as was necessary to embark it. There, concealed by the sailors, I deposited piece after piece as quietly as possible. In carrying the sails belonging to Captain Perroux, a circumstance occurred which might have been fatal to me. A few days before the massacre, a French sailor, who was working as sail maker, had died of the cholera. His alarmed companions wrapped the body in a sail, and then hurried on board their ships. My Indians now discovered the corpse, which was already in a state of putrefaction. Terrified at first, their terror soon changed to fury; for an instant I feared they would fall upon me.

"Your friends," they cried, "have left this body here purposely, that it might poison the air and increase the violence of the epidemic."

"What! you are afraid of a poor devil dead of the cholera!" I said to them, affecting to be as tranquil as possible; "never fear, I will soon rid you of him;" and, despite the aversion I felt, I covered the body with a small sail, and carried it down to the beach. There I made a rude grave, in which I placed it; and two pieces of wood, in the shape of a cross, for some days indicated the spot where lay the unhappy one, who probably had no prayers save mine.

It had been a busy and agitating day, but towards the evening I finished my task, and everything was embarked. I paid the Indians, and in addition gave them a barrel of spirits.

I did not fear their intoxication, being the only Frenchman there, and when it was dark I got into a boat, and towed a dozen casks of fresh water at her stern. Since the previous day I had not eaten; I felt worn out by fatigue and want of food, and threw myself down to rest upon the seats of the boat. Ere long a mortal chilliness passed through my veins, and I became insensible. In this state I remained more than an hour. At last I reached the *Cultivateur*, and was taken on board, and, by the aid of friction, brandy, and other remedies, was restored to consciousness. Food and rest quickly renovated my powers of mind and body, and the next day I was calm as usual among my comrades. I thought of my personal position; the events of the two last days made the review extremely simple. I had lost everything. A small venture of merchandise, in which I invested the savings of my previous voyages, had been intrusted to the captain for sale at Manilla. These goods were destroyed, together with all I possessed, at Cavite. There remained to me but the clothes I had on—a few old things I could wear only on board ship—and thirty-two dollars. I was but a littleric her than Bias. Unfortunatel I recollected that an English captain—whose ship I had seen in the roads—owed me something like a hundred dollars. In my present circumstances this sum appeared a fortune. The captain in question, from fear of the Indians, had dropped down as far as Maribélé, at the entrance of the bay, ten leagues from Cavite. To obtain payment it was necessary I should go on board his vessel. I borrowed a boat, and the services of four sailors, from Captain Perroux, and departed. I reached the ship at dusk. The unprincipled captain, who knew himself to be in deep water and safe from pursuit, replied that he did not understand what I was saying to him. I insisted upon being paid, and he laughed in my face. I was treated as a cheat. He threatened to have me thrown into the sea; in short, after a useless discussion, and at the moment when the captain called five or six of his sailors to execute his threat, I retreated to my boat. The night was dark, and as a violent and contrary wind had sprung up, it was impossible to regain the ship, so we passed the night floating upon the waves, ignorant as to the direction we were going. In the morning I discovered our efforts had been thrown away; Cavite was far behind us. The wind becoming calmer, we again commenced rowing, and two hours after noon reached the ship.

Meanwhile tranquillity was restored at Cavite and Manilla. The Spanish authorities took measures to prevent a recurrence of the frightful scenes I have detailed, and the priests of Cavite launched a public excommunication against all those who had attempted my life. I attributed this solicitude to the character of my profession, being in fact the only Æsculapius in the place. When I left the town the sick were obliged to content themselves with the hazardous presumptions of Indian sorcerers. One morning, I had almost decided upon returning to land, when an Indian, in a smartly decorated pirogue came alongside the *Cultivateur*. I had met this man in some of my shooting excursions, and he now proposed that I should go with him to his house, situated ten leagues from Cavite, near the mountains of Marigondon. The prospect of some good sport soon decided me to accept this offer. Taking with me my thirty-two dollars and double-barreled gun—in fact, my whole fortune—I intrusted myself to this friend, whose acquaintance I had just made. His little habitation was delightfully situated, in the cool shadow of the palm and yang-yang—immense trees, whose flowers spread around a delicious perfume. Two charming Indian girls were the Eves of this paradise. My good friend kept the promises he had made me on leaving the vessel; I was treated both by himself and family with every attention and kindness.

Hunting was my principal amusement, and, above all, the chase of the stag, which involves violent exercise. I was still ignorant of wild-buffalo hunting, of which, however, I shall have to speak later in my narrative; and I often requested my host to give me a taste of this sport, but he always refused, saying it was too dangerous. For three weeks I lived with the Indian family without receiving any news from Manilla, when one morning, a letter came from the first mate—who, on the death of the unfortunate Dibard, had taken the command of the *Cultivateur*—telling me he was about to sail, and that I must go on board at once if I wished to leave a country which had been so fatal to all of us. This summous was already several days old, and despite the reluctance I felt to quit the Indian's pleasant retreat, it was necessary that I should prepare to start. I presented my gun to my kind host, but had nothing to give his daughters, for to have offered them money would have been an insult. The next day I arrived at Manilla, still thinking of the cool shade of the palm and the perfumed flowers of the yang-yang. My first impulse was to go to the quay; but, alas! the *Cultivateur* had sailed, and I had the misery of beholding her already far away in the horizon, moving sluggishly before a gentle breeze towards the mouth of the bay. I asked some Indian boatmen to take me to the ship; they replied that it might be practicable if the wind did not freshen, but demanded twelve dollars to make the attempt. I had but twenty-five remaining. I considered for a few moments, should I not reach the vessel, what would become of me in a remote colony, where I knew no one, and my stock of money reduced to thirteen dollars, and with no articles of dress than those I had on—a white jacket, trousers, and striped shirt. A sudden thought crossed my mind: what if I were to remain at Manilla, and practise my profession? Young and inexperienced, I ventured to think myself the cleverest physician in the Philippine Islands. Who has not felt this self-confidence so natural to youth? I turned my back upon the ship, and walked briskly into Manilla.

Before continuing this recital, let me describe the capital of the Philippines.

Mouth of the Bay of Manilla.

CHAPTER II.

Description of Manilla—The two Towns—Gaiety of Binondoc—Dances—Gaming—Beauty of the Women—Their Fascinating Costume—Male Costume—The Military Town—Personal Adventures—My First Patient—His Generous Confidence—Commencement of my Practice—The Artificial Eye—Brilliant Success—The Charming Widow—Auspicious Introduction—My Marriage—Treachery and Fate of Iturbide—Our Loss of Fortune—Return to France postponed.

MANILLA and its suburbs contain a population of about one hundred and fifty thousand souls, of which Spaniards and Creoles hardly constitute the tenth part; the remainder is composed of Tagalocs, or Indians, Métis, and Chinese,

The city is divided into two sections—the military and the mercantile—the latter of which is the suburb. The former, surrounded by lofty walls, is bounded by the sea on one side, and upon another by an extensive plain, where the troops are exercised, and where of an evening the indolent Creoles, lazily extended in their carriages, repair to exhibit their elegant dresses and to inhale the sea-breezes. This public promenade—where intrepid horsemen and horsewomen, and European vehicles, cross each other in every direction—may be styled the Champs-Elysées, or the Hyde Park, of the Indian Archipelago. On a third side, the military town is separated from the trading town by the river Pasig, upon which are seen all the day boats laden with merchandize, and charming gondolas conveying idlers to different parts of the suburbs, or to visit the ships in the bay.

The military town communicates by the bridge of Binondoc with the mercantile town, inhabited principally by the Spaniards engaged in public affairs; its aspect is dull and monotonous; all the streets, perfectly straight, are bordered by wide granite footpaths. In general, the highways are macadamised, and kept in good condition. Such is the effeminacy of the people, they could not endure the noise of carriages upon pavement. The houses—large and spacious, palaces in appearance—are built in a particular manner, calculated to withstand the earthquakes and hurricanes so frequent in this part of the world. They have all one story, with a ground-floor; the upper part, generally occupied by the family, is surrounded by a wide gallery, opéned or shut by means of large sliding panels, the panes of which are thin mother-of-pearl. The mother-of-pearl permits the passage of light to the apartments, and excludes the heat of the sun. In the military town are all the monasteries and convents, the archbishopric, the courts of justice, the custom-house, the hospital, the governor's palace, and the citadel, which overlooks both towns. There are three principal entrances to Manilla—*Puerta Santa Lucia, Puerta Réal,* and *Puerta Parian.*

At one o'clock the drawbridges are raised, and the gates pitilessly closed, when the tardy resident must seek his night's lodging in the suburb, or mercantile town, called Binondoc. This portion of Manilla wears a much gayer and more lively aspect than the military section. There is less regularity in the streets, and the buildings are not so fine as those in what may be called Manilla proper; but in Binondoc all is movement, all is life. Numerous canals, crowded with pirogues, gondolas, and boats of various kinds, intersect the suburb, where reside the rich merchants—Spanish, English, Indian, Chinese, and Métis. The newest and most elegant houses are built upon the banks of the river Pasig. Simple in exterior, they contain the most costly inventions of English and Indian luxury. Precious vases from China, Japan ware, gold, silver, and rich silks, dazzle the eyes on entering these unpretending habitations. Each house has a landing-place from the river, and little bamboo palaces, serving as bathing-houses, to which the residents resort several times daily, to relieve the fatigue caused by the intense heat of the climate. The cigar manufactory, which affords employment continually to from fifteen to twenty thousand workmen and other assistants, is situated in Binondoc; also the Chinese custom-house, and all the large working establishments of Manilla. During the day, the Spanish ladies, richly dressed in the transparent muslins of India and China, lounge about from store to store, and sorely test the patience of the Chinese salesman, who unfolds uncomplainingly, and without showing the least ill-humour, thousands of pieces of goods before his customers, which are frequently examined simply for amusement, and not half a yard purchased. The balls and entertainments, given by the half-breeds of Binondoc to their friends, are celebrated throughout the Philippines. The quadrilles of Europe are succeeded by the dances of India, and while the young people execute the fandango, the bolero, the cachucha, or the lascivious movements of the bayadères, the enterprising half-breed, the indolent Spaniard, and the sedate Chinese, retire to the gaming saloons, to try their fortune at cards and dice. The passion for play is carried to such an extent, that the traders lose or gain in one night sums of 50,000 piasters (£10,000 sterling). The half-breeds, Indians, and Chinese, have also a great passion for cock-fighting; these combats take place in a large arena. I have seen £1,500 betted upon a cock which had cost £150; in a few minutes this costly champion fell, struck dead by his antagonist. In fine, if Binondoc be exclusively the city of pleasure, luxury, and activity, it is also that of amorous intrigues and gallant adventures. In the evening, Spaniards, English, and French, go to the promenades to ogle the beautiful and facile half-breed women, whose transparent robes reveal their splendid figures. That which distinguishes the female half-breeds (Spanish-Tagals, or Chinese-Tagals) is a singularly intelligent and expressive physiognomy. Their hair, drawn back from the face, and sustained by long golden pins, is of marvellous luxuriance. They wear upon the head a kerchief, transparent like a veil, made of the pine fibre, finer than our finest cambric; the neck is ornamented by a string of large coral beads, fastened by a gold medallion. A transparent chemisette, of the same stuff as the head-dress, descends as far as the waist, covering, but not concealing, a

Spanish Metis, or Half-Breeds.

bosom that has never been imprisoned in stays. Below, and two or three inches from the edge of the chemisette, is attached a variously coloured petticoat of very bright hues. Over this garment, a large and costly silk sash closely encircles the figure, and shows its outline from the waist to the knee. The small and white feet, always naked, are thrust into embroidered slippers, which cover but the extremities. Nothing can be more charming, coquettish, and fascinating, than this costume, which excites in the highest degree the admiration of strangers. The half-breed and Chinese Tagals know so well the effect it produces on the Europeans, that nothing would induce them to alter it.

While on the subject of dress, that of the men is also

Chinese Metis, or Half-Breeds.

worthy of remark. The Indian and the half-breed wear upon the head a large straw hat, black or white, or a sort of Chinese covering, called a *salacote;* upon the shoulders, the pine fibre kerchief embroidered; and round the neck, a rosary of coral beads; their shirts are also made from the fibres of the pine, or of vegetable silk; trousers of coloured silk, with embroidery near the bottom, and a girdle of red China crape, complete their costume. The feet, without stockings, are covered with European shoes.

The military town, so quiet during the day, assumes a more lively appearance towards the evening, when the inhabitants ride out in their very magnificent carriages, which are invariably conducted by postilions; they then mix with the walking population of Binondoc. Afterwards visits, balls, and the more intimate *réunions* take place. At the latter they talk, smoke the cigars of Manilla, and chew the betel,* drink glasses of iced *eau sucrée*, and eat innumerable sweetmeats; towards midnight those guests retire who do not stay supper with the family, which is always served luxuriously, and generally prolonged until two o'clock in the morning. Such is the life spent by the wealthy classes under these skies so favoured by Heaven. But there exists, as in Europe, and even to a greater extent, the most abject misery, of which I shall speak hereafter, throwing a shade over this brilliant picture.

I shall now return to my personal adventures. While I spoke with the Indians upon the shore, I had noticed a young European standing not many paces from me; I again met him on the road I took towards Manilla, and I thought I would address him. This young man was a surgeon, about returning to Europe. I partly told him the plans I wished to form, and asked him for some information respecting the city where I purposed locating myself. He readily satisfied my inquiries, and encouraged me in the resolution to exercise my profession in the Philippine Islands. He had himself, he said, conceived the same project, but family affairs obliged him to return to his country. I did not conceal the misfortune of my position, and observed that it would be almost impossible to pay visits in the costume, worse than plain, which I then wore.

"That is of no consequence," he replied; "I have all you would require: a coat almost new, and six capital lancets. I

* The betel is a species of pepper plant, the leaves of which are wrapped round areca nuts and the chunam—the latter is a kind of burnt-lime made of shells, and the areca nut is the fruit of a species of palm. The Indians, Chinese, half-breeds, and a great number of Creoles, continually chew this mixture, which is reputed to sweeten the breath and assist digestion.

will sell you these things for their cost price in France; they will be a great bargain." The affair was soon concluded. He took me to his hotel, and I shortly left it encased in a garment sufficiently good, but much too large and too long for me. Nevertheless, it was some time since I had seen myself so well clad, and I could not help admiring my new acquisition.

I had hidden my poor little white jacket in my hat, and I strode along the causeway of Manilla more proud than Artaban himself. I was the owner of a coat and six lancets; but there remained, for all my fortune, the sum of one dollar only; this consideration slightly tempered the joy that I felt in gazing on my brilliant costume. I thought of where I could pass the night, and subsist on the morrow and the following days, if the sick were not ready for me.

Reflecting thus I slowly wandered from Binondoc to the military town, and from the military town back to Binondoc,—when, suddenly, a bright idea shot across my brain. At Cavite I had heard spoken of a Spanish captain, by name Don Juan Porras, whom an accident had rendered almost blind. I resolved to seek him, and offer my services; it remained but to find his residence. I addressed a hundred persons, but each replied that he did not know, and passed on his way. An Indian who kept a small shop, and to whom I spoke, relieved my trouble: "If the senor is a captain," he said, "your excellency would obtain his address at the first barrack on your road." I thanked him, and eagerly followed his counsel. At the infantry barracks, where I presented myself, the officer on duty sent a soldier to guide me to the captain's dwelling: it was time, the night had already fallen. Don Juan Porras was an Andalusian, a good man, and of an extremely cheerful disposition. I found him with his head wrapped in a Madras handkerchief, busied in completely covering his eyes with two enormous poultices.

"Senor Captain," I said, "I am a physician, and a skilful oculist. I have come hither to take care of you, and I am fully convinced that I shall cure you."

"*Basta*" (enough is said), was his answer; "all the physicians in Manilla are asses."

This more than sceptical reply did not discourage me. I resolved to turn it to account. "My opinion is precisely the same as yours," I promptly answered; "and it is because I am strongly convinced of the ignorance of the native doctors, that I have made up my mind to come and practise in the Philippines."

"Of what nation are you, sir?"

"I am a Frenchman."

"A French physician!" cried Don Juan; "Ah! that is quite another matter. I ask your pardon for having spoken so irreverently of men of your profession. A French physician! I put myself entirely into your hands. Take my eyes, Senor Medico, and do what you will with them!"

The conversation was taking a favourable turn: I hastened to broach the principal question:

"Your eyes are very bad, Senor Captain," said I; "to accomplish a speedy cure, it is absolutely necessary that I should never quit you for a moment."

"Would you consent to come and pass some time with me, doctor?"

Here was the principal consideration settled.

"I consent," replied I, "but on one condition; namely, that I shall pay you for my board and lodging."

"That shall not part us—you are free to do so," said the worthy man; "and so the matter is settled. I have a nice room, and a good bed, all ready; there is nothing to do but to send for your baggage. I will call my servant."

The terrible word, "baggage," sounded in my ears like a knell. I cast a melancholy look at the crown of my hat—my only portmanteau—within which were deposited all my clothes—consisting of my little white jacket; and I feared Don Juan would take me for some runaway sailor trying to dupe him. There was no retreat; so I mustered my courage, and briefly related my sad position, adding that I could not pay for my board and lodging until the end of the month—if I was so fortunate as to find patients. Don Juan Porras listened to me very quietly. When my tale was told he burst into a loud laugh, which made me shiver from head to foot.

"Well," cried he, "I am well pleased it should be so; you are poor; you will have more time to devote to my malady, and a greater interest in curing me. What think you of the syllogism?"

"It is excellent, Senor Captain, and before long you will find, I hope, that I am not the man to compromise so distinguished a logician as yourself. To-morrow morning I will examine your eyes, and I will not leave you till I have radically cured them."

We talked for some time longer in this joyous strain, after which I retired to my chamber, where the most delightful dreams visited my pillow.

The next day I rose early, put on my doctoral coat, and entered the chamber of my host. I examined his eyes; they were in a dreadful state. The sight of one was not only destroyed, but threatened the life of the sufferer. A cancer had formed, and the enormous size it had attained rendered the result of an operation doubtful. The left eye contained many fibres, but there was hope of saving it. I frankly acquainted Don Juan with my fears and hopes, and insisted upon the entire removal of the right eye. The Captain, at first astonished, decided courageously upon submitting to the operation, which I accomplished on the following day with complete success. Shortly afterwards the inflammatory symptoms disappeared, and I could assure my host of a safe recovery. I then bestowed all my attention upon the left eye. I desired the more ardently to restore to Don Juan his vision, from the good effect I was convinced his case would produce at Manilla. For me it would be fortune and reputation. Besides, I had already acquired, in the few days, some slight patronage, and was in a position to pay for my board and lodging at the end of the month. After six weeks' careful treatment Don Juan was perfectly cured, and could use his eye as well as he did previous to his accident. Nevertheless, to my great regret, the Captain still continued to immure himself; his re-appearance in society, which he had forsaken for more than a year, would have produced an immense sensation, and I should have been considered the first doctor in the Philippines. One day I touched upon this delicate topic.

Senor Captain," said I, "what are you thinking about, to remain thus shut up between four walls, and why do you not resume your old habits? You must go and visit your friends, your acquaintances."

"Doctor," interrupted Don Juan, "how can I show myself in public with an eye the less? When I pass along the street all the women would say: 'There goes Don Juan the One-eyed!' No, no; before I leave the house you must get me an artificial eye from Paris."

"You don't mean that? It would be eighteen months before the eye arrived."

"Then here goes for eighteen months' seclusion," said Don Juan.

I persisted for upwards of an hour, but the Captain would not listen to reason. He carried his coquetry so far that, although I had covered the empty orbit with black silk, he had his shutters closed whenever visitors came; so that, as they always found him in the dark, none would credit his cure. I was very anxious to thwart Don Juan's obstinacy, as may well be imagined; I had not the time to waste, during eighteen months, in dancing attendance at fortune's door; therefore I determined to make this eye myself, without which the coquetish captain would not be seen. I took some pieces of glass, a tube, and set to work. After many fruitless attempts, I at last succeeded in obtaining the perfect form ot an eye; but this was not all—it must be coloured to resemble nature. I sent for a poor carriage-painter, who managed to imitate tolerably well the left eye of Don Juan. It was necessary to preserve this painting from contact with the tears which would soon have destroyed it. To accomplish this I had made by a jeweller a silver globe, smaller than the glass eye, inside which I united it by means of sealing-wax. I carefully polished the edges upon a stone, and after eight days' labour I obtained a satisfactory result. The eye which I had succeeded in producing was really not so bad after all. I was anxious to place it within the vacant orbit. It somewhat inconvenienced the Senor Don Juan, but I persuaded him that he would soon become accustomed to it. Placing across his nose a pair of spectacles, he examined himself in the looking-glass, and was so satisfied with his appearance that he decided on commencing his visits the following day.

As I had anticipated, the re-appearance in the world of

Captain Juan Porras made a great sensation, and soon the consequence was, that Senor Don Pablo, the eminent French physician—most especially the clever oculist—was much spoken of. From all quarters patients came to me. Notwithstanding my youth and inexperience, my first success gave me such confidence that I performed several operations upon persons afflicted with cataracts, which succeeded most fortunately. I no longer sufficed to my large connection, and in a few days, from the greatest distress, I attained perfect opulence: I had a carriage-and-four in my stables. I could not, however, notwithstanding this change of fortune, resign myself to leave Don Juan's house, out of gratitude for the hospitality he so generously offered me. In my leisure hours he kept me company, and amused me with the recital of his battle stories and personal adventures. I had already spent nearly six months with him, when a circumstance, which forms an epoch in my life, changed my existence, and compelled me to quit the lively captain. One of my American friends often called my attention in our walks towards a young lady in mourning, who passed for one of the prettiest senoras of the town. Each time we met her my American friend never failed to praise the beauty of the Marquesa de Las Salinas. She was about eighteen or nineteen years of age; her features were both regular and placid; she had beautiful black hair, and large expressive eyes; she was the widow of a colonel in the guards, who married her when almost a child. The sight of this young lady produced so lively an impression upon me, that I explored all the saloons at Binondoc, to endeavour to meet her elsewhere than in my walks. Fruitless attempts! The young widow saw nobody. I almost despaired of finding an opportunity of speaking to her, when one morning an Indian came to request me to visit his master. I got into the carriage and set off, without informing myself of the name of the sick person. The carriage stopped before the door of one of the finest houses in the Faubourg of Santa-Crux. Having examined the patient, and conversed a few minutes with him, I went to the table to write a prescription; suddenly I heard the rustling of a silk dress; I turned round—the pen fell from my hand. Before me stood the very lady I had so long sought after—appearing to me as in a dream! My amazement was so great that I muttered a few unintelligible words, and bowed with such awkwardness that she smiled. She simply addressed me to inquire the state of her nephew's health, and withdrew almost immediately. As to myself, instead of making my ordinary calls, I returned home; questioned Don Juan minutely about Madame de Las Salinas: he entirely satisfied my curiosity. He was acquainted with all the family of this youthful widow, and they were highly respected in the colony. The next morning, and following days, I returned to this charming widow, who graciously condescended to receive me with favour. These details being so completely personal, I pass them over. Six months after my first interview with Madame de Las Salinas, I asked her hand, and obtained it. I had therefore found, at more than five thousand leagues from my country, both happiness and wealth. I agreed that we should go to France as soon as my wife's property, the greater part of which lay in Mexico, should be realised. In the meantime my house was the rendezvous of foreigners, particularly of the French, who were already rather numerous at Manilla. At this period the Spanish government named me Surgeon-Major of the 1st Light Regiment, and of the first battalion of the militia of Panjanga.

Having been so successful in so short a time, I never once doubted but that fortune would continue to bestow her smiling favours upon me. I had already prepared everything for my return to France; for we hourly expected the arrival of the galleons that plied from Acapulco to Manilla, which were to bring my wife's fortune. Her fortune was no less than 700,000 francs (£28,000 sterling).

One evening, as we were taking tea, we were informed that the vessels from Acapulco had been telegraphed, and that the next morning they would be in; our piasters were to be on board; I leave you to guess if our wishes were not gratified. But, alas! how our hopes were frustrated: the vessels did not bring us a single piaster. This is what occurred: five or six millions were sent by land from Mexico to San Blas, the place of embarkation, and the Mexican government had the van escorted by a regiment of the line, commanded by Colonel Iturbide. On the journey he took possession of the van, and fled with his regiment into the independent states. It is well known that later Iturbide was proclaimed Emperor of Mexico, then dethroned, and at last shot, after an expedition that offers more than one analogy with that of Murat. The very day of the arrival of the vessels we learnt that our fortune was entirely lost, without even hopes of regaining the smallest part. My wife and self supported this event with tolerable philosophy. It was not the loss of our piasters that distressed us the most, but the necessity we were in to abandon, or at least to postpone, our journey to France.

Spanish Metis of the superior class.

CHAPTER III.

Continued Prosperity in Practice—Attempted Political Revolution—Desperate Street Engagement—Subjugation of the Insurgents—The Emperor of a Day —Dreadful Executions—Illness and Insanity of my Wife—Her Recovery and Relapse—Removal to the Country—Beneficial Results—Dangerous Neighbours — Repentant Banditti — Fortunate Escape — The Anonymous Friend—A Confiding Wife—Her Final Recovery, and our Domestic Happiness Restored.

DESPITE the misfortune I have alluded to, I kept up my house in the same style as before. My connection, and the different posts I occupied, permitted me to lead the life of a grandee belonging to the Spanish colonies; and probably I should have made my fortune in a few years, if

I had continued in the medical profession, but the wish for unlimited liberty caused me to abandon all these advantages for a life of peril and anxiety. At the same time do not let us anticipate too suddenly, and let the reader patiently peruse a few more pages about Manilla, and various events wherein I figured, either as actor or witness, before taking leave of a sybarite citizen's life

I was, as I said before, surgeon-major of the 1st Light Regiment of the line, and on intimate terms with the staff, and more particularly with Captain Novalès, a Creole by birth, possessing a courageous and venturesome disposition. He was suspected of endeavouring to excite his regiment to rebel in behalf of the Independence. An inquiry was consequently instituted, which ended without proof of the captain's culpability; nevertheless, as the governor still maintained his suspicious, he gave orders for him to be sent to one of the southern provinces, under the inspection of an alcaide. Novalès came to see me the morning of his departure, and complained bitterly of the injustice of the governor towards him, and added that those who had no confidence in his honour would repent, and that he would soon be back. I endeavoured to pacify him: we shook hands, and in the evening he went on board the vessel commissioned to take him to his destination. The night after Novalès departure, I was startled out of my sleep by the report of fire-arms. I immediately dressed myself in my uniform, and hastened to the barracks of my regiment. The streets were deserted; sentinels were stationed at about fifty paces apart. I understood that an extraordinary event had occurred in some part of the town. When I reached the barracks I was no little astonished to find the gates wide open, the sentry's box vacant, and not a soldier within. I went into the infirmary set apart for the special service of the cholera patients, and there a serjeant told me that the bad weather had compelled the vessel that was taking Novalès into exile to return into the port; that about one o'clock in the morning, Novalès, accompanied by Lieutenant Ruiz, came to the barracks, and having made himself certain of the votes of the Creole non-commissioned officers, put the regiment under arms, took possession of the gates, and proclaimed himself Emperor of the Philippines.

This extraordinary intelligence caused me some anxiety. My regiment had openly revolted; if I joined it, and were defeated, I should be considered a traitor, and, as such, shot; if, on the contrary, I fought against it, and the rebels proved victorious, I knew Novalès sufficiently well to be convinced that he would not spare me. Nevertheless I could not hesitate: duty bound me to the Spanish government, by which I had been so well treated. I left the barracks, rambling where chance might lead me. I shortly found myself at the head-quarters of the artillery; an officer behind the gate stood observing me. I went up to him, and asked him whether he was for Spain. Upon his answering me in the affirmative, I begged him to open the gate, declaring that I wished to join his party, and would willingly offer my services as surgeon to them. I went in, and took the commander's orders, which soon showed me how matters stood. During the night Ruiz went, in the name of Novalès, to General Folgueras, the commander during the absence of Governor Martinès, who was detained at his country house, a short distance from Manilla. He took the guard unawares, and seized the keys of the town, after having stabbed Folgueras; from thence he went to the prisons, set the prisoners at liberty, and put in their places the principal men of the public offices belonging to the colony. The 1st Regi ment was on Government Place, ready to engage in battle; twice it attempted to fall unexpectedly upon the artillery and citadel, but was driven back. Many expected assistance from without, and orders from General Martinès to attack the rebels. Very soon we heard a discharge of artillery: it was General Martinès, who, at the head of the Queen's Regiment, broke open Saint Lucy's Gate, and advanced into the besieged town. The body of the artillery joined the governor-general, and we marched towards Government Place. The insurgents placed two cannons at the corner of each street. Scarcely had we approached the palace, than we were exposed to a violent discharge of loaded muskets. The head chaplain of the regiment was the first victim. We were then engaged in a street, by the side of the fortifications, and from which it was impossible to attack the enemy with advantage. General Martinès changed the position of the attack, and in this condition we came back by the street of Saint Isabelle. The troops in two lines followed

Bridge of Manilla.

both sides of the street, and left the road free; in the mean time the Panpangas regiment, crossing the bridge, reached us by one of the opposite streets: the rebels were then exposed to the opposite attacks. They nevertheless defended themselves furiously, and their sharpshooters did us some harm. Novalès was everywhere, encouraging his soldiers by words, exploits, and example, while Lieutenant Ruiz was busy pointing one of the cannons, that swept the middle of the street we were coming up. At length, after three hours' contest, the rebels succumbed. The troops fell upon everything they found, and Novalès was taken prisoner to the governor's. As to Ruiz, although he had received a blow on his arm from a ball, he was fortunate enough to jump over the fortifications, and succeeded, for the time, in escaping; three days afterwards he was taken. The conflict was scarcely over, than a court-martial was held. Novalès was tried the first. At midnight he was outlawed; at two o'clock in the morning proclaimed Emperor; and at five in the evening shot. Such changes in fortune are not uncommon in Spanish colonies.

The court-martial, without adjourning, tried, until the middle of the following day, all the prisoners arrested with arms. The tenth part of the regiment was sent to the hulks, and all the non-commissioned officers were condemned to death. I received orders to be at Government Place by four o'clock, on which spot the executions were to take place; two companies of each battalion of the garrison, and all the staff, were to be present.

Towards five the doors of the town-hall opened, and between a double file of soldiers advanced seventeen non-commissioned officers, each one assisted by two monks of the order of Misericordia. Mournful silence prevailed, interrupted every now and then by the doleful beating of the drums, and the prayers of the agonising, chanted by the monks. The procession moved slowly on, and after some time reached the palace; the seventeen non-commissioned officers were ordered to kneel, their faces turned towards the wall. After a lengthened beating of the drums the monks left their victims, and at a second beating a discharge of muskets resounded: the seventeen young men fell prostrate on the ground. One, however, was not dead; he had fallen with the others, and seemed apparently motionless. A few minutes after the monks threw their black veils upon the victims: they now belonged to Divine justice. I witnessed all that had just happened. I stood a few steps from him who feigned death so well, and my heart beat with force enough to burst through my chest. Would that it had been in my power to lead one of the monks towards this unfortunate young man who must have experienced such mortal anguish; but, alas! after having been so miraculously spared, at the moment the black veil was about to cover him, an officer informed the commander that a guilty man had escaped being punished; the monks were arrested in their pious ministry, and two soldiers received orders to approach and fire upon the poor fellow.

I was indignant at this. I advanced towards the informer and reproached him for his cruelty; he wished to reply; I treated him as a coward, and turned my back to him. Express orders from my colonel compelled me to leave my house, to assist at this frightful execution; still, deep anxiety ought to have prevented me from so doing, as I will explain. On the eve when the battle was over, and the insurgents routed, the distress of my dear Anna came across my mind. It was now one o'clock in the afternoon, and she had received no tidings from me since three in the morning; might she not think me dead, or in the midst of the rebellion? Ah! if duty could make me forget for a moment she whom I loved more than life, now all danger was over her charming image returned to my mind. Dearest Anna! I beheld her pale, agitated; asking herself at each report of the cannon whether it rendered her a widow; when my mind became so agitated that I ran home to calm her fears. Having reached my house I went quickly up stairs, my heart beating violently; I paused for a moment at her door, then summoning a little courage I entered. Anna was kneeling down praying; hearing my footsteps she raised her head, and threw herself into my arms without uttering a word At first I attributed this silence to emotion, but, alas! upon examining her lovely face, I saw her eyes looked wild, her features contracted: I started back. I discovered in her all the symptoms of congestion of the brain. I dreaded lest my wife had lost her senses, and this fear alarmed me greatly. How fortunate it was that it lay in my power to relieve her. I had her placed in bed, and ministered myself to her wants. She was tolerably composed; the few words she uttered were inconsistent; she seemed to think that somebody was going to poison or kill her. All her confidence was placed in me. During three days the remedies I prescribed and administered were useless; the poor creature derived no benefit from them. I therefore determined to consult the doctors in Manilla, although I had no great opinion of their skill. They advised some insignificant drugs, and declared to me that there were no hopes, adding, as a philosophical mode of consolation, that death was preferable to the loss of reason. I did not agree on this point with these gentlemen: I would have preferred insanity to death, for I hoped that her madness would die away by degrees, and eventually disappear altogether How many mad people are cured, what numbers daily recover, yet death is the last word of humanity; and, as a young poet has truly said, is "the stone of the tomb."

Between the world and God a curtain falls! I determined to wage a war against death, and to save my Anna by having recourse to the most indisputable resources of science. I looked now upon my brotherhood with more contempt than ever, and, confident in my love and zealous will, I began my struggle with a destiny, tinged indeed with gloomy clouds. I shut myself up in the sick-chamber, and never left my wife. I had great difficulty in getting her to take the medicaments I trusted she would derive so much benefit from; I was obliged to call to my assistance all the influence I had over her, in order to persuade her that the draughts I presented to her were not poisoned. She did not sleep, but appeared very drowsy; these symptoms denoted very clearly great disorder of the brain. For nine days she remained in this dreadful state; during which time I scarcely knew whether she was dead or alive; at every moment I besought the Almighty to work a miracle in her behalf. One morning the poor creature closed her eyes. I cannot describe my feelings of anguish. Would she ever awake again? I leant over her; I heard her breathing gently, without apparent effort; I felt her pulse, it beat calmer and more regular; she was evidently better. I stood by her in deep anxiety. She still remained in a calm sleep, and at the end of half-an-hour I felt convinced that this satisfactory crisis would restore my invalid to life and reason. I sat down by her bed-side, and stayed there eighteen hours, watching her slightest movements. At length, after such cruel suspense, my patient awoke, as if out of a dream.

"Have you been long watching?" she said, giving me her hand: "Have I, then, been very ill? What care you have taken of me! Luckily you may rest now, for I feel I am recovered."

I think I have during my life been a sharer of the strongest emotions of joy or of sadness man can feel; but never had I experienced such real, heartfelt joy as when I heard Anna's words. It is easy to imagine the state of my mind in recollecting the bitter grief I was in for ten days; then can be understood the mental anguish I felt. Having witnessed such strange scenes for a considerable time, it would not have been surprising had I lost my senses. I was an actor in a furious battle; I had seen the wounded falling around me, and heard the death-rattle. After the frightful execution, I went home, and there still deeper grief awaited me. I had watched by the bed-side of a beloved wife, knowing not whether I should lose her for ever, or see her spared to me deprived of reason; when all at once, as if by a miracle, this dear companion of my life, restored to health, threw herself into my arms. I wept with her; my burning eyes, aching for want of rest, found at last some tears, but they were tears of joy and gladness. Soon we became more composed; we related to each other all that we had suffered. Oh! the sympathy of loving hearts! Our sorrows had been the same, we had shared the same fears, she for me and I for her. Anna's rapid recovery, after her renovating slumber, enabled her to get up; she dressed herself as usual, and the people who saw her could not believe she had passed ten days struggling between death and insanity—two gulphs, from which love and faith had preserved us.

I was happy; my deep sadness was speedily changed to gladness, even visible on my features. Alas! this joy was tran sitory, like all happiness; man here below is a continual prey to misfortune! My wife, at the end of a month, relapsed into her former sickly state; the same symptoms showed themselves again, with similar prospects, during the same space of time. I remained again nine days at her bed-side, and on the tenth a refreshing sleep brought her to her senses But this time, guided by experience, that pitiless mistress, who gives us lessons we should ever remember, I did not rejoice as I had done the month before. I feared lest this sudden cure might only be a temporary recovery, and that every month my poor invalid would relapse, until her brain becoming weaker and weaker, she would be deranged for life. This sad idea wounded my heart, and caused me such grief that I could not even dissimulate it before her who inspired it. I exhausted all the resources of medicine; all these expedients proved unavailable. I thought that perhaps, if I removed my poor invalid from the spot where the events had occurred that caused her disorder, her cure might be more easily effected; that perhaps bathing and country walks in the fine weather would contribute to hasten her recovery; therefore I invited one of her relations to accompany us, and we set out for Tierra-Alta, a delightful spot, a real oasis, where all things were assembled that could endear one to life. The first days of our settling there were full of joy, hope, and happiness. Anna got better and better every day, and her health very much improved. We walked in beautiful gardens, under the shade of orange-trees; they were so thick that even during the most intense heat we were cool under their shade. A lovely river of blue and limpid water ran through our orchard; I had some Indian baths erected there. We went out in a pretty, light, open carriage, drawn by four good horses, through beautiful avenues, lined on each side with the pliant bamboo, and sown with all the various flowers of the tropics. I leave you to judge, by this short account, that nothing that can be wished for in the country was wanting in Tierra-Alta. For an invalid it was a Paradise; but those are right who say there is no perfect happiness here below. I had a wife I adored, and who loved me with all the sincerity of a pure young heart. We lived in an Eden, away from the world, from the noise and bustle of a city, and far, too, from the jealous and envious. We breathed a fragrant air; the pure and limpid waters that bathed our feet reflecting, by turns a sunny sky, and one spangled with twinkling stars. Anna's health was improving: it pleased me to see her so happy. What, then, was there to trouble us in our lovely retreat? A troop of banditti! These robbers were distributed around the suburbs of Tierra-Alta, and spread desolation over the country and neighbourhood by the robberies and murders they committed. There was a regiment in search of them; this they little cared about. They were numerous, clever, and audacious; and, notwithstanding the vigilance of the government, the band continued their highway robberies and assassinations. In the house where I then resided, and which I afterwards left, Aguilar, the commander of the cavalry, who had replaced me as occupant, was fallen upon unexpectedly, and stabbed. Several years after this period, the government was obliged to come to some terms with these bandits, and one day twenty men, all armed with carbines and swords, entered Manilla. Their chieftain led them; they walked with their heads upright, their carriage was proud and manly; in this order they went to the governor, who made them a speech, ordered them to lay down their arms, and sent them to the archbishop that he might exhort them. The archbishop in a religious discourse implored of them to repent of their crimes, and become honest citizens, and to return to their villages. These men, who had bathed their hands in the blood of their fellow-creatures, and who had sought in crime—or rather, in every crime—the gold they coveted, listened attentively to God's minister, changed completely their conduct, and became, in the end, good and quiet husbandmen.

Now let us return to my residence at Tierra-Alta, at the period when the bandits were not converted, and might have disturbed my peaceful abode and security. Nevertheless, whether it was carelessness, or the confidence I had in my Indian, with whom I spent some time after the ravages occasioned with the cholera, and with whose influence I was acquainted, I did not fear the bandits at all. This Indian lived a few leagues off from Tierra-Alta; he came often to see me, and said to me on different occasions: "Fear nothing from the robbers, Senor Doctor Pablo; they know we are friends, and that alone would suffice to prevent them attacking you, for they would dread to displease me, and to make me their enemy." These words put an end to my fears, and I soon hăd an opportunity of seeing that the Indian had taken me under his protection.

If any of my readers for whom I write these souvonirs feel the same desire as I experienced to visit the cascades of Tierra-Alta, let them go to a place called Yang-Yang; it was near this spot where my Indian protector resided. At this part the river, obstructed in its course by the narrowness of its channel, falls from only one waterspout, about thirty or forty feet high, into an immense basin, out of which the water calmly flows onwards, to form, lower down, three other water falls, not so lofty, but extending over the breadth of the river, thereby making three sheets of water, clear and transparent as crystal. What beautiful sights are offered to the eyes of man by the all-powerful hands of the Creator! And how often have I remarked that the works of nature are far superior to those that men tire themselves to erect and invent!

As we went one morning to the cascades we were about to alight at Yang-Yang, when all at once our carriage was surrounded with brigands, flying from the soldiers of the line. The chief—for we supposed him to be so at first—said to his companions, not paying the slightest attention to us, nor even addressing us: "We must kill the horses!" By this I saw he feared lest their enemies should make use of our horses to pursue them. With a presence of mind which fortunately never abandons me in difficult or perilous cicumstances, I said to him: "Do not fear; my horses shall not be used by your enemies to pursue you: rely upon my word." The chief put his hand to his cap, and thus addressed his comrades: "If such be the case, the Spanish soldiers will do us no harm to-day, neither let us do any. Follow me!" They marched off, and I instantly drove rapidly away in quite an opposite direction from the soldiers. The bandits looked after me; my good faith in keeping my word was successful. I not only lived a few months in safety at Tierra-Alta, but many years after, when I resided in Jala-Jala, and, in my quality of commander of the territorial horse-guards of the province of Lagune, was naturally a declared enemy of the bandits, I received the following note:

"Sir,—Beware of Pedro Tumbaga; we are invited by him to go to your house and to take you by surprise; we remember the morning we spoke to you at the cascades, and the sincerity of your word. You are an honourable man. If we find ourselves face to face with you, and it be necessary, we will fight, but faithfully, and never after having laid a snare. Keep, therefore, on your guard; beware of Pedro Tumbago; he is cowardly enough to hide himself in order to shoot you."

Everybody must acknowledge I had to do with most polite robbers.

I answered them thus:

"You are brave fellows. I thank you for your advice, but I do not fear Pedro Tumbaga. I cannot conceive how it is you keep among you a man capable of hiding himself to kill his enemy; if I had a soldier like him, I would soon let him have justice, and without consulting the law."

A fortnight after my answer, Tumbaga was no more; a bandit's bullet disembarrassed me of him.

I will now return to the recital I have just interrupted. When I had left the bandits at Yang-Yang, I pulled up my horses and bethought me of Anna. I was anxious to know what impression had been produced on her mind from this un pleasant encounter. Fortunately my fears were unfounded; my wife had not been at all alarmed, and when I asked her if she was frightened, she replied: "Frightened, indeed! am I not with you?" Subsequently I had good proofs that she told me the truth, for in many perilous circumstances she always presented the same presence of mind. Whon I thought there was no longer any danger we retraced our steps and went home, satisfied with the conduct of the bandits towards us, for their manner of acting clearly showed us that they intended us no harm. I mentally thanked my Indian friend, for to him I attributed the peace our turbulent neighbours allowed us to enjoy. The fatal time was drawing near when my wife would again be suffering from another attack of that frightful malady brought on by Novalès revolt. I had hoped that the country air, the baths, and amusements of every kind would cure my poor invalid; my hopes were deceived, and, as in the preceding month, I had the grief once more to assist at a period of physical and mental suffering. I despaired: I knew not what course to pursue. I decided, however, upon remaining at Tierra-Alta. My dear companion was happy there on the days her health was better, and on the other days I never left her, endeavouring by every means that art and imagination could invent to fight against this fatal malady. At length my care, attempts, and efforts were successful, and at the periods the symptoms usually returned I had the happiness not to observe them, and believed in the certainty of a final cure. I then felt the joy one experiences after having for a long time been on the point of losing a very dear friend, who suddenly recovers. I now gave myself up without fear to the various pleasures Tierra-Alta offers.

Stag Hunting in the Marigondon Mountains.

CHAPTER IV.

Hunting the Stag—Indian Mode of Chasing the Wild Buffalo; its Ferocity—Dangerous Sport—Capture of a Buffalo—Narrow Escape of an Indian Hunter—Return to Manilla—Injustice of the Governor—My Resignation of Office—I Purchase Property at Jala-Jala—Retire from Manilla to Take Possession of my Domains—Chinese Legend—Festival of St. Nicholas—Quinaboutasan—Description of Jala-Jala—Interview with a Bandit Chief—Formation of a Guard—Preparations for Building—Visit to Manilla, and Return to Jala-Jala—Completion of my House—Reception of my Wife by the Natives—The Government of the Philippines—Character of the Tagaloc Indians—Unmerited Chastisement—A Curate Appointed—Our Labours at Civilisation—My Hall of Justice—Buffalo Hunting Expedition.

NATURALLY fond of hunting, I often went to the home of my Indian friend in the Marigondon mountains. Together we chased the stag, and killed the various kinds of birds which abound in these regions to such an extent that one may always choose between fifteen or twenty different species of pigeons, wild ducks, and fowl, and it frequently happened that I brought down five or six at a shot. The manner of killing wild fowl (a sort of pheasant) much amused me. We rode across the large plains, strewed with young wood, on good and beautiful horses, broken in for the purpose; the dogs raised the game, and, armed with whips, we endeavoured to knock the birds down at a single blow, which is not so difficult as might be imagined. When a number of the frightened flocks left the shelter of the wood we put our steeds to the gallop, and it became a veritable steeple-chase, such as amateur jockeys would much delight in. I also hunted the stag with the lance, on horseback; this sport is likewise very amusing, but, unfortunately, often attended with accidents. This is how they occur:—The horses employed are so well trained to the sport, that as soon as they perceive the stag it is no longer necessary, neither is it possible, to guide them; they pursue the animal at the top of their speed, and leap over every obstruction before them. The horseman carries a lance seven or eight feet long, which he holds in readiness to cast as soon as he thinks himself within reach of the stag. If he misses his aim the lance sticks in the ground, and it then requires great skill to avoid coming in contact with the opposite end, which often wounds either the hunter or the horse. I speak not of the falls to which one is liable from going at a furious gallop along unknown and uneven roads. I had already enjoyed this sport during my first sojourn at the Indian's, but, well as I acquitted myself, I was never able to gain his permission that I should assist at a chase far more dangerous, and which I might almost call a combat—that of the wild buffalo To all my questions my host had replied: "In this sport there is much to fear: I would not expose you to the risk." He avoided, also, taking me near that part of the plain touching upon the mountains of Marigondon, where these animals could generally be found. However, after repeated solicitation, I managed to obtain what I so ardently desired; the Indian only wished to know whether I was a good horseman, if I possessed dexterity; and when he had satisfied himself on these two points, we started one fine morning, accompanied by nine huntsmen and a small pack of dogs. In this part of the Philippines the buffalo is hunted on horseback, and taken with the lasso, the Indians not being much accustomed to the use of guns. In other parts fire-arms are used, as I shall have occasion to recount in another part of my narrative; but, in whichever case, there is little difference in the danger, for the one requires good riding and great skill, the other much presence of mind and a good gun.

The wild buffalo is quite different from the domesticated animal; it is a terrible creature, pursuing the hunter as soon as it gets sight of him, and, should he transfix him with its terrible horns, he would promptly expiate his rashness. My faithful Indian was much more anxious about my safety than his own. He objected to my taking a gun; he had little confidence in my skill with the lasso, and preferred that I should merely sit on horseback, unarmed and unencumbered in my movements; accordingly I set out, with a dagger for my sole weapon. We divided our party by threes, and rode gently about the plains, taking care to keep at a distance from the edge of the wood, lest we should be surprised by the animal we were seeking.

After riding for about an hour, we at last heard the baying of the dogs, and understood that the enemy was forced from its forest retreat. We watched with the deepest attention the spot where we expected him to break forth. He required a great deal of coaxing before he would show; at last there was a sudden crashing noise in the wood; branches were broken, young trees overthrown, and a superb buffalo showed himself, at about one hundred and fifty paces' distance. He was of a beautiful black, and his horns were of very large dimensions. He carried his head high, and snuffed the air as though scenting his enemies. Suddenly starting off at a speed incredible in so bulky an animal, he made for one of our groups, composed of three Indians, who immediately put their horses to a gallop, and distributed themselves in the form of a triangle. The buffalo selected one of them, and impetuously charged him. As he did so, another of the Indians, whom he passed in his furious career, wheeled his horse and threw the lasso he held ready in his hand; but he was not expert, and missed his aim. Thereupon the buffalo changed his course, and pursued the imprudent man who had thus attacked him, and who now rode right in our direction. A second detachment of three hunters went to meet the brute; one of them passed near him at a gallop, and threw his lasso, but was as unsuccessful as his comrade. Three other hunters made the attempt; not one of them succeeded. I, as a mere spectator, looked on with admiration at this combat—at those evolutions, flights, and pursuits, executed with such order and courage, and with a precision that was truly extraordinary.

I had often witnessed bull-fights, and often had I shuddered at seeing the *toreadors* adopt a similar method in order to turn the furious animal from the pursuit of the *picador*. But what comparison could possibly be established between a combat in an enclosed arena and this one in the open plain—between the most terrible of bulls and a wild buffalo? Fiery and hot-blooded Spaniards, proud Castilians, eager for perilous spectacles, go, hunt the buffalo in the plains of the Marigondon After much flight and pursuit, hard riding, and imminent peril, a dexterous hunter encircled the animal's horns with his lasso The buffalo slackened his speed, and shook and tossed his head, stopping now and then to try to get rid of the obstacle which impeded his career. Another Indian, not less skilful than his predecessor, threw his lasso with a like rapidity and success. The furious beast now ploughed the earth with his horns, making the soil fly around him, as if anxious to display his strength, and to show what havoc he would have made with any of us who had allowed themselves to be surprised by him. With much care and precaution the Indians conveyed their prize into a neighbouring thicket. The hunters uttered a shout of joy; for my part I could not repress a cry of admiration. The animal was vanquished; it needed but a few precautions to master him completely. I was much surprised to see the Indians excite him with voice and gesture until he resumed the offensive, and bounded from the ground with fury What would have been our fate had he succeeded in shaking off or breaking the lassos! Fortunately, there was no danger of this. An Indian dismounted, and, with great agility, attached to the trunk of a solid tree the two lassos that retained the savage beast; then he gave the signal that his office was accomplished, and retired. Two hunters approached, threw their lassos over the animal, and fixed the ends to the ground with stakes; and now our prey was thoroughly subdued, and reduced to immobility, so that we could approach him with impunity. With blows of their cutlasses the Indians hacked off his horns, which would so well have revenged him had he been free to use them; then, with a pointed bamboo, they pierced the membranes that separate the nostrils, and passed through them a cane twiste in the form of a ring. In this state of martyrdom they fastened him securely behind two tame buffaloes, and led him to the next village.

Here the animal was killed, and the hunters divided the carcass, the flesh of which is equal in flavour to beef. I had been fortunate in my first essay, for such encounters with these shaggy sovereigns of the plain do not always end so easily. A few days afterwards we renewed the sport, which, alas! terminated with an accident of too frequent occurrence. An Indian was surprised by a buffalo, at the moment the animal issued from the wood. With one blow from his horns the horse was impaled and cast to the earth, while his Indian rider fell near to him. The inequality of the ground offered some chance of the man escaping the notice of his redoubtable foe, until the latter, by a sudden movement of his head, turned the horse over upon his rider, and inflicted several blows with his horns, either of which would have proved fatal, but from the force becoming diminished in traversing the carcass of the horse. Fortunately some of the other sportsmen succeeded in turning the animal, and compelled him to abandon his victim. It was indeed time, for we found the poor Indian half dead, and terribly gored by the horns of the buffalo. We succeeded in stopping the blood which flowed copiously from his wounds, and carried him to the village upon a hastily constructed litter. It was only by considerable care and attention that his cure was eventually effected, and my friend the Indian strongly opposed my assisting at such dangerous sport for the future.

Anna's health was now completely re-established. I no longer dreaded the return of her fearful malady. During the space of several months I had enjoyed all the pleasures that Tierra-Alta afforded, and my affairs now requiring my presence at Manilla we set out for that city. Immediately after my arrival I was compelled, much to my regret, to resume my ordinary occupation; that is, to visit the sick from morning to night, and from night to morning. My profession did not well accord with my natural character, for I was not sufficiently philosophic to witness, without pain, the sufferings I was incapable of alleviating, and, above all, to watch the death-beds of fathers, of mothers, and of dearly loved children. In a word, I did not act professionally, for I never sent in my bills; my patients paid me when and how they could. To their honour, I am bound to say that I rarely had to complain of forgetfulness. Besides, my appointments permitted me to live sumptuously, to have eight horses in my stables, and to keep open house to my friends and the strangers who visited Manilla. Soon, however, what my friends designated a *coup-de-tête* caused me to lose all these advantages.

Every month I summoned a council of revision in the regiment to which I belonged. One day I brought forward a young soldier for rejection; all went well; but a native surgeon, long jealous of my reputation, was nominated by the governor to make inquiry and check my declaration. He naturally inserted in his report that I was deceived; that the malady of which I spoke was imaginary; and he succeeded in all this so well that the governor, enraged, condemned me in a penalty of six piasters. The following month I again brought forward the same soldier, as being incapable of performing his duties; a commission of eight surgeons was nominated; their decision was unanimous in my favour, and the soldier was accordingly discharged. This reparation not quite satisfying me, I presented an appeal to the governor, who would not receive it, upon the strange pretext that the decision of the medical committee could not annul his. I confess that I did not understand this argument. This method of reasoning, if reasoning it was, appeared to me specious in the extreme. Why allow the innocent to suffer, and the ignorant practitioner, who had contradicted my opinions and deceived himself, to escape? This injustice revolted me. I am a Breton, and I have lived with Indians—two natures which love only right and justice. I was so much annoyed by the governor's conduct towards me that I went to him, not to make another reclamation, but to tender my resignation of the important offices which I held. He received me with a specious smile, and told me that after a little reflection I should change my mind. The poor governor, however, was deceived, for, on leaving his palace, I went direct to the minister of finance and purchased the property of Jala-Jala. My course was marked out, my resolution unshakable. Although my resignation was not yet duly accepted, I began to act as though I was completely free. I had at the beginning informed Anna of the matter, and had asked her if she would reside at Jala-Jala. "With you I should be happy anywhere." Such was her answer. I was free, then, to act as I pleased, and could go wherever my destiny might lead me. I forthwith decided upon visiting the land that I had purchased.

For the execution of this project it was necessary to find a faithful Indian upon whom I could rely. From among my domestics I chose the coachman, a brave and discreet man, who was devoted to me. I took some arms, ammunition, and provisions. At Lapindan, a small village near the town of Santa Anna, I freighted a small boat worked by three Indians:

Passage-boat on the River Pasig.

and one morning, without making my project known to my friends, and without inquiring whether the governor had replaced me, I set out to take possession of my domains, respiring the vivifying and pure air of liberty. I ascended in my pirogue—which skimmed along the surface of the waters like a sea-gull—the pretty river Pasig, which issues from the lake of Bay, and traverses, on its way to the sea, the suburbs of Manilla. The banks of this river are planted with thickets of bamboo, and studded with pretty Indian habitations; above the large town of Pasig it receives the waters of the river St. Mateo, at the spot where that river unites itself with that of the Pasig. Upon the left bank are still seen the ruins of the chapel and parsonage of St. Nicholas, built by the Chinese, as the legend I am about to relate informs us

At an unknown epoch, a Chinese who was once sailing in a canoe, either upon the river Pasig, or that of St. Mateo, suddenly perceived an alligator making for his frail bark, which it immediately capsized. On his finding himself thus plunged in the water, the unfortunate Chinese, whose only prospect was that of making a meal for the ferocious animal, invoked the aid of St. Nicholas. You, perhaps, would not have done so, nor I either; and we should have been wrong, for the idea was a good one. The good St. Nicholas listened to the cries of the unhappy castaway, appeared to his wondering eyes, and with a stroke of a wand, like some benevolent fairy, changed the threatening crocodile into a rock, and the Chinese was saved. But do not imagine that the legend ends here; the Chinese are not an ungrateful people—China is the land of porcelain, of tea, and of gratitude. The Chinese who had thus escaped from the cruel fate that awaited him, felt desirous of consecrating the memory of the miracle; and, in concert with his brethren of Manilla, he built a pretty chapel and parsonage in honour of the good St. Nicholas. This chapel was for a long time officiated in by a bonze; and every year, at the festival of the saint, the rich Chinese of Manilla assembled there in thousands, to give a series of fêtes which lasted for fifteen days. But it happened that an archbishop of Manilla, looking upon this worship offered up by Chinese gratitude as nothing but paganism, caused both the chapel and parsonage to be unroofed. These harsh measures had no other result than to admit the rain into the buildings; but the worship due to St. Nicholas still continued, and remains to this day. Perhaps this arises from the attempt to suppress it!

At present, at the period when this festival takes place—

that is, about the 6th of November every year—a delightful view presents itself. During the night large vessels may be seen, upon which are built palaces actually several stories high, terminating in pyramids, and lit up from the base to the summit. All these lights are reflected in the placid waters of the river, and seem to augment the number of the stars, whose tremulous images dance on the surface of the waters: it is an extemporised Venice! In these palaces they give themselves up to play, to smoking opium, and to the pleasures of music. The *pévété*, a species of Chinese incense, is burning everywhere and at all times in honour of St. Nicholas, who is invoked every morning by throwing into the river small square pieces of paper of various colours. St. Nicholas, however, does not make his appearance; but the fête continues for a fortnight, at the termination of which the faithful retire till the year following.

And now that the reader is acquainted with the legend of the crocodile, of the Chinese, and of the good St. Nicholas, I will resume my voyage.

I sailed on peaceably upon the Pasig, proceeding to the conquest of my new dominions, and indulging in golden dreams. I gazed on the light smoke of my cigarette, without reflecting that my dreams, my castles in the air, must evaporate like it! I soon found myself in the lake of Bay. The lake occupies an extent of thirty leagues, and I greatly admired this fine sheet of water, bounded in the distance by mountains of fantastic forms. At length I arrived at *Quinaboutasan*—this is a Tagal word, which signifies "that which is perforated." Quinaboutasan is situated on a strait, which separates the island of Talem from the continent. We stopped for an hour in the only Indian hut there was in the place, to cook some rice and take our repast.

This hut was inhabited by a very old fisherman and his wife. They were still, however, able to supply their wants by fishing. At a later period I shall have occasion to speak of old Relempago, or the " Thunderer," and to recount his history. When I was in the centre of the sheet of water which separates Talem from Jala-Jala, I came in sight of the new domain which I had so easily acquired, and I could form some opinion of my acquisition at a glance. Jala-Jala is a long peninsula, extending from north to south, in the middle of the lake of Bay. This peninsula is divided longitudinally for the space of three leagues by a chain of mountains, which diminish gradually in height till they become mere hillocks. These mountains, are easy of access, and generally covered on one side with forests, and on the other with fine pasturage, abounding with waving and flexible grass, three or four feet high, which, agitated by the breeze, resembles the waves of the sea when in motion. It is impossible to find more splendid vegetation, which is watered by pure and limpid springs that gush from the mountain heights, and roll in a meandering course to join the waters of the lake. These pasture grounds constitute Jala-Jala the greatest game preserve in the island: wild boars, deer, buffaloes, fowls, quail, snipe, pigeons of fifteen or twenty different varieties, parrots—in short all sorts of birds abound in them. The lake is equally well supplied with aquatic birds, and particularly wild ducks. Notwithstanding its extent, the island produces neither noxious nor carnivorous animals; the only things to be apprehended are the civet cat, which only preys upon birds, and the monkeys, which issue in troops from the forests to ravage the fields of maize and sugar-cane. The lake, which abounds with excellent fish, is less favoured in this respect than the land, for it contains numerous crocodiles and alligators, of such immense size that in a few moments one of them can tear a horse to pieces, and swallow it in its monstrous stomach. The accidents they occasion are frequent and terrible, and I have seen many Indians become their victims, as I shall subsequently relate. I ought, doubtless, to have begun by speaking of the human beings who inhabited the forests of Jala-Jala, but I am a sportsman, and must therefore be excused for beginning with the game.

At the time I purchased it Jala-Jala was inhabited by some Malay Indians, who lived in the woods, and cultivated a few spots of ground. During the night they carried on the trade of piracy, and gave shelter to all the banditti of the neighbouring provinces. At Manilla this country had been described to me in the most gloomy colours. According to the citizens of that place it would not be long before I fell a victim to these robbers. My adventurous disposition, however, only made all these predictions, instead of frightening me, increase my desire to visit these men, who lived in an almost savage state. As soon as I had purchased Jala-Jala, I had laid down a line of conduct for myself, the object of which was to attach to me such of the inhabitants as were the most to be dreaded. I resolved to become the friend of these banditti, and for this purpose I knew that I must go amongst them, not like a sordid and exacting landlord but like a father. For the execution of my enterprise, everything depended on the first impression that I should make on these Indians, who had become my vassals. When I had landed, I directed my steps along the borders of the lake, towards a little hamlet composed of a few cabins. I was accompanied by my faithful coachman; we were both armed with a good double-barreled gun, a brace of pistols, and a sabre. I had taken the precaution of ascertaining from some fishermen the name of the Indian to whom I should especially address myself. This man, who was the most respected amongst his countrymen, was called in the Tagal language, "*Mabutiu-Tajo*," which may be translated the "bravest of the brave" he was a thorough-paced robber, a real piratical chief a fellow that would not hesitate to commit five or six murders in one expedition; but he was brave, and with a primitive people bravery is a quality before which they bow with respect. My conference with Mabutiu-Tajo was not long. A few words were enough to win me his favour, and to make him my faithful servant during the whole time I remained at Jala-Jala. This is the manner in which I spoke to him: "You are a great villain," I said; "I am the lord of Jala-Jala. I insist on your changing your conduct; if you refuse, I shall punish you for all your misdeeds. I have occasion for a guard: will you pledge me your honour to become an honest man, and I will make you my lieutenant?"

After these few words, Alila (this was the name of the robber) continued silent for a few moments, while his countenance displayed the marks of profound reflection. I awaited his answer with considerable anxiety and doubt as to what it would be.

"Master," he at length replied, with enthusiasm, presenting me his hand, and bending one knee to the ground: "I shall be faithful to you till death!"

His answer made me happy, but I did not let him see my satisfaction.

"Well and good," I replied; "to show you that I confide in you, take this weapon, and use it only against the enemy."

I gave him a Tagal sabre, which bore the following Spanish inscription, in large letters: "*No me sacas sin rason, ni me envainas sin honor.*" "Never draw me unjustly, and never sheath me with dishonour."

I translated this legend into the Tagaloc language: Alila thought it sublime, and vowed never to deviate from it.

"When I go to Manilla," I added, "I shall procure you a handsome uniform, with epaulettes; but you must lose no time in assembling the soldiers you will have to command, and who are to form my guard. Conduct me to the house of one of your comrades whom you think most capable of obeying you as serjeant." We went some distance from his cabin to the hut of one of his friends, who almost always accompanied him in his piratical excursions. A few words like those I had spoken to my future lieutenant produced a similar influence on his comrade, and induced him to accept the rank I offered him. We occupied the day in recruiting amongst the various huts, and in the evening we had a guard of ten effective men, infantry and cavalry, a number I did not wish to exceed.

Of these I took the command as captain; and thus, as will be seen, I went promptly to work. The following day I assembled the population of the peninsula, and, surrounded by my extempore guard, I chose a situation where I wished to found a village, and a site on which I wished my own habitation to be built. I ordered the heads of families to construct their huts on an allotment which I indicated, and I directed my lieutenant to employ as many hands as possible, to quarry stones, to cut down timber for the wood-work, and to prepare everything in short for my house. Having issued my orders, I departed for Manilla, promising to return soon. When I reached home, I found them in a state of inquietude, for, as nothing had been heard of me, it was thought I had fallen a prey to the crocodiles, or a victim to the pirates. The recital of my journey, and the description I gave of Jala-Jala, far from disgusting my wife with the idea I had conceived of inhabiting that country, made her, on the contrary, impatient to visit our estate, and to establish herself there. It was, however, a farewell she was taking of the capital—of its fêtes, its assemblies, and its pleasures.

I paid a visit to the governor. My resignation had been considered as null and void: he had preserved all my places for me. I was touched by this goodness. I sincerely thanked him, but told him that I was really in earnest, that my resolution was irrevocably fixed, and that he might otherwise dispose of my employments. I added, that I only asked him for one favour, that of commanding all the local gendarmerie of the province of La Lagune, with the privilege of having a personal guard, which I would form myself. This favour was instantly granted, and a few days after I received my commission. It was not ambition that suggested to me the idea of asking for this important post, but sound reason. My object was to establish an authority for myself at Jala-Jala, and to have in my own hands the power of punishing my Indians, without recurring to the justice of the alcaid, who lived ten leagues away from my dominions.

Wishing to be comfortably settled in my new residence, I drew out a plan of my house. It consisted of a first-floor, with five bed-chambers, a large hall, a spacious drawing-room, a terrace, and bathing rooms. I agreed with a master-mason and a master carpenter for the construction of it; and having obtained arms and uniforms for my guard, I set out again. On arriving I was received with joy by my Indians. My lieutenant had punctually executed my orders. A great quantity of material was prepared, and several Indian huts were already built.

This activity gave me pleasure, as it evinced a desire for my gratification. I immediately set my labourers to work, ordering them to clear away the surrounding wood, and I soon had the pleasure of laying the foundation of my residence; I then went to Manilla. The works lasted for eight months, during which time I passed backwards and forwards continually from Manilla to Jala-Jala, and from Jala-Jala to Manilla. I had some trouble, but I was well repaid for it when I saw a village rise from the earth. My Indians constructed their huts on the places I had indicated; they had reserved a site for a church, and, until this should be built, mass was to be celebrated in the vestibule of my mansion. At length, after many journeys to and fro, which gave great uneasiness to my wife, I was enabled to inform her that the castle of Jala-Jala was ready to receive its mistress. This was a pleasing piece of intelligence, for we were soon to be no longer separated.

I quickly sold my horses, my carriages, and useless furniture, and freighted a vessel to convey to Jala-Jala all that I required. Then, having taken leave of my friends, I quitted Manilla, with the intention of not returning to it but through absolute necessity. Our journey was prosperous, and on our arrival, we found my Indians on the shore, hailing with cries of joy the welcome advent of the "*Queen of Jala-Jala*," for it was thus they called my wife.

We devoted the first days after our arrival to installing ourselves in our new residence, which it was necessary to furnish, and make both useful and agreeable; this we accordingly effected. And now that years have elapsed, and I am far removed from that period of independence and perfect liberty, I reflect on the strangeness of my destiny. My wife and I were the only white and civilised persons in the midst of a bronzed and almost savage population, and yet I felt no apprehension. I relied on my arms, on my self-possession, and on the fidelity of my guards. Anna was only aware of a part of the dangers we incurred, and her confidence in me was so great, that when by my side she knew not what it was to fear When I was well established in my house, I undertook a difficult and dangerous task, that of establishing order amongst my Indians, and organizing my little town according to the custom of the Philippine islands. The Spanish laws, with reference to the Indians, are altogether patriarchal. Every township is erected, so to speak, into a little republic. Every year a chief is elected, dependant for affairs of importance on the governor of the province, which latter, in his turn, depends on the governor of the Philippine islands. I confess that I have always considered the mode of government peculiar to the Philippines as the most convenient and best adapted for civilization. The Spaniards, at the period of their conquest, found it in full operation in the isle of Luzon.

I shall here enter into some details. Every Indian population is divided into two classes, the noble and the popular. The first is composed of all Indians who are, or have been *cabessas de barangay*, that is to say, collectors of taxes, which situation is honorary. The taxes established by the Spaniards are personal. Every Indian of more than twenty-one years of age pays, in four instalments, the annual sum of three francs; which tax is the same to the rich and the poor. At a certain period of the year, twelve of the cabessas de barangay become electors, and assembling together with some of the old inhabitants of the township, they elect, by ballot, three of their number, whose names are forwarded to the governor of the Philippines. The latter chooses from amongst these names whichever he pleases, and confides to him for one year the functions of *gobernadorcillo*, or deputy-governor. To distinguish him from the other Indians, the deputy-governor bears a gold-headed cane, with which he has a right to strike such of his fellow-citizens as may have committed slight faults. His functions partake at the same time of those of mayor, justice of the peace, and examining magistrate. He watches over good order and public tranquillity; he decides, without appeal, suits and differences of no higher importance than sixteen piasters (£3 6s. 8d.). He also institutes criminal suits of high importance, but there his power ceases. The documents connected with these suits are sent by him to the governor of the province, who, in his turn, transmits them to the royal court of Manilla. The court gives judgment, and the alcaid carries it into execution. When the election for deputy-governor takes place, the assembled electors choose all the officials who are to act under him. These are alguazils, whose number is proportioned to the population; two witnesses, or assistants, who are charged with the confirmation of the acts of the deputy-governor—for without their presence and sanction his acts would be considered null and void; a *jouès de palma*, or palm judge, with the functions of rural guard; a vaccinator, bound to be always furnished with vaccine matter, for new-born children; and a schoolmaster, charged with public instruction; finally, a sort of gendarmerie, to watch banditti and the state of the roads within the precincts of the commune and the neighbouring lands. Men, grown up, and without employment, form a civic guard, who watch over the safety of the village. This guard indicates the hours of the night, by blows struck upon a large piece of hollow wood. There is in each town a parochial house, which is called Casa Réal, where the deputy-governor resides. He is bound to afford hospitality to all travellers who pass through the town, which hospitality is like that of the Scotch mountaineers—it is given, but never sold. During two or three days, the traveller has a right to lodging, in which he is supplied with a mat, a pillow, salt, vinegar, wood, cooking vessels, and—paying for the same—all descriptions of food necessary for his subsistence. If, on his departure, he should even require horses and guides to continue his journey, they are procured for him. With respect to the prices of provisions, in order to prevent the abuses so frequent amongst us, a large placard is fixed up in every Casa Réal, containing a tariff of the market prices of meat, poultry, fish, fruit, &c. In no case whatever can the deputy-governor exact any remuneration for the trouble he is at.

Such were the measures that I wished to adopt, and which, it is true, possessed advantages and disadvantages. The greatest inconvenience attending them was undoubtedly that of placing myself in a state of dependence upon the deputy-governor, whose functions gave him a certain right, for I was his administrator. It is true that my rank, as commandant of all the gendarmerie of the province, shielded me from any injustice that might be contemplated against me. I knew very well that, beyond military service, I could inflict no punishment on my men without the intervention of the deputy-governor; but I had sufficiently studied the Indian character to know that I could only rule it by the most perfect justice and a well-understood severity. But whatever were the difficulties I foresaw, without any apprehension of the troubles and dangers of every description that I should have to surmount, I proceeded straightforward towards the object I had traced out for myself. The road was sterile and encumbered with rocks; but I entered

Tagal Indians pounding rice.

upon it with courage, and I succeeded in obtaining over the Indians such an influence, that they ultimately obeyed my voice as they would that of a parent. The character of the Tagaloc is extremely difficult to define. Lavater and Gall would have been very much embarrassed by it; for both physiognomy and craniology would be, perhaps, equally at a loss amongst the Philippines.

The natural disposition of the Tagal Indian is a mixture of vices and virtues, of good and bad qualities. A worthy priest has said, when speaking of them: "They are great children and must be treated as if they were little ones."

It is really curious to trace, and still more so to read, the moral portrait of a native of the Philippine islands. The Indian keeps his word, and yet—will it be believed?—he is a liar. Anger he holds in horror, he compares it to madness; and even prefers drunkenness, which, however, he despises. He will not hesitate to use the dagger to avenge himself for injustice; but what he can least submit to is an insult, even when merited. When he has committed a fault, he may be punished with a flogging; this he receives without a murmur, but he cannot brook an insult. He is brave, generous, and a fatalist. The profession of a robber, which he willingly exercises, is agreeable to him, on account of the life of liberty and adventure it affords, and not because it may lead to riches. Generally speaking, the Tagalocs are good fathers and good husbands, both these qualities being inherent. Horribly jealous of their wives, but not in the least of the honour of their daughters; and it matters little if the women they marry have committed errors previous to their union. They never ask for a dowry, they themselves provide it, and make presents to the parents of their brides. They dislike cowards, but willingly attach themselves to the man who is brave enough to face danger. Play is their ruling passion, and they delight in the combats of animals, especially in cock-fighting. This is a brief compendium of the character of the people I was about to govern. My first care was to become master of myself. I made a firm resolution never to allow a gesture of impatience to escape me, in their presence, even in the most critical moments, and to preserve at all times unshaken calmness and *sang-froid*. I soon learned that it was dangerous to listen to the communications that were made to me, which might lead me to the commission of injustice, as had already happened under the following circumstances.

Two Indians came one day to lodge a complaint against one of their comrades, living at some leagues' distance from Jala-Jala. These informers accused him of having stolen cattle. After I had heard all they had to say, I set off with my guard to seize upon the accused, and brought him to my residence. There I endeavoured to make him confess his crime, but he denied it, and said he was innocent. It was in vain I promised him if he would tell the truth to grant him his pardon, for he persisted even in the presence of his accusers. Persuaded, however, that he was telling me falsehoods, and disgusted with his obstinacy in denying a fact which had been sworn to me, with every appearance of sincerity, I ordered him to be tied upon a bench, and receive a dozen strokes of a whip. My orders were executed; but the culprit denied the charge, as he had done before. This dogged perseverance irritated me, and I caused another correction to be administered to him the same as the first. The unfortunate man bore his punishment with unshaken courage: but in the midst of his sufferings he exclaimed, in penetrating accents: "Oh! sir, I swear to you that I am innocent; but, as you will not believe me, take me into your house. I will be a faithful servant, and you will soon have proofs that I am the victim of an infamous calumny." These words affected me. I reflected that this unfortunate man was, perhaps, not guilty after all. I began to fear I had been deceived, and had unknowingly committed an act of injustice. I felt that private enmity might have led these two witnesses to make a false declaration, and thus induce me to punish an innocent man. I ordered him to be untied. "The proof you demand," I said to him, "is easily tried. If you are an honest man, I shall be a father to you; but if you deceive me, do not expect any pity from me. From this moment you shall be one of my guard; my lieutenant will provide you with arms." He thanked me earnestly, and his countenance lit up with sudden joy. He was installed in my guard. Oh! human justice! how fragile, and how often unintelligible art thou! Some time after this event, I learnt that Bazilio de la Cruz—this was the name of the man—was innocent The two wretches who had denounced him had fled, to avoid the chastisement they merited. Bazilio kept his promise, and during my residence at Jala-Jala he served me faithfully and without malice or ill-will. This fact made a lively impression on me; and I vowed that for the future I would inflict no punishment without being sure of the truth of the charge alleged. I have religiously kept this vow—at least I think so; for I have never since ordered a single application of the whip until after the culprit had confessed his crime.

I have before said that I had expressed a wish to have a church built in my village, not only from a religious feeling, but as a means of civilisation: I was particularly desirous of having a curate at Jala-Jala. With this view I requested Monseigneur Hilarion, the archbishop, whose physician I had been, and with whom I was on terms of friendship, to send me a clergyman of my acquaintance, and who was at that time unemployed. I had, however, much difficulty in obtaining this nomination. "Father Miguel de San-Francisco," the archbishop replied, "is a violent man, and very headstrong: you will never be able to live with him." I persisted, however; and as perseverance always produces some result, I at length succeeded in having him appointed curate at Jala-Jala. Father Miguel was of Japanese and Malay descent. He was young, strong, brave, and very capable of assisting me in the difficult circumstances that might occur; as, for example, if it were

Father Miguel.

necessary to defend ourselves against banditti. Indeed I must say that, in spite of the anticipations, and I may add the prejudices, of my honourable friend the archbishop, I kept him with me during the whole time of my abode at Jala-Jala, and never had the slightest difference with him. I can only reproach him with one thing to be regretted, which is that he did not preach sufficiently to his flock. He gave them only one sermon annually, and then his discourse was always the same, and divided into two parts: the first was in Spanish, for our edification, and the second in Tagaloc, for the Indians. Ah! how many men have I since met with who might well imitate the worthy curate of Jala-Jala! To the observations I sometimes made he would reply: "Let me follow my own course, and fear nothing. So many words are not necessary to make a good Christian." Perhaps he was right. Since my departure from the place the good priest is dead, bearing with him to the tomb the regret of all his parishioners.

As may be seen, I was at the beginning of my labour of civilisation. Anna assisted me with all her heart, and with all her intelligence, and no fatigue disheartened her. She taught the young girls to love that virtue which she practised so well herself. She furnished them with clothes, for at this period the young girls from ten to twelve years of age were still as naked as savages. Father Miguel de San Francisco was charged with the mission more especially belonging to his sacred character. The more readily to disseminate through the colony that instruction which is the beneficent parent of civilisation, the young people were divided into squads of four at a time, and went by turns to pass a fortnight at the parsonage. There they learned a little Spanish, and were moulded to the customs of a world which had been hitherto unknown to them. I superintended everything in general. I occupied myself in works of agriculture, and giving proper instruction to the shepherds who kept the flocks I had purchased to make use of my pasturage. I was also the mediator of all the differences which arose amongst my colonists. They preferred rather to apply to me than to the deputy-governor; and I succeeded at last in obtaining over them the influence I desired. One portion of my time, and this was not the least busy, was occupied in driving the banditti from my residence and its vicinity. Sometimes I set off for this purpose before daybreak and did not return until night; and then I always found my wife good, affectionate, and devoted to me: her reception repaid me for the labours of the day. Oh, felicity almost perfect! I have never forgotten you! Happy period! which has left indelible traces in my memory, you are always present to my thoughts! I have grown old, but my heart has ever continued young in recollecting you.

In our long chit-chat of an evening we recounted to each other the labours of the day, and everything that occurred to us. This was the season of sweet mutual confidence. Hours too soon vanished, alas! Fugitive moments, you will never return! It was also the time when I gave audience; real bed of justice, imitated from St. Louis, and thrown open to my subjects. The door of my mansion admitted all the Indians who had anything to communicate to me. Seated with my wife at a great round table, I listened, as I took my tea, to all the requests that were made to me, all the claims that were laid before me. It was during these audiences that I issued my sentences. My guards brought the culprits before me, and, without departing from my ordinary calmness, I admonished them for the faults they had committed; but I always recollected the error I had committed in my sentence against poor Bazilio, and I was, therefore, very circumspect I first listened to the witnesses; but I never condemned until I heard the culprit say:

"What would you have, sir? It was my destiny. I could not prevent myself from doing what I did."

"Every fault merits chastisement," I would reply; "but choose between the deputy-governor and me—by which do you wish to be chastised?"

The reply was always the same.

"Kill me, if you will, master; but do not give me up to my own countrymen."

I awarded the punishment, and it was inflicted by my guards. When this was over, I presented the Indian with a cigar, as a token of pardon. I uttered a few kind words to him to induce him not to commit any fresh faults, and he went away without bearing any malice to his judge. I had, perhaps, been severe, but I had been just; that was enough. The order and discipline I had established were a great support for me in the minds of the Indians; they gave me a positive influence over them. My calmness, my firmness. and my justice—those three great qualities without which no government is possible—easily satisfied these natures, still untrained and unsophiscated. But one thing, however, disquieted them. Was I brave? This is what they were ignorant of, and frequently asked of one another. They spurned the idea of being commanded by a man who might not be intrepid in the face of danger. I had indeed made several expeditions against banditti, but they had produced no result, and would not serve as proofs of my bravery in the eyes of the Indians. I very well knew that they would form their definite opinion upon me from my conduct in the first perilous extremity we should encounter together. I was therefore determined to undertake anything, that I might show myself at least equal to the best and bravest of all my Indians: everything was comprised in that. I felt the imperious necessity of showing myself not only equal but superior in the struggle, by preserving my self-possession.

An opportunity at length offered.

The Indians look upon buffalo hunting as the most dangerous of all their wild sports, and my guards often said they would rather stand naked at twenty paces from the muzzle of a carbine than at the same distance from a wild buffalo. The difference they said is this, that the ball of a carbine may only wound, but the horn of a buffalo is sure to kill. I took advantage of the terror they had of this animal, and one day declared, with the utmost possible coolness, my intention to hunt one. They then made use of all their eloquence to turn me from my project; they gave me a very picturesque, but a very discouraging description of the dangers and difficulties I should have to encounter, especially as I was not accustomed to that sort of warfare,—and such a combat is, in fact, a struggle for life or death. But I would listen to nothing. I had spoken the word: I would not discuss the point, and I looked upon all their counsels as null and void. My decision was right; for these kind counsels, these frightful pictures of the dangers I was about to incur, had no other object than to entrap me; they had concerted amongst themselves to judge of my courage by my acceptance or refusal of the combat. My only answer was to give orders for the hunt. I took great care that my wife should not be informed of our excursion, and I set off, accompanied by half a score Indians, nearly all of whom were armed with muskets. Buffalo hunting is different in the mountains from what it is in the plains. On the plain one only requires a good horse, with address and agility in throwing the lasso; but in the mountains it requires something more: and, above all, the most extraordinary coolness and self-possession are essentially necessary.

This is the way in which it is done: the hunter takes a gun on which he can depend, and places himself in such a position that the buffalo must see him on issuing from the wood. The moment the animal sees him, he rushes on him with the utmost velocity, breaking, rending, and trampling under foot every obstacle to the fury of his charge; he rushes on as if about to crush the enemy, then stops within some paces for a few seconds, and presents his sharp and threatening horns. This is the moment that the hunter should fire, and lodge his ball in the forehead of the foe. If unfortunately his gun misses fire, or if his coolness fails him, if his hand trembles, or his aim is bad, he is lost—Providence alone can save him! This was, perhaps, the fate that awaited me; but I was resolved to tempt this cruel proof, and I went forward with intrepidity—perhaps to death. We at length arrived on the skirts of an extensive wood, in which we felt assured there were buffaloes, and here we halted. I was sure of my gun, and I conceived I was equally so of my self-possession; I therefore determined that the hunt should be conducted as if I had been a simple Indian. I placed myself at the spot where it was fully expected that the animal would come out, and I forbade anyone to remain near me. I ordered everyone to his proper place, and I then stood alone on the open ground, about two hundred paces from the borders of the forest, to await an enemy that would show me no mercy if I missed him. It is, I confess, a solemn moment, when one stands between life and death by the more or less certainty of a gun, or the greater or less steadiness of the arm that holds it. I was, however, perfectly tranquil. When all were at their posts two hunters entered the forest, having first thrown off some of their clothing, the more readily to climb up trees in case of danger: they had no other arms than a cutlass, and were accompanied by the dogs. A dead silence continued for upwards of half-an-hour; everyone listening for the slightest noise, but nothing was heard. The buffalo continues a long time frequently without betraying his lair; but at the end of the half-hour we heard the repeated barking of the dogs, and the shouts of the hunters: the animal was aroused from his cover. He defended himself for some time against the dogs, till at length, becoming furious, he sprang forward with a bound towards the skirts of the forest. In a few minutes after, I heard the crashing of the branches and the young trees that the buffalo rent asunder in the terrible velocity of his course. His advance could only be compared to the galloping of several horses—to the rushing noise of some frightful monster—or, I might almost say, of some furious and diabolical being. Down he came like an avalanche; and at this moment, I confess, I experienced such lively emotions that my heart beat with extraordinary rapidity. Was it not death—aye, and frightful death—that was perhaps approaching me? Suddenly the buffalo made his appearance. He stopped for an instant; gazed, as if frightened, around him; sniffed up the air of the plain which extended in the distance; then, with distended nostrils, head bent, and horns projected, he rushed towards me, terrible and furious. The moment was come. If I had longed for an opportunity of showing off my courage and *sang-froid* to the Indians, these two precious qualities were now put to a severe test. There I was, face to face with the peril I had courted; the dilemma was one of the most decided and unavoidable that could possibly be: conqueror or conquered, there must be a victim—the buffalo or me, and we were both equally disposed to defend ourselves.

It would be difficult for me to state exactly what was passing in my mind, during the brief period which the buffalo took in clearing the distance that lay between us. My heart, so vividly agitated while the ferocious animal was rushing through the forest, now beat no longer. My eyes were fixed upon him, my gaze was rivetted on his forehead in such a manner that I could see nothing else. My mind was concentrated on one object alone, in which I was so absorbed, that I could actually hear nothing, though the dogs were still bark-

LA GIRONIERE'S FIRST SHOT AT A BUFFALO.—*Page* 93.

ing at a short distance, as they followed their prey. At length, the buffalo lowered his head, presented his sharp-pointed horns, stopped for a moment, then, with a sudden plunge, he rushed upon me, and I fired. My ball pierced his skull, and I was half saved. The animal fell within a pace of me, like a mass of rock, so loud, and so heavy. I planted my foot between his two horns, and was preparing to fire my second barrel, when a long and hollow bellowing indicated that my victory was complete—the monster had breathed his last sigh. My Indians then came up. Their joy was succeeded by admiration; they were in ecstacy; I was everything they could wish for. All their doubts had vanished with the smoke of my rifle, when, with steady aim, I had shot the buffalo. I was brave; I had won their confidence; I had stood the test. My victim was cut up in pieces, and borne in triumph to the village As the

Horns of the Buffalo

victor, I took his horns; they were six feet long. I have since deposited them in the museum of Nantes. The Indians, those imaginative beings, called me thenceforward, "*Malamit Oulou*," Tagal words, which signify "cool head."

I must confess, without vanity, that the proof to which my Indians had subjected me was sufficiently serious to give them a decided opinion of my courage, and to satisfy them that a Frenchman was as brave as themselves. The habit I subsequently acquired of hunting convinced me that but little danger is really incurred when the weapon is a good one, and the self-possession does not fail. Once every month I indulged in this exercise, which imparts such lively sensations; and I recognised the facility with which one may lodge a ball in a plain surface, a few inches in diameter, and at a few paces distance. But it is no less true that our first huntings were very dangerous. Once only I permitted a Spaniard named Ocampo to accompany us. I had taken the precaution to station two Indians at his side; but when I quitted them to take up my own post, he imprudently sent them away, and soon after, the buffalo started from the wood, and rushed upon him. He fired both his barrels, and missed the animal; we heard the reports and ran towards him, but it was too late! Ocampo was no longer in existence. The buffalo had gored him through and through, and his body was ploughed up with frightful wounds. But no such accident ever took place again; for when strangers came to witness our buffalo hunts, I made them get up in a tree, or on the crest of a mountain, where they might remain as spectators of the combat, without taking any part in it, or being exposed to any danger.

And now that I have described buffalo hunting in the mountains, I must return to my colonising labours.

My House at Jala-Jala.

CHAPTER V.

Description of my House at Jala-Jala—Storms, Gales, and Earthquakes—Reforming the Banditti — Card-playing — Tagal Cock-fighting — Skirmishes with Robbers — Courage of my Wife — Our Domestic Happiness — Visits from Europeans—Their Astonishment at our Civilisation—Visit to a Sick Friend at Manilla—Tour through the Provinces of the Ilocos and Pangasinan Indians—My Reception by the Tinguians—Their Appearance and Habits—Manners and Customs—Indian Fête at Laganguilan y Madalag—Horrible Ceremonies to Celebrate a Victory—Songs and Dances—Our Night-watch—We Explore our Cabin—Discovery of a Secret Well—Tomb of the Tinguian Indians.

AS I have previously said, my house possessed every comfort that could possibly be desired. It was built of hewn stone, so that in case of an attack it could serve as a small fortress. The front overlooked the lake, which bathed with its clear and limpid waters the verdant shore within a hundred steps from my dwelling; the back part looked upon woods and hills, where the vegetation was rich and plentiful. From our window we could gaze upon those grand majestic scenes which a beautiful tropical sky so frequently affords. At times, on a dark night, the summits of the hills suddenly shone with a weak.faint light, which increased by degrees; then the bright moon gradually appeared, and illuminated the tops of the mountains, as large beacon-fires would have done; then again, calm, peaceful, and serene, she reflected her soft poetic light over the bosom of the lake, as tranquil and unruffled as herself. It was indeed an imposing sight. Towards evening, Nature at times showed herself in all her commanding splendour, infusing a secret terror into the very soul. Everything bore evidence of the sacred influence of the Divine Creator. At a short distance from our house we could perceive a mountain, the base of which was in the lake and the summit in the clouds. This mountain served as a lightning conductor to Jala-Jala: it attracted the thunder. Frequently heavy black clouds, charged with electricity, gathered over this elevated point, looking like other mountains trying to overturn it; then a storm began, the thunder roared tremendously, the rain fell in torrents; every minute frightful claps were heard, and the total darkness was scarcely broken by the lightning that flashed in long streams of fire, dashing from the top and sides of the mountain enormous blocks of rock, that were hurled into the lake with a fearful crash. It was an admirable exemplification of the power of the Almighty! Soon the calm was restored, the rain ceased, the clouds disappeared, the fragrant air bore on its yet damp wings the perfume of the flowers and aromatic plants, and Nature resumed her ordinary stillness. Hereafter I shall have occasion to speak of other events that happened at certain periods, and were still more alarming, for they lasted twelve hours.

These were gales of wind, called in the Chinese seas *Tay-Foung*. At several periods of the year, particularly at the moment of the change of the monsoon,* we beheld still more terrifying phenomena than our storms—I allude to the earthquakes. These fearful convulsions of nature present a very different aspect in the country from what they do in cities. If in towns the earth begins to quake, everywhere we hear a terrible noise; the edifices give way, and are ready to fall down; the inhabitants rush out of their houses, run along the streets, which they encumber, and try to escape. The screams of frightened children and women bathed in tears are blended with those of the distracted men; all are on their knees, with clasped hands, their looks raised to Heaven, imploring its mercy with sobbing voices. Everything totters, is agitated; all dread death, and terror becomes general. In the country it is totally different, and a hundred times more imposing and terrific. For instance, in Jala-Jala, at the approach of one of these phenomena, a profound, even mournful stillness pervades nature. The wind no longer blows; not a breeze nor even a gentle zephyr is perceptible. The sun, though cloudless, darkens, and spreads around a sepulchral light. The atmosphere is burdened with heavy and sultry vapours. The earth is in labour. The frightened animals quietly seek shelter from the catastrophe they foresee. The ground shakes; soon it trembles under their feet. The trees move, the mountains quake upon their foundations, and their summits appear ready to tumble down. The waters of the lake quit their bed, and inundate the country. Still louder roaring than that produced by the thunder is heard: the earth

* During six months the winds blow continually from the north-east, and during the other six months from the north-west: these two periods are termed north-east monsoon and north-west monsoon.

quivers; everywhere its motion is simultaneously felt. But after this the convulsion ceases, everything revives. The mountains are again firm upon their foundations, and become motionless; the waters of the lake return by degrees to their proper reservoir; the heavens are purified and resume their brilliant light, and the soft breeze fans the air; the

Herd of Wild Buffaloes.

wild buffaloes again scour the plain, and other animals quit the dens in which they had concealed themselves; the earth has resumed her stillness, and nature recovered her accustomed imposing calm.

I have not sought to enter upon those minute descriptions, too tedious generally for the reader; I only wished to give an idea of the various panoramas that were unfolded to our eyes whilst at Jala-Jala.

I now return to the details of my ordinary life.

As I had killed a wild buffalo when hunting, I had given sufficient proofs of my skill, and my Indians were devoted to me, because they had confidence in me. Nothing more now pre-occupied me, and I spent my time in superintending some necessary alterations. Shortly the woods and forests adjoining my domain were cut down, and replaced by extensive fields of indigo and rice. I stocked the hills with horned cattle, and a fine troop of horses with delicate limbs and haughty mien; I also succeeded in dispersing the banditti from Jala-Jala. I must say a great many of them abandoned their wandering sinful lives; I received them on my land, and made good husbandmen of them. How was it that I had collected such a number of recruits? In a strange manner, I will admit, and worthy of relating, as it will show how an Indian allows himself to be influenced and guided, when he has confidence in a man whom he looks upon as his superior. I frequently walked in the forests alone, with my gun under my arm. Suddenly a bandit would spring out, as if by enchantment, from behind a tree, armed from top to toe, and advance towards me.

"Master," said he to me, putting one knee to the ground, "I will be an honest man; take me under your protection!"

I asked him his name; if he had been marked out by the high court of justice, I would answer him severely:

"Withdraw, and never present yourself again before me; I cannot forgive you, and if I meet you again, I must do my duty."

If he was unknown to me, I would kindly say to him.

"Follow me."

I would take him home, and then tell him to lay down his arms; and after having preached to him, and exhorted him to persist in his resolution, I would point out to him the spot in the village where he might build his cabin, and, in order to encourage him, I would advance him some money to support himself until he became transformed from a bandit into an agriculturist. I congratulated myself each day on having left an open door to repentance, since by my cares I restored to an honest and laborious life, people who had gone astray and been perverted. I endeavoured also to persuade the Indians to abandon their vicious wild customs, without being too severe towards them; to obtain much from them I knew it was necessary to give way a little. The Indians are passionately fond of cards and cock-fighting, as I have said before; therefore, in order not to debar them entirely from these pleasures, I allowed them to play at cards three times a year—the day of the village festival, upon my wife's birthday, and upon my own. Woe to the one who was caught playing out of the times prescribed above; he was severely punished. As to the cock-fights, I allowed them on Sundays and holidays, after Divine service. For this purpose I had public arenas built. In these arenas, in presence of two judges, whose decrees were without appeal, the spectators laid heavy wagers. There is nothing more curious than to witness a cock-fight. The two proud animals, purposely chosen and trained for the day of the contest, come upon the battle-field armed with long, sharp, steel spurs They bear themselves erect; their deportment is bold and warlike; they raise their heads, and beat their sides with heir wings, the feathers of which spread in the form of the proud peacock's fan. They pace the arena haughtily, raising their armed legs cautiously, and darting angry looks at each other, like two old warriors in armour ready to fight before the eyes of an assembled court. Their impatience is violent, their courage impetuous; shortly the two adversaries fall upon and

Tagal cock-fighting

attack each other with equal fury; the sharp weapons they wear inflict dreadful wounds, but these intrepid combatants appear not to feel the cruel effects. Blood flows; the champions only appear the more animated. The one that is getting weak raises his courage at the idea of victory; if he draw back, it is only to recruit his strength, to rush with more ardour than ever upon the enemy he wishes to subdue. At length when their fate is decided, when one of the heroes, covered with blood and wounds, falls a victim, or runs away, he is declared vanquished, and the battle is ended.

The Indians assist with a sort of ferocious joy at this amusement. Their attention is so captivated by it that they do not utter a word, but follow with particular care the most minute details of the conflict. Almost all of them train up a cock, and treat him for several years with comical tenderness, when one reflects that this animal, taken as much care of as a child, is destined by its master to perish the first day it fights. I also found that it was necessary to provide some amusement compatible with the tastes, manners, and habits of my former bandits, who had led for so long a space of time such a wandering vagabond life. For this purpose I allowed hunting on all parts of my estate, conditionally, however, that I should take beforehand, as tithe, a quarter of any stag or wild boar they should kill. I do not think that ever a sportsman—one of those men reclaimed from the paths of vice to those of virtue—failed in this engagement, or endeavoured to steal any game. I have often received seven or eight haunches of venison in a day, and those who brought them were delighted to be able to offer them to me.

The church I had laid the foundation of was progressing rapidly; the population of the township was daily increasing; and everything succeeded according to my wishes. I had still occasional difficulties with the hardened robbers who surrounded me; but I pursued them without intermission, for it was to my interest to remove them from the neighbourhood of my residence. Frequently they annoyed me by the alarms that they gave us. These resolute, determined men arrived in gangs to

Tagal Indians.

besiege our house. My guards surrounded me, and we occasionally fought skirmishes, which always terminated in our favour. Providence has unfathomable secrets. I was never struck by a ball from a bandit. I bear the scars of seventeen wounds; but these wounds were made with naked blades. It could be said of me, as in I know not which Scotch ballad: "Did not the Devil's soldiers pass through the balls, instead of the balls passing through them" Yet I have often been fired at; sometimes the barrel of a gun has been pointed at my chest, and that at a few paces from me. My clothes have been torn by the bullet, but my body has always escaped harm.

One morning I was cautioned to put myself on my guard, because some banditti had met together at a few leagues from my house, and intended attacking it. Hearing this, I armed my people, and set out to meet the band that was coming to assail me, so as to anticipate their attack. At the place that had been indicated to me I found nobody, and passed the day in exploring the neighbourhood, in hopes of meeting the bandits, but my search was useless. Suddenly the thought struck me that a secret enemy had imposed upon me, and that, at the moment I was going to face imaginary danger, perhaps my house I had left would be suddenly attacked. I trembled —I shivered all over. I gallopped off, and reached home in the middle of the night. My fears were but too well-founded. I had fallen into a snare. I found my servants armed, watching, with my wife at their head. "What are you doing here?" I exclaimed, going up to her. "I am keeping watch," she replied, with great presence of mind; "I was told that the advice given to you was false; that you would not find the robbers where you expected, and that, during your absence, they would come here." This act of heroism proved to me what courage and energy God had given to a woman apparently so delicate. The banditti did not attack us: was there not some guardian angel watching over my dwelling?

We were more than a year at Jala-Jala without seeing a European. One would have thought that we had withdrawn ourselves entirely from the civilised world, and that we were going to live for ever with the Indians. Our mountains had so bad a reputation, that nobody dared expose themselves to the thousand dangers they feared to encounter in the locality. We were therefore alone, yet still very happy. It was, perhaps, the most pleasant time I spent in my life. I was living with a beloved and loving wife; the good work I had undertaken was performed under my eyes; the comfort and happiness, the natural results of such good work, spread themselves among my vassals, who daily became more and more devoted to me. How could I have regretted quitting the pleasures and entertainments of a town, where those diversions and pleasures are bought by lies, hypocrisy, and deceit—those three vices oı civilised society? However, the terror spread around by the banditti was not great enough to keep away the Europeans entirely; and one morning some people,* mad enough to dare to visit a mad man—such was the name given to me at Manilla, when I left to go and live in the country—came to see me, armed to their very teeth. The surprise of these venturesome visitors is impossible to be described, when they found us at Jala-Jala, calm, and in perfect safety. Their astonishment increased when they went entirely through our colony; and on their return to town they gave such an account of our retreat, and of the entertainments they found there, that shortly after we received more visits, and I had not only to give hospitality to friends, but likewise to strangers. If, now and then, our affairs compelled us to go to Manilla, we very soon came back to our mountains and forests, for there only Anna and myself were happy. Very great reasons alone could induce us to leave our pleasant abode; however, a slight event occurred that obliged us to quit it for a short time. I was informed that one of my friends, who had acted as witness to my marriage, was seriously ill.† What the greatest pleasure, the most heartfelt joy, the most splendid banquet, could not obtain from me, friendship exacted. At this sad intelligence I determined at once upon going to Manilla, to give my advice to the sick man, whose family had solicited my aid; and as my absence might be

* At their head was Don Josè Fuentès, my constant friend.

† Don Simon Fernandez, *Oidor* at the Court Royal.

Ilocos Indians.

prolonged, I packed up my things, and we left, our hearts sadder than ever at having to quit Jala-Jala on so melancholy an errand. Upon my arrival there, I was told that my friend had been taken from Manilla to Boulacan, a province to the north of that town, where it was hoped the country air would hasten his recovery. I left Anna at her sister's, and went off to join Don Simon, whom I found convalescent; my presence was almost useless, and the journey I had made resulted in shaking affectionately my former comrade by the hand, whom I would not leave until convinced that he was entirely recovered.

In order to utilise my time, I decided upon making a tour to the north into the provinces of Ilocos and Pangasinan. I had my reasons for so doing: I wished, if possible, to make an excursion to the Tinguians and Igorrots, wild populations, who were much talked of, but little known. I wished to study them myself. I took the precaution not to confide this idea to anybody, for then, indeed, people would not have known what name to give my folly. I made my preparations, and set out with my faithful lieutenant, Alila, who never left me, and who was justly styled *Mabouti-Tao*. We were mounted upon good horses, that carried us along like gazelles to Vigan, the chief town of the province of South Ilocos, where we left the animals. From there we took a guide, who conducted us on foot to the east, close to a small river called Abra (opening). This river is the only issue by which we could penetrate to the Tinguians. It winds around high mountains of basalt; its sides are steep; its bed is encumbered with immense blocks of rock, fallen from the sides of the mountains, which render it impossible to walk along its banks. To reach the Tinguians, it is necessary to have recourse to a slight skiff, that can easily pass through the current and the most shallow parts. My guide and my lieutenant soon contrived to make a small raft of bamboos; when it was finished we embarked, Alila and myself, our guide refusing to accompany us. After much trouble and fatigue, casting ourselves often into the water to draw our raft along, we at length got clear of the first range of mountains, and perceived, in a small plain, the first Tinguian village. When we reached there we got out, and went towards the huts we had distinguished in the distance. I allow it was acting rather foolishly to go and thus expose ourselves, in the midst of a colony of ferocious and cruel men whose language we did not know; but I relied upon my usual good fortune. I will add that I had taken divers objects with me to give as presents, trusting to meet some inhabitant speaking the Tagaloc language. I walked on, then, without troubling myself about what would become of us. In a few minutes we reached the nearest cabins, and the inhabitants gave us at first an unwelcome reception. Frightened at seeing us approach, they advanced towards us, armed with hatchets and spears; we waited for them without recoiling in the least. I spoke to them by signs, and showed them some necklaces of glass beads, to make them understand we were friendly disposed. They deliberated among themselves, and when they had held their consultation, they beckoned us to follow them. We obeyed. They led us to their chief, who was an old man. My generosity was greater towards him than it had been to his subjects. He appeared so delighted with my presents, that he immediately put us at our ease, by making us understand that we had nothing to fear, and that he took us under his special protection.

This pleasing reception encouraged us.

I then set about examining with attention the men, women, and children who surrounded us, and who seemed as much astonished as ourselves. My amazement was very great when I beheld tall men, slightly bronzed, with straight hair, regular features, aquiline noses, and really handsome, elegant women. Was I really among savages? I should rather have thought I was among the inhabitants of the south of France, had it not been for the costume and language. The only clothing the men wore was a sash, and a sort of a turban, made out of the bark of the fig tree. They were armed, as they always are, with a long spear, a small hatchet, and a shield. The women also wore a sash, and a small narrow apron that came down to their knees. Their heads were ornamented with pearls, coral beads, and pieces of gold, twisted among their hair; the upper parts of their hands were painted blue; their wrists adorned with interwoven bracelets, spangled with glass beads—these bracelets reached the elbow, and formed a kind of half-plaited sleeve. On this subject I learnt a remarkable fact. These interwoven bracelets squeeze the arm very much; they are put on when the women are quite young, and they prevent the development of the flesh to the advantage of the wrist and hand, which swell and become dreadfully big; this is a mark of beauty with the Tinguians, as a small foot is with the Chinese, and a small waist with the European ladies. I was quite astonished to find myself in the midst of this population, where there was no reason whatsoever to be alarmed. One thing only annoyed me; it was the odour that these people spread around them, which could be smelt even at a distance However, the men and women are cleanly, for they are in the habit of bathing twice daily. I attributed the disagreeable smell to their sash and turban, which they never leave off, but allow to fall into rags. I remarked that the reception given me by the chief gained us the good-will of all the inhabitants, and I accepted, without hesitation, the hospitality proffered us. This was the only means of studying well the manners and customs of my new hosts.

The territory occupied by the Tinguians is situated about 17 degrees north latitude, and 27 degrees west longitude; it is divided into seventeen villages. Each family possesses two habitations, one for the day and the other for the night. The abode for the day is a small cabin, made of bamboos and straw, in the same style as most Indian huts; the one for the night is smaller, and perched upon great posts, or on the top of a tree, about sixty or eighty feet above the ground. This height surprised me, but I understood this precaution when I knew that thus, under shelter at night, the Tinguians are saved from the nocturnal attacks of the Guinanès, their mortal enemies, and defend themselves with the stones which they throw from the tops of the trees.* In the middle of each village there is a large shed, in which are held the assemblies, festivities, and public ceremonies. I had been already two days in the village of Palan (this was the name of the place where I stopped at), when the chiefs received a message from the small town of Laganguilan y Madalag, that lies far off to the east. By this message the chiefs were informed that the inhabitants of this district had fought a battle, and that they had been victorious.

The inhabitants of Palan hearing this news screamed with joy; it was quite a tumult when they heard that a fête would be given in commemoration of the success at Laganguilan y Madalag. All wished to be present—men, women, children; all desired to go to it. But the chiefs chose a certain number of warriors, some women, and a great many young girls: they made their preparations and set out. It was too favourable an opportunity for me not to avail myself of it, and I earnestly begged my hosts to allow me to accompany them. They consented, and the same night we set out on our journey, being in all thirty in number. The men wore their arms, which are composed of a hatchet, that they call *aligua*, a sharp-pointed spear of bamboo, and a shield; the women were muffled up in their finest ornaments. I remarked that these garments were cotton materials, of showy colours. We walked one behind another, according to the custom of the savages. We went

* The most bitter enemies of the Tinguians are a race of cruel, blood-thirsty savages, who inhabit the interior of the mountains. They have also to fear the Igorrots, who live nearer, but who are less savage.

through many villages, the inhabitants of which were also going to the fête; we crossed over mountains, forests, torrents, and at last, at break of day, we reached Laganguilan y Madalag. This small town was the scene of much rejoicing. On all sides the sound of the gong and tom-tom were heard. The first of these instruments is of a Chinese shape; the second is in the form of a sharp cone, covered over at the bottom with a deer's skin.

Towards eleven o'clock, the chiefs of the town, followed by all the population, directed their steps towards the large shed. There everyone took his place on the ground, each party, headed by its chiefs, occupying a place marked out for it beforehand. In the middle of a circle formed by the chiefs of the warriors were large vessels, full of *basi*, a beverage made with the fermented juice of the sugar-cane; and four hideous heads of Guinans entirely disfigured—these were the trophies of the victory. When all the assistants had taken their places, a champion of Laganguilan y Madalag took one of the heads and presented it to the chiefs of the town, who showed it to all the assistants, making a long speech comprehending many praises for the conquerors. This discourse being over, the warrior took up the head, divided it with strokes of his hatchet, and took out the brains. During this operation, so unpleasant to witness, another champion got a second head, and handed it to the chiefs, the same speech was delivered, then he broke the skull to pieces in like manner, and took out the brains. The same was done with the four bleeding skulls of the subdued enemies. When the brains were taken out, the young girls pounded them with their hands into the vases containing the liquor of the fermented sugar-cane; they stirred the mixture round, and then the vases were taken to the chiefs, who dipped in their small osier goblets, through the fissures of which the liquid part ran out, and the solid part that remained at the bottom they drank with ecstatic sensuality. I felt quite sick at this scene, so entirely new to me. After the chieftains' turn came the turn of the champions. The vases were presented to them, and each one sipped with delight this frightful drink, to the noise of wild songs. There was really something infernal in this sacrifice to victory.

We sat in a circle and these vases were carried round. I well understood that we were about undergoing a disgusting test. Alas! I had not long to wait for it. The warriors planted themselves before me, and presented me with the basi and the frightful cup. All eyes were fixed upon me. The invitation was so direct, to refuse it would perhaps be exposing myself to death! It is impossible to describe the interior conflict that passed within me. I would rather have preferred the carbine of a bandit five paces from my chest; or await, as I had already done, the impetuous attack of the wild buffalo. What a perplexity! I shall never forget that awful moment. It struck me with terror and disgust; however, I contained myself, nothing betraying my emotion. I imitated the savages, and, dipping the osier goblet into the drink, I approached it to my lips, and passed it to the unfortunate Alila, who could not avoid this infernal beverage. The sacrifice was complete; the libations were over, but not the songs. The basi is a very spirituous and inebriating liquor, and the assistants, who had partaken rather too freely of this horrible drink, sang louder to the noise of the tom-tom and the gong, while the champions divided the human skulls into small pieces destined to be sent as presents to all their friends. The

THE BRAIN FEAST OF THE TINGUIAN INDIANS.—*Page* 112.

distribution was made during the sitting, after which, the chiefs declared the ceremony over. They then danced. The savages divided themselves into two lines, and howling, as if they were furious madmen or terribly provoked, they jumped about, laying their right hand upon the shoulder of their partners, and changing places with them. These dances continued all day; at last night came on, each inhabitant retired with his family and some few guests to his aerial abode, and soon afterwards tranquillity was restored.

We cannot help feeling astonished, when we are in Europe—in a good bed, under a warm eider-down coverlet, the head luxuriously reclining upon good pillows—when we reflect on the singular homes of the savages in the woods. How often have I represented to myself these families—roosting eighty feet above ground, upon the tops of trees. However, I know that they sleep as quietly in those retreats, open to every wind, as I in my well-closed and quiet room. Are they not like the birds who repose at their sides upon the branches? Have they not Nature for a mother, that admirable guardian of all she has made, and do they not also close their eyelids under the tutelary looks of the Supreme Father of the universe?

My faithful Alila retired with me into one of the low-storied cabins to pass the night, as we had been in the habit of doing while staying with the Tinguians. For our better security we were accustomed to watch one another alternately; we never both slept at the same time. Without being timid, ought we not to be prudent? This night it was my turn to go to sleep the first. I went to bed, but the impressions of the day had been too strong: I felt no inclination to sleep. I therefore offered to relieve my lieutenant of his watch; the poor fellow was like myself—the heads of the Guinans kept dancing before his eyes. He beheld them pale, bloody, hideous; then torn, pounded, broken to pieces; then the shocking beverage of the brains, that he also so courageously swallowed, came back to his mind, and he suffered sufficiently to make him repent our visit. "Master," said he to me, looking very much grieved, "why did we come among these devils? Ah! it would have been much better had we remained in our good country of Jala-Jala." He was not perhaps in the wrong, but my desire to see extraordinary things gave me a courage and a will he did not partake of. I answered him thus: "Man must know all, and see all it is possible to see. As we cannot sleep, and that we are masters here, let us make a night visit; perhaps we shall find things that are unknown to us. Light the fire and follow me, Alila." The poor lieutenant obeyed without answering a word. He rubbed two pieces of bamboo one against the other, and I heard him muttering between his teeth:

"What cursed idea has the master now? What shall we see in this miserable cabin—with the exception of the *Tic-balan,** or *Assuan?* † We shall find nothing else." During the Indian's reflections the fire burnt up. I lit, without saying a word, a cotton wick, plastered over with elemi gum, that I always carried with me in my travels, and I began exploring. I went all through the inside of the habitation without finding anything, not even the Tic-balan, or Assuan, as my lieutenant imagined. I was beginning to think my search fruitless, when the idea struck me to go down to the ground-floor of the cabin, for all the cabins are raised about eight or ten feet above ground, and the under part of the floor, closed with bamboos, is used as a store: I descended. Anyone who could have

* Evil Spirit. † A malicious divinity of the Tagalocs.

seen me—a white man, a European, the child of another hemisphere—wander by night, with a taper in my hand, about the hut of a Tinguian Indian, would have been really surprised at my audacity, and I may almost say, my obstinacy, in seeking out danger while pursuing the wonderful and unknown. But I went on, without reflecting on the strangeness of my conduct: as the Indians say: "I was following my destiny." When I had reached the ground, I perceived in the middle of a square, inclosed with bamboos, a sort of trap, and I stopped quite pleased. Alila looked at me with astonishment. I lifted up the trap, and saw a rather deep well; I looked into it with my light, but could not discover the bottom of it. Upon the sides only, at a depth of about six or seven yards, I thought I distinguished some openings that I took for entrances into sub terraneous galleries. What had I now discovered? Was I, like Gil Blas, about to penetrate into the midst of an assemblage of banditti, living in the internal parts of the earth; or should I find, as in the tales of the "Arabian Nights," some beautiful young girls, prisoners of some wicked magician? Indeed, my curiosity increased in proportion to my discoveries. "There is something strange here," said I to my lieutenant; "light a second match, I will go down to the bottom of the well." Hearing this order, my faithful Alila shrunk back in dismay, and ventured to say to me, in a frightfully dismal tone:

"Why, master, you are not content to see what is upon the earth, you must also see what is inside of it!"

This simple observation made me smile. He continued: "You wish to leave me alone here; and if the souls of the Guinans whose brains I have just drank come to fetch me, what will become of me? You will not be here to defend me!

My lieutenant would not have been frightened at twenty

banditti, he would have struggled against every one of them until death; but his legs trembled, his voice faltered, he was terrified at the idea of remaining alone in this cabin, exposed to the view of the spirit of a Guinan, which would come and ask him to restore his brains! Whilst he addressed me these complaints, I had leant my back against one side of the well, my knees were applied against the other, and down I went. I had already descended about four yards, when I felt some rubbish falling upon me. I raised my head, and saw Alila coming down too. The poor fellow would not remain alone. "Well done," said I to him, "you are becoming curious too; you will be rewarded, believe me, for we shall see fine sights." And I continued my under-ground research. After proceeding six or seven yards I reached the opening I had remarked from above, and stopped. I placed my light before me, and espied a corner, where sat the dried black corpse of a Tinguian in the same state as a mummy. I said nothing; I waited for my lieutenant, anxious as I was to enjoy his surprise. When he was aside of me: "Look, look," I exclaimed; "what is that?" He was stupified. "Master," said he at last, "I entreat of you to leave this place; let us get out of this cursed hole! Take me to fight against the Tinguians of the village—I am quite willing to do that—but do not remain among the dead! What should we do with our arms, if they suddenly appeared to ask us why we are here?" "Be quiet," I answered him; "we shall go no farther." I felt satisfied that this well was a tomb, and that lower down I should see some more Tinguians in a state of preservation. I respected the abode of the dead, and came up, to Alila's great satisfaction. We put everything in its place, and returned to the upper story of the cabin. I soon fell asleep, but my lieutenant could not: the thoughts of the mummy and horrible beverage kept him awake.

Guinan Indians.

CHAPTER VI.

Visit to Manabo—Conversation with my Guide—Religion of the Tinguians—Their Marriage Ceremony—Funereal Rites—Mode of Warfare—I take leave of the Tinguians—Journey to the Igorrots—Description of them—Their Dwellings—A Fortunate Escape—Alila and the Bandits—Recollections of Home—A Majestic Fig-tree—Superstition of Alila—Interview with an Igorrot—The Human Hand—Nocturnal Adventure—Consternation of Alila—Probable Origin of the Tinguians and Igorrots.

THE following morning, before dawn, our hosts began to descend from their high regions, and we left our temporary abode, to make preparations for our departure. I had resided long enough at Laganguilan y Madalag. I was desirous of visiting Manabo, a large village, situated at a short distance from Laganguilan. I availed myself of the presence of the inhabitants of Manabo, who had come to assist at the Brain Feast—this was the appellation I had given to this savage fête—and I set out with them. Among the troop there was one who had spent some time among the Tagalocs; he spoke their language a little, and I knew it tolerably well. I profited by this fortunate occurrence, and during the whole of the way I conversed with this savage, and questioned him upon the habits, customs, and manners of his fellow-countrymen. One point particularly pre-occupied me. I was unacquainted with the religion of these people, so very curious to study. Until then I had seen no temple; nothing that bore resemblance to an idol; I knew not what God they worshipped. My guide, chatty for an Indian, gave me quickly every information necessary. He told me that the Tinguians have no veneration for the stars; they neither adore the sun, nor moon, nor the constellations; they believe in the existence of a soul, and pretend that after death it quits the body, and remains in the family. As to the god that they adore, it varies and changes form according to chance and circumstances. And here is the reason: When a Tinguian chief has found in the country a rock, or a trunk of a tree, of a strange shape—I mean to say, representing tolerably well either a dog, cow, or buffalo—he informs the inhabitants of the village of his discovery, and the rock, or trunk of a tree, is immediately considered as a divinity—that is to say, as something superior to man. Then all the Indians repair to the appointed spot, carrying with them provisions and live hogs. When they have reached their destination they raise a straw roof above the new idol, to cover it, and make a sacrifice by roasting hogs; then, at the sound of instruments, they eat, drink, and dance until they have no provisions left. When all is eaten and drank, they set fire to the thatched roof, and the idol is forgotten until the chief, having discovered another one, commands a new ceremony.

With regard to the morals of the Tinguians, my guide informed me that the Tinguian has generally one legitimate wife, and many mistresses; but the legitimate wife alone inhabits the conjugal house, and the mistresses have each of them a separate cabin. The marriage is a contract between the two families of the married couple. The day of the ceremony, the man and wife bring their dowry in goods and chattels; the marriage portion is composed of china vases, glass, coral beads, and sometimes a little gold powder. It is of no profit to the married couple, for they distribute it to their relations. This custom, my guide observed to me, has been established to prevent a divorce, which could only take place in entirely restituting all the objects that were contributed at the marriage by the party asking for divorce—a rather skilful expedient for savages, and worthy of being the invention of civilised people. The relatives thus become much interested in preventing the separation, as they would be obliged to restitute the presents received; and, if one of the couple persisted in requesting it, they would prevent him or her by making away with one of the objects furnished, such as a coral necklace, or a china vase. Without this wise measure, it is to be supposed that a husband, with mistresses, would very often endeavour to obtain a divorce. My fellow-traveller enlightened me upon all the points that I wished to investigate. The government, said he to me, after resting himself for a few minutes, is very patriarchal. It is the oldest man who com mands.—As at Lacedæmonia, thought I, for there old age was honoured.—The laws are perpetuated by tradition, as the Tinguians have no idea of writing. In some instances they apply the punishment of death. When the fatal sentence has been pronounced, the Tinguian who has merited it must escape, if he wishes to avoid it, and go and live in the forests; for, the old men having spoken, all the inhabitants are bound to perform their orders. Society is divided into two classes, as with the Tagalocs, the chiefs and the commonalty. Whoever possesses and can exhibit to the public a certain number of china vases is considered a chief. These jars constitute all the wealth of the Tinguians. We were still conversing about the natives of the country when we reached Manabo. My guide had scarcely ceased talking all the way from Laganguilan.

My attention was now attracted by some flames that were issuing from under a cabin, where a large fire was burning. Around it many people were sitting, howling like wolves.

"Ah! ah!" said my guide, seemingly very pleased; "here is a funeral. I did not tell you anything about these ceremonies; but you will judge for yourself of what they are. It will be time enough to-morrow. You must be tired. I will take you to my day-cabin, and you may repose yourself without any danger of the Guinans, for a funeral compels a great many people to be on the watch all night."

I accepted the offer made to me, and we took possession of the Tinguian cabin. It was my turn to take the first watch, and my poor Alila, a little more at his ease, fell into a sound sleep. I followed his example, after my watch, and we did not wake up until it was broad daylight.

We had scarcely finished our morning repast, composed of honey-potatoes, palms, and dried venison, when my guide o the preceding day came to conduct me to the spot where the funeral of the deceased was about to take place. I followed him, and placing ourselves a few steps from the *cortége*, we assisted at a strange sight. The deceased sat in the middle of his cabin upon a stool; underneath him, and at his side, fires were burning in enormous chafing-dishes; at a short distance about thirty assistants were seated in a circle. Ten or twelve women formed another circle; they were seated nearer to the corpse, close by which the widow was also placed, and who was distinguished by a white veil, that covered her from head to foot. The women brought some cotton, with which they wiped off the moisture that the fire caused to exude from the corpse, which was roasting by degrees. From time to time one of the Tinguians spoke, and pronounced, in a slow, harmonious tone of voice, a speech, which he concluded by a sort of laugh, that was imitated by all the assistants; after which they stood up, eat some pieces of dried meat, and drank some basi; they then repeated the last words of the orator, and danced.

I endured—such is the word—this sight for an hour; but I did not feel courage enough to remain in the cabin any longer. The odour that exhaled from the corpse was unbearable. I went out, and breathed the fresh air; my guide followed me, and I begged him to tell me what had occurred from the beginning of the illness of the deceased.

"Willingly," he answered me.

Delighted to breathe freely, I listened with interest to the following recital:

"When Dalayapo," said the narrator, "fell sick, they took him to the grand square, to apply severe remedies to him; that is to say, all the men of the village came in arms, and, to the sound of the gong and the tom-tom, they danced around the sick man from the rising to the setting of the sun. But this grand remedy had no effect—his illness was incurable. At the setting of the sun they placed our friend in his house, and no more heed was paid to him: his death was certain, as he would not dance with his fellow-countrymen."

I smiled at the remedy and the reasoning, but I did not interrupt the narrator.

"For two days Dalayapo was in a state of suffering; then, at the end of those two days, he breathed no more; and, when that was perceived, they immediately put him on the bench where we saw him just now. Then the provisions that he possessed were gathered together to feed the assistants, who paid him all due honours. Each one made a speech in his praise: his nearest relations began the first, and his body was surrounded with fire to dry it up. When the provisions are consumed, the strangers will leave the cabin, and only the widow and a few relations will wait until the body is thoroughly dried. In a fortnight's time he will be placed in a large hole that is dug under his house. He will be put in a niche, or aperture, in the wall, where already his deceased relatives' remains are deposited, and then all is over."

This hole, thought I, must be similar to the one I went into the other night at Laganguilan.

The explanation that I had just received completely satisfied me, and I did not request to be present again at the ceremony. I resolved, since I was very comfortably seated, under the shade of a *balété*, upon availing myself of the obliging disposition of my guide, to ask him to inform me, suddenly changing the conversation all the while, how his tribe managed to wage war on the Guinans, their mortal enemies.

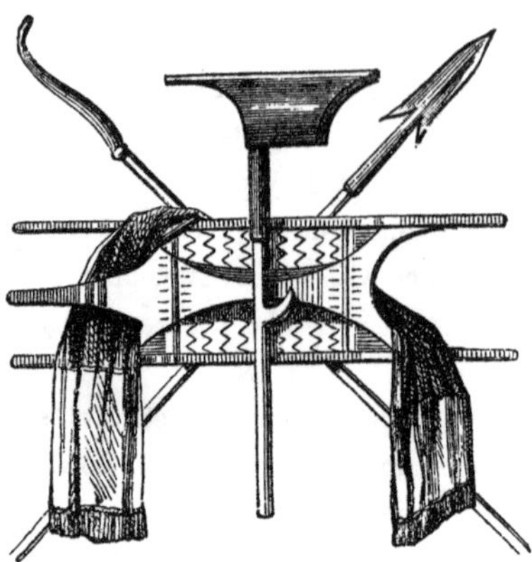

Weapons of the Tinguian Indians.

"The Guinans," said he to me, without drawing in any way on my patience, "wear the same arms as we do. They are neither stronger, nor more skilful, nor more vigorous. We have two modes of fighting them. Sometimes we give them a grand battle at mid-day, and then we meet them face to face, under a burning sun; at other times, during some dark night, we creep in silence to their dwelling-places, and if we be able to surprise any of them we cut off their heads, which we take away with us, and then we get up a feast, such as you have already witnessed."

That word "feast" recalled to my mind the sanguinary orgie, or carousing, I had been present at, and particularly the share I had taken in it, so that I felt I was blushing and growing pale by turns. The Indian took no heed of it, and went on thus:

"In the grand battles all the men belonging to a village are compelled to take up arms, and to march against the foe.

It is generally in the midst of a wood that the two armies meet. As soon as they come in sight of each other they set up crying and howling on both sides. Each man then rushes upon his enemy, and upon this shock depends the fate of the victory; for one of the armies is always panic-struck, and scampers away; then it is that the other pursues it, and kills as many as possible, taking care to preserve the heads, which they bring home with them."*

"Why it is a hide-and-seek fight, the consequences of which are, however, very cruel," I said. My Indian was of the same opinion, and rejoined:

"In general the conquerors are ever those who are cleverest in concealing themselves, in order to surprise their enemies, and who then dash on them bawling and howling."

Here my guide stopped short, the fight having no longer any interest for him; and then, perceiving I questioned him no longer, he left me to myself, when I returned to my habitation and Alila, who was sick enough of Manabo. For my own part I had seen enough of the Tinguians, and besides I thought I had observed that they seemed not too well pleased with the long stay I had made among them. I passed over in my mind the brain feast, so I resolved upon leaving. I therefore went to take leave of the elders. Unfortunately I had nothing to offer them, but I promised them many presents, when I should get back among the Christians—and then I left them.

The satisfaction of my faithful lieutenant was at its height when we started for home. Not being disposed to go back by the same way I had come, I determined upon keeping more to

* It is on account of this cruel custom of beheading their victims that the Spaniards have given to these savages the name of "*corta cabezas*," 'decapitators."

the east, crossing over the mountains, and upon taking the sun as my guide. This road seemed preferable to me, inasmuch as I was about to traverse a country inhabited by a few Igorrots, that other species of the savage tribe I was not acquainted with. The mountains we crossed over were crowned with magnificent forests. Now and then we perceived lovely fertile valleys below our feet, and the grass was so high and thick-set, that it was with great difficulty we could pass through it. During our journey, my lieutenant kept a sharp look-out, wishing to kill some game for our support. As for myself, I was indeed far from thinking of the pleasure of shooting, so great was my contemplation of the admirable panoramic views that we met with every moment; and I was too much enraptured with the virgin and fruitful soil that spread itself so incommensurately around us to think even of eating. But my faithful Alila was less an enthusiast than I was myself: however, in return, he was more prudent. At the close of the day on which we started he killed a stag; so we halted on the brink of a stream, cut off some palm-tree strips, in guise of rice and bread, and set about eating the roasted liver of the animal. Our repast was truly a copious one. Ah! how often since that time, when seated before a richly served table—having before me delicious and *recherché* viands, and that in dining-rooms where the atmosphere was balmy and perfumed by the aroma arising from the highly flavoured dishes—how often, I say, have I regretted the supper I partook of with Alila in the forest, after a day's ramble on the mountains! Nay, what mortal could forget such hours—such places?

Our repast over, we made our bed of some branches we lopped off from the trees, and which we joined together on the very moist soil in the interior of the vast forest, and there we slept soundly till the morrow, without fear, and particularly without having any sombre or disagreeable dreams At the dawn of day we were on foot again, all Nature seeming to wake up with ourselves. Oh! how fine and calm did she appear to us! The vapours that arose from her breast covered her all over with a veil, like a young virgin at her waking; and then this veil by degrees would break up into pieces, which pieces, gently balanced on the morning breeze, would disappear, and be lost on the tops of the trees or the summits of the rocks. On we walked for a long time, till at last, towards the middle of the day, we came to a small plain inhabited by the Igorrots. We found, in all, three cabins, or huts, so that the population was far from being large. At the door of one of these cabins I saw a man, of about sixty years of age, and a few women. As we had arrived from behind the huts we took the savages by surprise, so that they had no time to fly at our approach: we were in the midst of them.

I assumed the line of conduct I had pursued on arriving at Palan, but as I had no more coral beads or coloured glass. I presented them with a part of our stag, making them understand at the same time that we came with the most friendly intentions. From that moment there was established between us a very curious sort of mimic conversation, during which I was able to examine at my ease the new race of beings I saw around me. I perceived that the costume of the Igorrots was pretty nearly the same as that of the Tinguians, the ornaments excepted, but their features and physiognomy were quite different. The men were smaller, their breasts being exceedingly broad, their heads immensely big, their limbs developed, their strength herculean; their shape was not so handsome as that of the savages I had just left; their colour of a dark bronze, very dark indeed; their noses are less aquiline, their eyes yellow and fully open—*a la Chinoise*. The women's shape was also very protuberant, their complexion dark, their hair long, and combed up—*a la Chinoise*. Unfortunately it was impossible for me, with all my mimicry, to obtain the information I wished for, so I was obliged to content myself with visiting the cabin, which was a real hut, having but the ground-floor. The surrounding parts were closed in by very thick piles, covered with a roof in the form of a bee-hive. There was but one issue, through which it was impossible to have either egress or ingress, except in crawling on all-fours. In spite of this difficulty I would see the interior of this Indian dwelling; so, having made a sign to my lieutenant to keep watch, I penetrated into the hut. The Igorrots seemed quite surprised at my so doing, but they made no opposition to it. I found myself within an obnoxious hole, or hovel, through a small opening in the summit of which the daylight peeped in and the smoke crept out. The floor was thickly covered with dust, and it was upon such a soft couch that the whole family laid down to rest. In one of the corners I perceived some bamboo lances, a few cocoa-nuts divided into two parts, so as to serve as cups, a heap of good-sized round pebbles, that were used in case of attack, and a few pieces of wood, of very common workmanship, that served as pillows.

I soon got out of such a den, from which I was driven by the nauseous smell it contained in its every part, but I had been able to see everything in it. I then inquired, by signs, of the Igorrot, the way I should go, in order to join the Christians. He fully understood me, showed me the road with his finger, and we then proceeded on our journey. As I journeyed on, I remarked here and there fields of *patates* and sugar-cane, which of course must have been the only husbandry of those miserable savages. After about an hour's journey we were near running into a very great danger. On entering into a vast plain we saw an Igorrot, flying away as quickly as possible. He had remarked us, and I attributed his flight to fear, when suddenly I heard the sound of the tom-tom and gong, and saw, at the same time, twenty men armed with lances, rapidly advancing towards us. I felt that a fight was about to ensue, so I told my lieutenant to fire at the group, so as to injure none of them.

Alila fired: his bullet passed over the heads of the savages, who were so astonished at the detonation that they suddenly halted, and examined us attentively. I prudently took ad vantage of their surprise, and an immense forest presenting itself on our right, we entered it, leaving the village on our left, but the savages did not follow us into it.

During the whole of this scene my lieutenant did not utter a word. I had already remarked that when in pre sence of danger he became dumb, but when he had lost sight of the Igorrots his speech and loquacity returned to him.

"Master," said he to me, in a very dissatisfied tone, "how I do regret not having fired directly into the middle of those miscreants!"

"And why so?" asked I.

"Because I am certain I should have killed one of them at least."

"Well?"

"Well, master, our journey would not have terminated without our sending at least one soul of a savage to the devil."

"Ah! Alila," said I; "so you have become wicked and naughty, have you?"

"No, no, no, master," replied he; "but I cannot conceive why you are so kind and compassionate to that infernal race. You, who pursue and persecute the *Tulisans*,* who are a hundred times better than these wretches are, and who are Christians besides."

"What!" cried I; "brigands, robbers, and assassins better than poor primitive beings, who have no one to guide and conduct them to the path of virtue!"

"Oh, master!" replied my lieutenant, and most sententiously this time; "Oh! the brigands, as it pleases you to call them, are in nowise what you think them. The Tulisan is not an assassin. When he takes away life it is only when he is compelled, in defence of his own, and if he do kill, why it is always *de bon cœur*."

"Oh! oh!" said I; "and the robberies—how do you explain them?"

"If he rob, why it is only to get possession of a little of the superfluity of the rich, and that he divides among the poor—that's all. Now, master, do you know what use the Tulisan makes of his plunder?"

"No, indeed, master Alila," answered I, smilingly.

"Well, he keeps nothing of it for himself," said my lieutenant, with great pride; "in the first place he gives a part of it to the priest, to have masses said for him."

"Indeed! it is mighty edifying—go on."

"And then he gives another part of it to his mistress, or *bonne amie*, because he loves her, and likes to see her finely dressed out; and as for the remainder, why, faith! he spends it among his friends. You may therefore see, master, that the Tulisan possesses himself of the superfluity of one person to

* Banditti.

satisfy several other persons with it.* Oh! but he is far, very far indeed, from being so wicked as those savages, who kill you without saying a word to you, and then eat up your brains—fie!" And here Alila heaved a deep sigh, for the brain feast was ever present to his mind. His conversation so interested me, his system was so curious, and he himself so frank in drawing it out, that I almost forgot the Igorrots in listening to him.

We pursued our road through the wood, keeping as much as possible to the south, in order to get near the province of Batangas, where I was to meet my poor patient, who no doubt was very uneasy about my long absence. When I started I said not a word about my project, and had I done so it is most likely I should have been thought as no longer belonging to this world. The recollection of my wife, whom I had left at Manilla, and who was far from supposing me to be among the Igorrots, inspired me with the most anxious desire of returning home to my family as quick as possible. Absorbed in my thoughts, and carried away by my reflections, I walked silently along, without even casting a glance upon the luxuriant vegetation all around us. I must indeed have been very much pre-occupied, for a virgin forest between the tropics, and particularly in the Philippine islands, is in nowise to be compared with our European forests. I was aroused from my pensiveness, and recalled to the remembrance of my whereabouts, by the noise of a torrent, and I gratefully admired nature in her gigantic productions. I looked up, and before me I perceived an immense *baléte*, an extraordinary fig-tree, that thrives in the sombre and mysterious forests of the Philippines, and I stopped to admire

* "The nakedness of the poor might be clothed out of the trimmings of the vain."—Dr. Goldsmith's "Vicar of Wakefield."—Tr.

it. This immense tree springs from a seed similar to the seed of the ordinary fig-tree; its wood is white and spongy, and in a few years it grows to an extraordinary size. Nature, who has had foresight in all things, and who allows the young lamb to leave its wool on the bushes for the timid bird to pick it up and build its nest with—Nature, I say, has shown herself in all her genius in the fig-tree of the Philippine islands, which grows so rapidly and so immensely. The branches of this tree generally spring from the base of the trunk; they extend themselves horizontally, and, after forming an elbow or curve, rise up perpendicularly; but, as I said before, the tree is spongy, and easily broken, and the branch, while forming the curve, would inevitably be broken, did not a ligament, which the Indians call a drop of water—*goutte d'eau*—fall from the tree and take root in the earth; there it swells, and grows in proportion with the size of the branch, and acts to it as a living prop. Besides which, around the trunk, and at a considerable distance from the ground, are natural supports, which rise up in points or spirals to about the middle of the trunk. Has not the Grand Architect of the world foreseen everything?

The appearance presented by the balété is very frequently indescribably picturesque; and this is so true that, within a space of some hundred paces in diameter—which these gigantic fig-trees usually occupy—one may see by turns grottoes, halls, chambers, that are often furnished with natural seats, formed out of and by the roots themselves. No! no vegetation is more diversified, nor more extraordinary! This tree sometimes grows out of a rock, where there is not an inch of earth; its long roots run along the rock, encompass it, and then plunge into the neighbouring brook. It is indeed a masterpiece of nature—a *chef d'œuvre*—which, however, is very ordinary in the virgin forests of the Philippine islands.

"Here," said I to my lieutenant, "is a good spot for us to spend the night on."

He recoiled some paces.

"What!" said he; "do you wish to stop here, master?"

"Certainly," replied I.

"Oh! but you don't see that we are in still more danger here than in the midst of the Igorrots!"

"And why, then, are we in danger?" asked I.

"Why? why? Do you not know that the Tic-balan dwells in the large balétés. If we stop here you may be very sure that I shan't sleep a moment, and that we shall be tormented the whole night."

I smiled, which my lieutenant perceiving:

"Oh! master," said he, most dolefully, "what should we do with an evil spirit that fears neither bullet nor dagger?"

The terror of the poor Tagal was really too great for me to resist him, so I yielded, and we took up our quarters for the night at a place much less to my own taste, but much more to Alila's. The night passed away like many others—I mean, perfectly well, and we woke up to resume our journey through the forest.

We had been walking about two hours, when, on leaving the wood, and entering on a plain, we met an Igorrot, mounted upon a buffalo, face to face. The encounter was somewhat curious. I levelled my gun at the savage: my lieutenant took hold of the animal by the long leather strap, and I made a sign to the Igorrot not to stir: then—always in my mimic language—I asked if he were alone. I understood from him that he was accompanied by no fellow-traveller, and that he was going northwards, in the opposite direction to our own But Alila, who decidedly had a grudge against the savages, was most anxious to lodge a ball in this fellow's head. However, I strenuously opposed such a project, and ordered him to let go the bridle.

"But, master," said he, "allow me at least to see what these jars contain."

Around the neck of the Igorrot's buffalo were strung three or four jars, covered with leaves of the banana tree.

My lieutenant, without even waiting for my answer, applied his nose to them, and discovered, to his infinite satisfaction, that they contained a deer or stag ragout, which sent forth a certain perfume; so, still without consulting me, he undid the smallest of the jars, struck the buffalo a blow with the but-end of his gun, and, letting go the animal at the same time, exclaimed:

"Go, you rascal—go!"

The Igorrot, finding himself free, fled as quick as the beast could carry him, and we re-entered the woods, taking care to avoid the openings, for fear of being surprised by too large a number of savages.

Towards four o'clock we halted to take our repast. This wished-for moment was impatiently expected by my lieutenant, as the savage's jar sent forth a very savoury smell. At last the desired moment arrived: we sat down on the grass. I stuck my poignard into the jar, which Alila had brought up to the fire, and I withdrew—an entire human hand!* My poor lieutenant was as stupified as I was myself, so we remained a few minutes without saying a word. At last I gave a vigorous

* The Igorrots, however, according to the reports of the Indians, are not anthropophagi; perhaps the one in question had received these ragouts from some other savages—the Guinans, for instance.

kick to the jar, and smashed it in pieces, so that the human flesh it contained was scattered over the ground, while still I held the fatal hand on the point of my dagger.

That hand horrified me; yet I examined it most carefully, and it appeared to me to have been the hand of a child of an Ajetas, a species of savages that inhabit the mountains of Nueva-Exica and Maribèles, of which race I shall have an opportunity of speaking during the course of this work. I took some strips of palm-tree, roasted in the burning embers; Alila did the same, and we set out, not in the best of humours, in search of another resting-place for the night.

Two hours after sun-rise we issued from the forest and entered upon the plain. From time to time—that is, from distance to distance—we met with rice-fields, cultivated after the Tagal manner, and then did my lieutenant exclaim most joyously to me:

"Master, we are now in Christian ground."

He was right; the road was becoming more easy. We followed on a narrow pathway, and towards evening arrived in front of an Indian cabin, at the door of which a young girl was sitting, while abundant tears trickled down her sorrowful countenance. I drew near her, and inquired into the cause of her grief. On hearing my question she rose up, and without replying to my queries, conducted us into the interior of the habitation, where we beheld the inanimate body of an old woman, whom we learned was the mother of the young girl; the brother of the latter had gone to the village in quest of the relations of the deceased, to aid them in transporting the corpse to its final destination.

This scene affected me very much. I did my best to console the poor young girl, and solicited hospitality for the night, which was instantly granted. To be in company with a dead body nowise affrighted me; but I bethought of Alila, so superstitious and so fearful with regard to ghosts and evil spirits.

"Well," said I to him; "are you not afraid to spend the night near a corpse?"

"No, master," replied he, courageously; "this dead person is a Christian soul, which, far from wishing us evil, will watch over us."

I was really astonished at the answer of the Tagaloc, at his calmness and security: the rogue had his own motives for thus speaking to me. The Indian huts in the plains, are never composed of more than one room; the one we were in was scarcely large enough to hold us all four; however, we one and all managed as well as we could. The deceased occupied the back part; a small lamp, placed by her head, threw out a feeble light, and beside her lay the young Indian girl. I had established my quarters at a short distance from the bed of death, and my lieutenant was nearest the door, left open purposely to dispel the heat and foul air.

Towards two o'clock in the morning I was waked up by a shrill voice, and I felt at the same time that some one was passing over me, and uttering cries that soon were heard outside the cabin. I immediately stretched out my hand towards the place where Alila had lain down, but that place was empty; the lamp was out, and the darkness complete.

This made me very uneasy. I called to the young girl, who answered me that she had heard, like me, cries and noise, but she was ignorant of the cause. I snatched up my gun and sallied forth, calling out to my lieutenant; but to no purpose. No one answered; the stillness of death reigned all around. I then set out, walking over the fields at hazard, calling out now and then Alila's name. I had not, perhaps, gone a hundred paces when I heard the following words, pronounced most timidly, proceeding from a tree by which I was passing:

"I am here, master."

It was Alila himself. I drew nigh, and saw my lieutenant ensconced behind the trunk of the tree, and trembling like one of its leaves.

"What then has happened to you?" I inquired; "and what are you doing there?"

"Oh! master," said he to me; "pray forgive me! Bad thoughts got the better of me; it was the young Indian girl inspired me with them, and the demon blew them into my inner man. I—I—I—drew nigh, during the night, to the young girl's resting-place, and when I saw you fast asleep—I put out the lamp."

"Well, and then—" said I, most impatiently and angrily.

"And then—I wished to take a kiss from the young girl; but, at the very moment I drew nigh, the old dead woman took her daughter's place, so I only met with a cold and icy face, and at the same moment two long arms stretched out to seize upon me. Oh! it was then I gave such a cry—and I fled! fled! fled! but the old woman pursued me—yes, the corpse tracked me behind; and she has only just now disappeared, on hearing the sound of your voice. I then hid behind this tree, where you now see me, in a piteous plight."

The fright of the Tagal and his mistake made me almost laugh out; but I severely reprimanded him for the bad intention he had of abusing the hospitality that had been so graciously afforded us: he repented, and begged of me to excuse him. He was, I should think, sufficiently punished by his fright. I wished to take him back to the cabin with me; but for no consideration would he return. I therefore left my gun in his charge, and went back to the house of mourning, where I found the poor young girl just as frightened as he was. I soon made her acquainted with the adventure; so thanking her for her kind hospitality, and morning coming on, I returned to Alila, who was most impatiently expecting me.

The hope of seeing soon again our relations, our homes, our friends, gave us new courage, and before sunset we arrived at an Indian village, without anything remarkable having taken place: this was to be our last stage.*

* It would be difficult to establish from what nations the divers species of men who inhabit the interior of Luzon originally came. The Tinguians, from their fine shape, their colour, their eyes, their almost aquiline nose, the value they set upon china vases, their music, and finally from their habits, would appear to be the descendants of the Japanese. It is most likely that at a very distant period some junks from the Japan coasts, hurried along by strong northern winds, may have been wrecked upon the Luzon shores, and that their crews, seeing no possibility of returning to their native country, as well as to avoid the Malayan population that was in possession of the beaches,—it is possible, I say, that the shipwrecked persons withdrew into the interior of the mountains, the difficulty of access to which protected them from all invasion.

The Japanese sailors, who are merely coasters, sail about with their wives, as I had an opportunity of witnessing on board many junks, whither I went through mere curiosity. Those same junks, beaten by the tempest, had steered for shelter to the eastern coast of Luzon, where they anchored for four months, waiting for the return of the monsoon; and had they not met with a protecting government, their crews would have been compelled to fly into the mountains, as I suppose the Tinguians had been obliged to do. The latter having some women with them, must have procured others from among the neighbouring population, and as they inhabit the finest and healthiest country in the world, their number must have considerably increased. They are now spread over sixteen villages: Palan, Jalamey, Mabuantoc, Dalayap, Lanquiden, Baac, Padanquitan y Pangal, Campasan y Danglas, Lagayan, Ganagan, Malaylay, Bucay, Gaddani, Laganguilan y Madalag, Manab, Palog y Amay.

The Igorrots, whom I had less opportunities of studying, seem to be the descendants of the remains of the grand naval army of the Chinese

Inhabitants of Boulacan

After this long and interesting journey I arrived at Quingua, a village in the province of Boulacan, where I had left my friend in convalescence.

Lima-On, who, after attacking Manilla, on the 30th November, 1574, had taken refuge in the province of Pangasinan, in the gulf of Lingayan, where he was a second time defeated, and his fleet completely destroyed. A part of the crew escaped into the mountains of Pangasinan, where the Spaniards could not pursue them.

The Igorrot has long hair, eyes *à la Chinoise*, a flat nose, thick lips, high cheek bones, broad shoulders, strong and nervous limbs, and bronze colour; he greatly resembles the Chinese of the southern provinces of the Celestial Empire.

I could obtain no information as to extraction concerning the Guinans, another people of savages, ferocious and cruel, who live in the neighbourhood of the Tinguians.

I keep back for a future period a description of the Ajetas, or Negritos, the aborigines of Luzon.

Manilla Fishing Raft.

CHAPTER VII.

I return to Jala-Jala—An Excursion on the Lake—Relempago's Narrative—Re-organisation of my Government—A Letter from my Brother Henry—His Arrival—He joins me in the Management of my Plantations—Cajoui, the Bandit: Anten-Anten—Indian Superstition—A Combat with the Bandit—His Death—A Piratical Descent—My Lieutenant is Wounded—I extract the Ball, and cure him.

MY prolonged absence from home caused great uneasiness. Very fortunately my wife remained at Manilla, and was totally ignorant of the journey I had recently undertaken.

My patient had not exactly followed the prescribed regimen, so that his distemper had increased, and he was impatiently expecting to return and die, he said, in his house: his wishes were complied with. A few days after my arrival we set out and arrived the next day at Manilla, where my poor friend rendered his last sigh in the middle of his family. This event damped, of course, the pleasure I should have enjoyed in beholding my wife once more.

A few days after the demise of our friend we embarked, and set sail for Jala-Jala.

We glided most agreeably upon the lake until we left the strait of Quinanbutasan, but, once there, we met with so violent an east wind, and the water of the lake was so ruffled, that we were obliged to re-enter the strait, and cast anchor near the cabin of the old fisherman, Relempago, whom I have already noticed.

Our sailors landed to prepare their supper; as for ourselves, we remained in our boat, where we stretched ourselves at our ease, the old fisherman, as he sat doubled up in the Indian fashion, amusing us in the best way he could by the narration of brigand stories.

I interrupted him all on a sudden, saying to him:

"Relempago, I should prefer hearing the history of your own personal adventures; do, therefore, relate your misfortunes to us."

The old fisherman heaved a sigh, and then, unwilling to disoblige me, began his story in the poetical terms so familiar to the Tagal tongue, and which it is almost impossible to reproduce by a translation:

"Lagune is not my native place," said he; "I was born in the island of Zébou, and was at the age of twenty what is called a fine young man; but, pray believe me, I was by no means proud of my physical advantages, and I preferred being the first fisherman of my village. Nevertheless, my comrades were jealous of me, and all that because the young girls would look at me with a certain complaisant air, and seemed to find me to their liking."

I could not but smile at this frank avowal of the old man, which he perceiving, continued:

"I tell you these things, sir," replied he, "because at my age one can speak of them without fearing to appear ridiculous—it is so long ago. And besides, allow me to inform you that I relate to you such things, not from vanity—Oh, no! but merely to furnish you with an exact recital. Besides, the sly and roguish looks that young girls threw at me, as I passed through the village, flattered me in no manner. I was in love with Theresa, sir; yes, I was passionately in love with her, and my love was returned, for fondly did she love me; a look from any other but from her was totally indifferent to me. Ah! Theresa was the prettiest lass in the village! but, poor soul! she has done like myself—she has greatly altered; for years are an enormous weight, which bends and breaks you down in spite of yourself, and against which there is no way of struggling.

"When, seated as I am at present, I bethink me of the fine by-gone days of my youth—of the strength, the courage, that we used to find in our mutual affection—Oh! I shed tears of regret and sensibility. Where are now those fine—those happy days? Gone, gone, gone! they have fled before the piercing and terrible winds that forerun the storms and the hurricanes. Like the day, life has its dawn; like the day, also, it has its decline!"

Here the poor old fisherman made a pause, and I was loth to interrupt him in his meditation. There then ensued a profound silence, that lasted several minutes. Suddenly Relempago seemed to start from a dream, and passing his hand over his forehead, looked at us for some time, as if to excuse himself for those few moments of mental absence, and then he continued as follows:

"We had been brought up together," said he, "and had been affianced as soon as we had grown up. Theresa would have died rather than belong to any other, and, as I shall here after prove it, I would have accepted any condition, even the most unfavourable one rather, than abandon the friend of my heart. Alas! it is almost always with our tears that we trace our painful way through life. Theresa's relations were opposed to our union; they even put forward vain and frivolous pretexts; and whatever efforts I made to bring them to decide upon bestowing her affianced hand on me, I never could succeed. And yet they well knew that, like the palm tree, we could not live without each other, and we were to be separated, it would be condemning us to die. But our tears, our prayers, our griefs, were only heard by senseless people, and we were labouring under the most poignant grief, while no one would understand or sympathise with our sorrow. I was beginning to lose all courage, when one morning there came into my mind the pious thought of offering to the Infant Jesus, in the church of Zébou, the first pearl I should fish up. I therefore repaired earlier than usual to the sea-shore, implored the Almighty to grant me his protection, and to have me married to my beloved Theresa. The sun was just beginning to dart his burning rays upon the earth, and was gilding the surface of the waters. Nature was awaking from her transitory sleep, and every living being or object was singing in its language a hymn to the Creator.

"With a beating heart I began diving to the bottom of the

sea, in search of the pearl which I so ardently wished for, but my searches and struggles were completely fruitless at first. Had anyone been near me at that moment he would have easily read my disappointment in my face. Nevertheless, my courage failed me not. I began again, but with no better success. 'Oh, Lord!' cried I, 'thou hearest not then my prayers, my supplications! Thou wilt not then accept for thy beloved son the offering that I destine for him.'* For the sixth time I plunged, and brought up from the bottom of the sea two enormous oysters. Oh! how my heart leaped with joy! I opened one of them, and found it contained a pearl so large that never in my life had I seen one like it. My joy was so great that I set-to dancing in my pirogue, as if I had lost my reason. The Lord, then, did vouchsafe to protect me, since He enabled me to accomplish my vow. With a joyful heart I retraced my steps to my dwelling, and, not wishing to fail in my word, I took my magnificent pearl to the curate of Zébou.

"The reverend father," continued the old fisherman, "was delighted with my present. That pearl was worth 5,000 piasters (or 25,000 francs, *i. e.*, £1,000 English money), and you must have admired it—you, as well as all other persons who attend the church—for the Infant Jesus always holds it in his hand. The curate thanked and congratulated me on my very good idea.

"'Go home in peace, brother,' said he to me; 'go home in peace. Heaven will not forget thy meritorious action—yea, the disinterestedness of thy good work, and sooner or later thy desires will be hearkened to.'

* According to Indian tradition, and to Spanish tradition likewise, the Infant Jesus of Zébou existed before the discovery of the Philippines. After the conquest the Infant was found upon the sea-shore; the Spanish conquerors deposited it in the cathedral, where it performed great miracles.

"I left the holy man with my heart joyful indeed, and I hastened to inform Theresa of the pastor's consoling words: we rejoiced like two children together. Ah! true indeed it is to say that youth has been endowed by the Almighty with every privilege, particularly with that of hope. At the age of twenty if the heart think that it may live in hope, away with all cares immediately; and, as the morning breeze sips up the drops of moisture that have been left by the storm in the chalice of flowers, so does hope dry up the tears that moisten the eyes of the young, and drive away the sighs that inflate and oppress the breast. So sure were we that our tribulations would ere long be over, that we no longer thought of our by gone sorrow! In the spring-time of life grief leaves no more trace after it than the nimble foot of the wily Indian on the strand, when the sea-wind has blown over it.

"The inhabitants of the village, seeing us so joyful, so purely happy, were envious of our lot, and Theresa's relations could no longer find any pretext for opposing our being united. We were now in full sight of connubial bliss; our boat of life was gently rocked by a very mild wind; we were singing the return-home hymn, not supposing, alas!-that we were going to be dashed against a breaker! Our young Indians foresee not in the morning the storm that is to assail them in the evening. The buffalo cannot avoid the lasso, and most often, in order to avoid it, he anticipates the danger. I roved about, I may say heedlessly thoughtless of the precipice before my feet. Misfortune marked me for her own when I least expected it.

"One evening, on my return from fishing, at the moment when I was repairing to Theresa's, there to repose myself after my fatigues of the day, I saw one of my neighbours advancing towards me. That man had always shown me the greatest affection, so that on seeing him thus advance, my limbs began to tremble, and the pulsations of my heart gradually ceased. His face was pale, and entirely altered. His haggard eyes threw forth flashes of terror, and his voice was trembling and agitated.

" '*Los Moros** have made a descent upon the coast,' said he to me.

" 'Good Heavens!' exclaimed I, covering my face with my hands.

" 'They surprised some persons of the village, and carried them off prisoners.'

" 'And Theresa?' exclaimed I.

" 'Carried off with the others,' he replied.

"I heard no more of this revelation, and for some minutes —like the warrior pierced to the heart by a poisoned arrow— I was completely deprived of all consciousness.

"When I came back to myself tears flooded my face, and brought me some relief: but suddenly I resumed my courage, and felt that no time was to be lost. I ran to the shore where I had left my pirogue, which I unfastened, and, as quickly as oars could pull me, I pursued the Malays, not in the hope of wresting Theresa from them, but resolved upon partaking of her captivity and misfortune. We better endure the sufferings we have to undergo when we are two together than when we are alone. He who had brought me the fatal tidings saw me start, and thought I had lost my senses; the fact is, my countenance bore all the traces of mental alienation. Methought I was inspired by the grand master-spirit; my pirogue bounded along the troubled waters of the ocean as if it possessed wings. One would have said that I had twenty

* The Malays.

rowers at my disposal, and I cleft the waves with the same rapidity as the halcyon's flight, when wafted away by the hurricane. After a short time's laborious and painful rowing I at last came in view of the corsairs who were carrying away my treasure. At the sight my strength was renewed again, and I was soon up with them. When I was side by side with them I informed them, in words the most feeling, and which sprang from my poor lacerated heart, that Theresa was my wife, and that I would prefer being a slave with her to abandoning her. The pirates listened to my voice, stifled by my tears, and took me on board, not from commiseration, but from cruelty. In fact, I was a slave more added to their numbers: why should they have repulsed me? A few days after that fatal evening we arrived at Jolo. There the division of the slaves was made, and the master into whose hands we fell took us away with him. Was it, then, to undergo a like destiny that I had dived so early in the morning for a pearl for the Infant Jesus of Zébou? Yes, was it for this that I had made a vow to bring him the first pearl I should find? Notwithstanding my profound sorrow I murmured not, neither did I regret my offering. The Lord was the master! His will should be done."

Here Relempago paused, and looked towards Heaven with a smile of angelic resignation, and we then remarked upon his face the furrows traced by the deep sorrows of his life. The wind was still blowing with violence, and our boat was dancing on the waves; our sailors had finished their repast, and, in order to listen to the fisherman's tale of woe, had taken up their place by his side. Their features wore an expression of the most innocent attention; so, having made a sign to the narrator, he resumed his story as follows:—

'Our captivity lasted two years, during which time we had to endure very great sufferings. Very often would my master take me away with him to a lake in the interior of the island, and these absences lasted for whole months together, during which time I was perforce separated from my Theresa, my dear wife; for, not having been able to get united by a clergyman, we had joined ourselves, under the all-benevolent and protecting eye of the Almighty! On my return, I used to find my poor companion still the same good, faithful, devoted. and affectionate friend, whose courage sustained my own.

"One circumstance decided me upon taking an audacious resolution. Theresa was in an interesting situation! Oh! what would not my joy have been had I been at Zébou, in the midst of our family and of our friends! What happiness should I not have felt at the idea of being a father! Alas! in slavery, that very same thought froze my blood with terror, and I firmly resolved upon snatching both mother and child from the tortures of captivity. In one of our excursions I had been wounded in the leg, and this wound came greatly to my aid. One day my master set out for the borders of the grand lake, and, knowing I had a bad leg, left me at Jolo. I availed myself of this opportunity to put into execution a project that I had formed for a long time, that of flying with Theresa. The task was a daring one, but the desire of freedom doubles one's strength and increases one's courage, so I did not hesitate for a moment. When night had lowered, my dear Theresa took a road I had pointed out to her, I went by another one, and we both arrived at the sea-shore at a short distance from each other. There we jumped into a pirogue, and threw ourselves upon the protection of Divine mercy!

"We rowed vigorously the whole night, and never in my life shall I forget that mysterious flight. The wind blew rather violently, the night was dark, and the stars insensibly lost their vivid brightness. Every moment we thought we heard behind us the noise of our pursuers, and our hearts beat so loud and so violently that they could be heard in the midst of the silence that reigned around all nature.

"Day at last appeared: we descried by degrees, in the mist of the morning, the rocks that lined the shore, and we could see far enough in the distance that no one was pursuing us. Then were our hearts filled with cheering hope, and we continued rowing towards the north, in order to land on some Christian isle.

"I had taken with me some cocoa-nuts, but they were a very small resource, and we had been at sea three whole days without eating anything, when, exhausted by fatigue and want, we fell upon our knees and invoked the pity, compassion, and succour of the Infant Jesus of Zébou. Our prayer over, we felt our strength completely exhausted; the oars fell from our hands, and we lay down in the bottom of the pirogue, decided upon dying in each other's arms.

"Our weakness gradually increased, and finally we swooned away, the pirogue all the while dashing heedlessly on with the waves

"When we recovered from our fainting fit—I know not how long it lasted—we found ourselves surrounded by Christians, who, having perceived us in our light skiff, had come to our aid, conveyed us to their hospitable dwelling, and took the most pious care of us. We had not long been disembarked when Theresa was taken with the pains of labour, and was confined of a very diminutive, sickly child. I went down on my knees before the innocent little creature that had sc miraculously escaped from slavery, and prayed for it—it was a boy!"

Here the poor old fisherman heaved a heavy sigh, while tears were fast falling upon his shrunken hands.

We one and all respected this painful recollection of the poor old man.

"Our convalescence was very long indeed," said Relempago; "at last our health was sufficiently restored to permit of us leaving the isle of Negros, where the Infant Jesus had so miraculously caused us to land, and we came to settle here, on the side of this large lake, which, being situated in the interior of the isle of Luçon, afforded me the means of pursuing my avocation of fisherman without in any way fearing the Malays, who might very easily have captured us again at Zébou.

"My first care—yes, the dearest act of my life—on arriving, was to have our marriage celebrated in the church of Moron. I had promised it to God, and I would not fail in the promise I had made Him who reads all hearts. After that I built the little cottage you see hard-by, and my existence glided on most peacefully. The fishing trade went on prosperously. I was still a young man, active and intelligent, and sold my fish very easily to the vessels passing through the strait. My son had by this time become a fine young man."

"Of course he resembled his father," said I, recollecting the beginning of the old man's tale, but my remark could not excite a smile upon his countenance.

"Oh! the lad was a good fisherman," continued he, "and happily did we all three live together, till a dreadful mis fortune befell us. The Infant Jesus had no doubt forsaken us, or perhaps the Almighty was displeased with us; but I am far from murmuring. He has visited us most severely, since He has overwhelmed us with grief of such a strong nature, that it must accompany us to our last resting-place!"

And here the poor old man's tears trickled down his weather-beaten cheeks once more, in abundance, in bitterness, and in sorrow.

Ah! how right was the Italian poet, when he said:—

"Nought lasteth here below but tears!"

The voice of Relempago was stifled by his sobbing; however, he made one more effort, and continued thus:

"One night—a fine moonlight night—we set our nets in a certain part of the strait, and as we felt some difficulty in drawing them up, the lad plunged into the water to ascertain what obstacle we had to contend with, and to set all to rights. I was in my pirogue, leaning over the side, waiting for his return, when all of a sudden I thought I saw, through the silvery beams of the lamp of night, a large spot of blood spreading itself over the surface of the water. Fear took possession of me, and I quickly hauled up my nets. My hapless child had seized upon and become entangled in them—but, alas! when he came to the surface he was a corpse!"

"What! your son?" cried I.

"My poor dear José-Maria," said he, "had his head bitten off by a cayman that had got entangled in our nets. Ever since that night—that fatal night!—Theresa and I offer up our prayers to the Omnipotent, imploring Him to take us to himself; for, alas! nothing now has any charms for us here below. The first of us that will depart for that bourn from whence no traveller returns will be interred by the survivor beside our beloved child—there, under that little hillock yonder, which is surmounted by a wooden cross, in front of my humble cottage; and the last of us two to leave this valley of tears will no doubt meet with some charitable Christian hand, to place our mortal remains beside the bodies of those we loved so tenderly during our hapless pilgrimage here below."

Here Relempago ceased his painful history, and, that he might give a free course to his grief and tears, he rose up, and bowed us his adieu, which we returned to him with hearts oppressed with sympathetic sorrow.

The wind had ceased blowing, and the attentive sailors were awaiting our orders, so that in a few moments afterwards we were sailing towards Jala-Jala, where we landed before sunset.

On the morrow of my arrival I entered on the business of my little government, to which my absence had been far from useful or favourable, so that I was obliged to suppress many abuses that had crept into it while I had been away. Some slight corrections, joined to an active and incessant surveillance, or inspection, soon established once more the most perfect order and discipline; so that, from that moment, I was at liberty to devote all my time and attention to the cultivation of my lands.

We were now at the beginning of the winter—the rainy and windy season. No stranger had dared crossing the lake, to come and visit us, so that, alone with my dear wife, our days glided most happily and tranquilly away, for we knew not what *ennui* was or meant: our mutual affection was so great that our own presence was sufficient company for each other.

This delightful solitude was soon interrupted by a fortunate and unforeseen event. A letter from Manilla—a very rare circumstance at Jala-Jala—reached me, informing me that my eldest brother, Henry, had just arrived there; that he had put up at my brother-in-law's; and that he was expecting me with all imaginable impatience. I was not aware that he had left France to come and see me, so that such news, and his sudden, as well as unexpected, arrival, surprised and overjoyed me.

I was once more to see one of my dearest relations – a brother whom I had always tenderly loved. Ah! he who has never quitted his home, his family, and his early attachments, will with difficulty understand the emotions I experienced on receiving this agreeable letter. When the first transports of my joy were somewhat allayed, I resolved to set out at once for Manilla. Preparations for my departure were speedily made. I chose my lightest canoe, and my two strongest Indians, and a few minutes after, having embraced my beloved Anna, I was scudding over the waters of the lake, slowly—too slowly for my impatience, as I wished to be able to give wings to my fragile skiff, and to traverse the distance that separated me from my brother as rapidly as my thoughts: no journey ever appeared to me so long, and nevertheless my two robust rowers exerted all their strength to favour my wishes. At length I arrived, and immediately hastened to my brother-in-law's, and there I threw myself into Henry's arms. Our emotions were such that for some time we could not speak; the abundant tears we shed alone showed the joy of our hearts. When the first transport was over, I asked him questions beyond number. Not one member of my family was forgotten; the smallest details concerning these beloved beings were to me of the greatest interest. We passed the remainder of the day and the following night in incessant and interesting conversation

The next day we started for Jala-Jala. Henry was eager to become acquainted with his sister-in law, and I to make the dear companion of my life a sharer in my happiness. Excellent Anna! my joy was joy for you—my happiness was your delight! You received Henry as a brother, and this sisterly attachment was always, on your part, as sincere as your affection for me had ever been.

After a few days spent in the most agreeable conversation about France, and about all those beloved friends who remained there, feelings of sadness that I could with difficulty repress became intermingled with my joy. I thought of our numerous family, so far distant, and so scattered over the globe. My youngest brother was, to my great regret, dead at Madagascar. My second brother, Robert, resided at Porto-Rico; and my two brothers-in-law, both captains of vessels, engaged in long voyages, were gone to the Indies. My poor mother and my poor sisters were alone, without protectors, without support: what sad moments of fear and anxiety you must have spent in your solitude! Ah! how I should have rejoiced to have you near me; but, alas! a whole world separated us, and the hope of seeing you again one day could alone scatter the clouds that darkened occasionally the happy days adorned by the presence of my brother.

After some time of rest, Henry asked to join me in my labours. I then made him acquainted with my mode of cultivation, and he took upon himself the management of the plantations and of their products. I reserved to myself the regulation of my Indians, the charge of the flocks, and that of putting down the bandits.

I had frequent quarrels, and even incessant conflicts, with these turbulent Indians; but I never boasted of these petty engagements, in which I was often obliged to take a most active part. On the contrary, I recommended strict silence to my attendants, for I did not wish to cause anxiety to my excellent Anna, nor to give my brother the desire of accompanying me. I did not like to expose him to the dangers I ran myself, as I had not equal hopes of safety for him. I relied upon my star, and really, to a certain degree, all modesty aside, I think that the bandits' balls respected me. When I was engaged in contests in the plain, or in some of the skirmishes, the danger was not great; but it was quite a different thing when it was necessary to fight hand to hand, which happened more than once; and I cannot forbear the pleasure of relating one of those circumstances that made me say just now *the bandits' balls respected me.*

One day I was alone with my lieutenant, having both of us only our daggers, and we were coming back to our habitation, and passing through a thick forest, situated at the end of the lake. Alila said to me: "Master, this neighbourhood is much frequented by Cajoui." Cajoui was known as the chief of a most daring gang of brigands. Among his numerous atrocities he had amused himself, on that very day, by drowning twenty of his fellow-countrymen. I then determined to free the country of the odious assassin, and the advice of my lieutenant induced me to take a narrow path, that led us to a hut concealed in the midst of the woods. I told Alila to remain below, and to watch, while I went to endeavour to reconnoitre the persons who inhabited it. I went up by the small ladder that leads to the interior of the Tagalese huts; a young Indian woman was there, quite alone, and very busy plaiting a mat. I asked her for some fire to light my cigar, and returned to my lieutenant. Having accidentally cast my eyes upon the exterior of the hut, it appeared much larger than it did inside. I ran up again quickly, and looked all round the place in which the young girl was, and observed at the extremity of it a small door, covered over by a mat. I gave it a strong push, and at the moment, Cajoui, who, with his carbine on cock, was waiting for me behind the door, fired straight at me. The fire and the smoke blinded me, and by a most inconceivable chance the ball slightly grazed my clothes without wounding me. Alila, knowing I had no fire-arms, hearing the report, thought I was killed. He ran up to the top of the steps, and found me enveloped in a cloud of smoke, with my dagger in my hand, trying to find my enemy, who seeing me still standing erect, after he had shot at me, thought, no doubt, I had about me some *anten-anten*—a certain diabolic incantation that, according to the Indian belief, makes a man invulnerable to all sorts of fire-arms. The bandit was frightened, jumped out of a window, and ran away as fast as he could across the forest.

Alila could not believe what had happened to me; he felt all over my body, in order to convince himself that the ball had not passed through me. When he was quite sure that I had not received a wound, he said to me.

Master, if you had not had the anten-anten about you you would have been killed."

My Indians always believed I was possessed of this secret, as well as of many others. For instance, when they often saw me go for twenty-four, even for thirty-six hours, without eating or drinking, they became persuaded that I could live in that manner for an indefinite period; and one day, a good Tagalese padre, in whose house I chanced to be, almost went upon his knees while begging me to communicate to him the power I possessed, as he said, to live without food.

The Tagals have retained all their old superstitions. However, thanks to the Spaniards, they are all Christians; but they understand that religion nearly in the way that children do. They believe that to attend on Sundays and festival days at the Divine offices, and to go to confession and to communion once a year, is sufficient for the remission of all their sins. A little anecdote that occurred to me will show how far they understand evangelical charity.

One day two young Indians stole some poultry from one of their neighbours, and they came to sell them to my major-domo for about sixpence. I had them called before me, to administer a lecture, and to punish them With the utmost simplicity they made me this answer:

"It is true, master, we have done wrong, but we could not do otherwise; we are to go to communion to-morrow, and we had not money enough to get a cup of chocolate."

It is a custom with them to take a cup of chocolate after communion, and it was considered by them a greater sin to miss taking that than to commit the trifling theft of which they were guilty.

Two evil-doing demons play an important part among them, and in which all believed before the conquest of the Philippine islands. One of those malevolent demons is the Tic-balan which I have already mentioned, who dwells in the forests, in the interior of the large fig-trees. This demon can do every possible harm to anyone who dares not to respect him, or who does not carry certain herbs about his person, every time an Indian passes under one of these fig-trees he makes a movement towards it with his hand, saying: "*Tavit-po*,' Tagal words, signifying: "Lord! with your permission!" The lord of the place is the Tic-balan.

The other demon is called Azuan. She presides especially over parturitions in an evil manner, and an Indian is often seen, when his wife is in labour, perched upon the roof of his hut, with a sabre in his hand, thrusting the point into the air, and striking on all sides with the edge, to drive away, as he says, the Azuan. Sometimes he continues this manœuvring for hours, until the labour is over. One of their beliefs—and one that Europeans might envy—is, that when a child that has not reached the age of reason dies, it is happy for all the family, since it is an angel that has gone to heaven, to be the protector of all its relations. The day of the interment is a grand fête-day; relations and friends are invited; they drink, they dance, and they sing all night in the hut where the child died. But I perceive that the superstitions of the Indians are drawing me from my subject. I shall have occasion, further on, to describe the manners and customs of these singular people.

I now resume my statement, at the moment when my lieutenant tried to assure me that I had some anten-anten, and that consequently I could not be wounded by a shot fired at me.

He then addressed the young girl, who had remained in the corner, more dead than alive.

"Ah! cursed creature!" said he to her; "you are Cajoui's mistress: now your turn is come!"

At this moment he advanced towards her with his dagger in his hand. I ran between him and the poor girl, for I knew he was capable of killing anyone, particularly after I had been attacked in a manner that had placed me in danger.

"Wretch!" said I to him, "what are you going to do?"

"No great things, master; only to cut off the hair and ears of this vile woman, and then send her to tell Cajoui that we shall soon catch him!"

It cost me much trouble to prevent him from executing his plan. I was obliged to use all my authority, and to allow him to burn the cabin, after the terrified young girl, thanks to my protection, had fled into the forest.

My lieutenant was right in sending word to Cajoui that we should catch him. Some months after, and several leagues from the place where we had set fire to his cabin, one day, when three men of my guard accompanied me, we discovered, in the thickest part of the wood, a small hut. My Indians rushed forward in quick time to surround it; but almost all round it there was found a morass, covered over with sedges and bushes, when all three sunk in the mud, up to their middle. As I did not run as fast as they did I perceived the danger, and went round the marsh, so as to reach the cabin by the only accessible way. Suddenly I found myself face to face with Cajoui, and near enough almost to touch him. I had my dagger in my hand: he also had his—the struggle began. For a few seconds we aimed many strokes at each other, which each of us tried to avoid as well as he could. I think, however, that fortune was turning against me; the point of Cajoui's poignard had already entered rather deeply into my right arm, when with my left hand I took from my belt a large-sized pistol. I discharged it full at his breast: the ball and the wadding went through his body. For a few seconds Cajoui endeavoured still to defend himself; I struck him with all my force, and he fell at my feet; I then wrested from him his dagger, which I still retain. My people came out of the mud-hole and joined me. Compassion soon replaced the animosity we bore against Cajoui. We made a sort of litter; I bandaged his wound, and we carried him more than six leagues in this manner to my habitation, where he received all the care his state required. Every moment I expected him to die; every quarter of an hour my people came to tell me how he was; and they kept saying to me:

"Master, he cannot die, because he has the anten-anten upon him; and it is very lucky that you have some of it too, and that you fired at him, for our arms would have been of no avail against him."

I laughed at their simplicity, and expected from one minute to another to hear that the wounded man had breathed his last, when my lieutenant brought me, quite joyously, a small manuscript, about two inches square, saying to me:

"Here, master, is the anten-anten I found upon Cajoui's body."

At the same time one of my men announced his death.

"Ah!" said Alila, "if I had not taken the anten-anten from him he would be still alive."

I searched the small book through and through; prayers and invocations that had not much sense were therein written in the Tagalese language. A good friar who was present took it out of my hands. I imagined that he had the same curiosity as I had, but by no means; he rose up and went into the kitchen, and in a short time after came out and told me that he had made an *auto-da-fé* of it. My poor lieutenant almost cried with vexation, for he considered the little book to be his property, and thought that in possession of it he would be invulnerable. I should also have wished to have kept it, as a curious specimen of Indian superstition. The next day I had much trouble to persuade my stout friend, Father Miguel, to bury Cajoui in the cemetery. He maintained that a man who died with the anten-anten upon him ought not to receive Christian burial. To make him accede to my wishes it was necessary to tell him that the anten-anten had been taken from Cajoui before his death, and that he had time to repent.

A few days after Cajoui's death it was my faithful Alila's turn to encounter danger, not less imminent than that to which I had been exposed, at the time of my combat with the bandit chief. But Alila was brave, and, although he had no anten anten, fire-arms did not frighten him.

Large vessels—real Noah's arks—freighted by various merchants, sailed every week from the town of Pasig for that of Santa-Cruz, where every Thursday a large market was held. Eight daring and determined brigands went on board one of these vessels: they hid their arms among the bales of goods. The ship was scarcely out at sea when they seized them, and a horrible scene of slaughter ensued. All who endeavoured to resist them were butchered, even the pilot was thrown overboard; at length, finding no more resistance, they plundered the passengers of the money they had upon them, took every article of value they could find, and, loaded with their booty, they steered the vessel to a deserted spot on the shore, where they landed.

I had been informed of this nefarious enterprise, and went with haste to the spot where they landed. Unfortunately I arrived too late, for they had already escaped to the mountains, after they had divided the spoil. Notwithstanding the slight hope I entertained of overtaking them, I set off in pursuit, and after a long march I met an Indian, who informed me that one of the bandits, not so good a walker as the others, was not far off, and that if I and my guards ran quickly we might overtake him. Alila was the best runner—he was as fleet as a deer; so I told him: "Set out, Alila, and bring me that runaway, either dead or alive."

My brave lieutenant, to be less encumbered in the race, left his gun with us, took a long spear, and went off. Shortly after we had lost sight of him we heard the report of fire-arms; we knew it must be the brigand firing upon Alila, and we all thought that he was killed or wounded. We hastened forward, in the hopes of arriving in time to render him assistance; but we soon saw him coming leisurely towards us; his face and clothes were covered with blood, the spear in his right hand, and in his left the hideous head of the bandit, which he carried by the hair—as Judith had formerly done with that of Holophernes. But my poor Alila was wounded, and my first care was to examine if the wound was serious. When I was satisfied it was not dangerous, I asked him for the details of his combat.

"Master," said he to me, "shortly after I left you I perceived the bandit; he saw me also, and ran off as quickly as he could, but I ran faster than he, and was soon close to him. When he lost all hopes of escaping he turned upon me and presented his pistol; I was not alarmed, and advanced towards him at all risk. The pistol was fired, and I felt myself wounded in the face; this wound did not stop me. I darted at him and pierced his body with my spear; but, as he was too heavy for me to bring to you, I cut off his head, and here it is."

When I had congratulated Alila upon his success, I examined his wound, and found that a fragment of a ball, cut into four pieces, had hit him upon the cheek, and was flattened on the bone. I extracted it, and a speedy cure followed.

Now, as I have almost terminated, and shall not return to, my numerous adventures with the bandits, I resume the continuation of my ordinary life at Jala-Jala.

The House of La Planche.

CHAPTER VIII.

Death of my Brother Robert—Our Party at Jala-Jala—Illness and Last Moments of my Friend Bermigan—Recovery and Departure for France of Lafond—Joachim Balthazard: his Eccentricity—Tremendous Gale of Wind—Narrow Escape in Crossing the Lake—Safe Return to Jala-Jala—Destruction of my House and the Village by a Typhoon—Rendezvous with a Bandit—Ineffectual Attempts to Reform Him—His Death—Journey to Tapuzi—Its Inaccessibility—Government of the Tapuzians—Morality and Religious Character of their Chief—Their Curiosity at Beholding a White Man—Former Wickedness and Divine Punishment—We bid Adieu to the Tapuzians, and Return to Jala-Jala.

AT this period a sad event plunged my house into mourning. Letters from my family announced to me that my brother Robert had returned from Porto-Rico, but that soon after a serious illness had carried him to the grave. He died in the arms of my mother and sisters, in the small house of La Planche, where, as I said before, we had all been brought up.

My excellent Anna, wept with us, and exerted every means that interesting affection could suggest to alleviate the grief my brother Henry and myself experienced from this melancholy bereavement. A few months afterwards a new source of sorrow fell to our lot. Our little social party at Jala-Jala consisted of my sister-in-law; of Delaunay, a young man from St. Malo, who had come from Bourbon to establish at Manilla some manufactories for baking sugar; of Bermigan, a young Spaniard; and my friend, Captain Gabriel Lafond, like myself, from Nantes. He had come to the Philippine islands on board the *Fils de France*, had passed some years in South America, and had occupied several places of distinction in the navy, as captain-commandant, until at last, after many adventures and vicissitudes, he came with a small fortune to Manilla, where he bought a vessel, and set sail for the Pacific Ocean, to fish for the *balaté* or sea-worm. He had scarcely reached the island of Tongatabou when the vessel struck upon the rocks that surround this island; he saved himself by swimming to the shore, having lost everything. From thence he went to the Marianne islands, where grief and bad food caused him to fall ill; he returned to Manilla, labouring under dysentry. I had him brought to my house, and whilst there attended to him with all the care a fellow-countryman and a good friend endowed with sterling and amiable qualities, deserved. Our evenings were spent in amusing and instructive conversation. As we had all travelled a great deal, each had somethimg to relate. During the day the invalids kept company with the ladies, while my brother and myself followed our respective avocations. But soon, alas! a shocking event disturbed the calm that reigned at Jala-Jala. Bermigan fell so dangerously ill, that a few days sufficed to convince me there was no hope of saving him. I shall never forget the fatal night: we were all assembled in the drawing-room, grief and consternation were in every heart and pourtrayed in every countenance; in an adjoining room a few short steps from us, we heard the death-rattle of poor Bermigan, who had only a few minutes to live. My excellent friend, Lafond, whom sickness had reduced almost to the last stage, broke silence, and said: "Well! poor Bermigan goes to-day, and in a few days, perhaps to-morrow, it will be my turn. Just see! my dear Don Pablo; I may almost say that I no longer exist. Look at my feet—my body! I am a mere skeleton; I can scarcely take any food. Ah! it is better to be dead than live like this!"

I was so persuaded that his forebodings would not be delayed in being realized, that I scarcely dared to utter the smallest consolation or any hopes. Who could then have told me that he and I alone were to survive all those who surrounded us, full of life and health? But, alas! let us not here anticipate future events.

Poor Bermigan breathed his last. Our house at Jala-Jala was no longer untouched by the hand of Death—a human being had expired therein; and on the following day, in sadness and silence, we all proceeded to the cemetery, to inter the body of our friend, and to render him the last proofs of our respect. The body was laid at the foot of a large cross, which is placed in the centre of the grave-yard. For many days sadness and silence prevailed in our home at Jala-Jala.

Some time afterwards I had the gratification to see the efforts I employed for my friend Lafond were successful. By means of the strong remedies I administered his health was speedily restored, his appetite returned, and he was soon able to set sail for France. He is now residing in Paris, married to a woman possessed of every quality necessary to make a man happy, and is the father of three children. Holding an honourable position, and enjoying public esteem, he has never forgotten the six months he spent at Jala-Jala, for ingratitude never sullied his noble, loving, and devoted heart. A sincere attachment still subsists between us, and I am happy thus to assure him that he is, and ever will be, to me a valued friend.*

As I have now mentioned several persons who resided for some time at Jala-Jala, I must not forget one of my colonists, Joachim Balthazard, a native of Marseilles, as eccentric a man as I have ever known. When Joachim was young, he set sail from Marseilles. When he arrived at Bourbon, his name not being on the crew's list, he was arrested, and put on board the *Astrolabe*, which was then making a voyage round the world. He deserted at the Marianne islands, and came to the Philippines in the greatest distress, and addressed himself to some good friars, in order, as he said, to effect his conversion and his salvation. He lived among them, and at their expense, for nearly two years; afterwards he opened a coffee-house at Manilla, and spent in pleasure and debauchery a large sum of money that a fellow-countryman and I had advanced him. He afterwards built upon my grounds a large straw edifice, that had more the appearance of a huge magazine than of a house. There he kept a kind of seraglio, adopted all the children which his numerous wives gave him, and, with his own family, made his house not unlike a mutual school. Whenever he was weary of either of his wives he called one of his workmen, saying to him in the most serious manner:

"There is a wife that I give you; be a good husband, treat her well: and you, woman, this is your husband, be faith

* See Appendix, No. 1.

ful to him. Go, may God bless you! Be off, and let me never see you again."

He was generally without a farthing, or all of a sudden rich with heavy sums, that were spent in a few days. He borrowed from everybody, and never paid them back; he lived like a real Indian, and was as cowardly as a half-drowned chicken. His light-coloured hair, sallow complexion, and beardless face, gave him the nick-name among the Indians of *Onela-Dogou*, Tagalese words, that signify "one who has no blood."

As I was one day crossing over the lake in a small canoe with him and two Indians, we were assailed by one of those extraordinary gales of wind, which in the Chinese seas are called *Tay-Foung* (typhoon). These gales of wind. though extremely rare, are tremendous. The sky is covered with the heaviest clouds; the rain pours in torrents; the day-light disappears, almost as much as in the densest fog; and the wind blows with such fury that it throws down everything it reaches in its course.*

We were in our canoe; the wind had scarcely begun to blow with all its violence than Balthazard commenced to invoke all the saints in Paradise. Almost in despair, he cried out aloud

"Oh, God! have mercy upon me, a wretched sinner! Grant me the grace that I may have an opportunity of confessing my sins, and of receiving absolution!"

All these lamentations and appeals served only to frighten my two Indians, and most undoubtedly our position was critical enough for us to endeavour to retain our presence of mind, so

* I experienced two such gales during my residence at Jala-Jala—the one I am now speaking of, and another to which I shall afterwards allude.

as to attend to the management of our little boat, which from one moment to another was in danger of being swamped. However, I was certain that, being provided with two large beams of bamboos, it could keep its position in the current between two waters and not capsize, if we had the precaution and strength to scud before the wind, and not turn the side to a wave, for in such case we should all have been drowned. What I foresaw, happened. A wave burst upon us; for a few minutes we were plunged in the deep, but when the wave passed over we came above water. Our canoe was swamped between the currents, but we did not abandon it; we put our legs under the seats, and held them fast; the half of our body was above water. But every time that a wave came towards us it passed over our heads, and then went off, giving us time to breathe until another wave came and dashed over us. Every three or four minutes the same manœuvring took place. My Indians and I used all our strength and skill to scud on before the wind. Balthazard had ceased his lamentations; we all kept silence; from time to time I only uttered these words:

"Take courage, boys, we shall reach the shore."

Our position then became much worse, for night set in. The rain continued to pour in torrents, the wind increased in fury. From time to time we received some light from globes of fire, like what the sailors call "Saint Elmo's fire." While these rays of light continued I looked as far around me as I could, and only perceived an immense body of water in furious agitation. For nearly two hours we were tossed about by the waves that drove us towards the beach, and, at a moment when we least expected it, we found ourselves driven into the midst of an extensive grove of lofty bamboos. I then knew that we were over the land, and that the lake had inundated the country for several miles around. We were up to our breasts in water, and it was not in our power to pass through the inundation. The darkness was too great to allow us to go in any direction; our canoe was no longer of any use to us, as it was entangled among the bamboos. We climbed up the trees as well as we could, even to the height where the bamboos end in sharp points; our bodies were much torn by the sharp thorns growing on the small branches; the rain continued to pour without intermission; the wind still blowed, and each gust caused the bamboos to bend, the flexible branches of which tore our bodies and faces. I have suffered a great deal in the course of my life, but no night ever appeared to me so long and cruel as this! Joachim Balthazard then recovered his speech, and, in a trembling, broken voice, said to me:

"Ah! Don Pablo, do write I beg of you, to my mother, and tell her the tragical end of her son!"

I could not help answering him: "You cowardly rascal! Do you think, then, that I am more at my ease than you are? Hold your tongue, otherwise I shall make you turn diver, so that I may never hear you again." Poor Joachim then knew what to do, and did not utter a word; only from time to time he made us aware of his trouble by his deep moans.

The wind, which was blowing from the north-west, towards four o'clock in the morning suddenly changed to the east, and shortly afterwards gave over. It was almost daylight: we were saved. We could at last see one another; all four of us looked in a wretched condition; our clothes being torn to pieces. Our bodies were lacerated, and covered with deep scratches. The cold had penetrated into the very marrow of our bones, and the long bath we had taken had wrinkled the skin; we looked just like drowned people taken out of the water, where they had been for some hours. Nevertheless, crippled as we were, we slipped down from the bamboos, and were soon bathing in the waters of the lake. The effect was healthful and agreeable: it seemed like a warm bath at 30 degrees of heat.

We were quite restored by this mild temperature. We got our canoe out of the grove, where fortunately it had been caught so fast that neither the waves nor the currents could drive it any farther. We again set it afloat, and soon succeeded in reaching an Indian hut, where we dried ourselves, and recruited our strength. Calm was now re-established; the sun shone in all its splendour, but everywhere traces of the typhoon were visible. In the course of the day we reached Jala-Jala, where our arrival caused great joy. They knew at home that I was on the lake, and everything led them to presume that I had perished. My good and dear Anna threw herself into my arms in tears; she had been in such anxiety for my safety, that for some moments the tears that flowed down her cheeks alone expressed her joy at again seeing me.

Balthazard returned to his seraglio. As long as he was under my protection the Indians respected him, but after my departure from Jala-Jala he was assassinated; and all those who knew him agreed that he had deserved his fate for more than one cause.

As I have mentioned this typhoon, I am going to anticipate a little, in describing, as briefly as possible, a still more frightful one than that which I experienced in my slight canoe and in the bamboo grove.

I had just completed some pretty baths upon the lake opposite my house. I was quite satisfied and proud of procuring this new pleasure for my wife. On the very day that the Indians had added the last ornaments to them, towards evening a western wind began to blow furiously; by degrees the waters of the lake became agitated, and shortly we no longer doubted but that we were going to have a typhoon.

My brother and I stayed some time examining, through the panes of glass, whether the baths would resist the strength of the wind, but in a heavy squall my poor edifice disappeared like a castle made of cards. We withdrew from the window, and luckily too, for a heavier squall than that which had destroyed the baths burst in the windows that faced to the west. The wind drove through the house, and opened a way for itself, by throwing down all the wall over the entrance-door. The lake was so agitated that the waves went over my house, and inundated all the apartments. We were not able to remain there any longer. By assisting each other, my wife, my brother, a young Frenchman who was then staying at Jala-Jala, and myself, succeeded in reaching a room on the ground-floor; the light came from a very small window; there, in almost total darkness, we spent the greater part of the night, my brother and I leaning our shoulders against the window, opposing with all our strength that of the wind, which threatened to force it in. In this small room there were several jars of brandy: my excellent Anna poured some into the hollow of her hand, and gave it us to drink, to support our strength and to warm us. At break of day the wind ceased, and calm re-appeared. All the furniture and decorations of my house were broken and shattered to pieces; all the rooms were inundated, and the store-rooms were full of sand, carried there by the waters of the lake. Soon my house became an asylum for my colonists, who had all spent a wretched night, and were without shelter.

The sun soon shone splendidly; the sky was cloudless; but my sadness was extreme when, from a window, I examined the disasters produced by the typhoon. There was no village! Every hut was levelled to the ground. The church was thrown down—my store-houses, my sugar factory, were entirely destroyed; there was then nothing more than heaps of ruins. My fine cane-fields were altogether destroyed, and the country, which previously had appeared so beautiful, seemed as if it had passed through a long wintry season. There was no longer any verdure to be seen; the trees were entirely leafless, with their boughs broken, and portions of the wood were entirely torn down; and all this devastation had taken place within a few hours. During that and the following day the lake threw up, upon the shore, the bodies of several unfortunate Indians who had perished. The first care of Padre Miguel was to bury the dead, and for a long time afterwards there were to be seen, in the grave-yard of Jala-Jala, crosses, with the inscription: "*An unknown who died during the typhoon.*" My Indians began immediately to rebuild their huts, and I, as far as possible, to repair my disasters.

The fertile nature of the Philippine islands speedily effaced the aspect of mourning which it had assumed. In less than eight days the trees were completely covered with new leaves, and exhibited themselves as in a brilliant summer, after the frightful winter had passed over. The typhoon had embraced a diameter of about two leagues, and, like a violent hurricane, had upset and shattered everything it met during its course.

But enough of disasters: I return to the epoch when the death of poor Bermigan caused affliction to us all.

All was prosperity in my dwelling: my Indians were happy; the population of Jala-Jala increased every day; I was beloved and respected. I had rendered great service to the Spanish government by the incessant warfare I carried on against the bandits; and I may say that even amongst them I enjoyed a high reputation. They looked upon me, indeed, as their enemy, but in the light of a brave enemy, incapable of committing any act of baseness against them, and who carried on an honourable warfare; and the Indian character was so well known to me, that I did not fear they would play me any low tricks, or would treacherously attack me. Such was my conviction, that around my house I was never accompanied by day or by night. I traversed without fear all the forests and mountains, and I often even treated with these honourable bandits, as one power does with another, by not disdaining the invitations sometimes sent to me to come to a certain place, where, without fear of surprise, they could consult me, or even invoke my assistance. This sort of rendezvous was always held in the night, and in very lonely places. On their side, as well as on mine, a promise given of not doing any injury to each other was religiously observed. In these nocturnal conversations, held without witnesses, I often brought back to a life of peace mistaken men, whom the turbulence of youth had thrown into a series of crimes, which the laws would have visited with most severe punishment. Sometimes, however, I failed in my attempts, and especially when I had to do with proud and untameable characters, such as are to be found among men who never have had any other guide but natural instinct. One day, among others, I received a letter from a half-breed, a great criminal, who infested the neighbouring province of Laguna; he told me that he wished to see me, and begged me to come alone in the middle of the night to a wild spot, where he would also come alone: I did not hesitate to go to the place appointed. I found him there as he had promised me. He told me that he wished to change his mode of life, and to dwell on my estate. He added, that he had never committed any crime against the Spaniards, but only against the Indians and the half-breeds. It would have been impossible for me to have received him without compromising myself. I proposed to place him in the house of a friar, where he might remain concealed for several years, until his crimes were forgotten, and then he could enter into society. After a moment's reflection, he replied:

"No, that would be to lose mv liberty. To live as a slave! I would prefer to die."

I then proposed to him to go to Tapuzi, a place where the bandits, when hotly pursued, were enabled to conceal themselves with impunity.—(I shall very soon have occasion to speak of this village.)—The half-breed, with an insignificant gesture, replied:

"No; the person I wish to take with me would not come there. You can do nothing for me, adieu!"

He then pressed my hand, and we separated. Some days afterwards, a hut in which he was seen, near Manilla, was surrounded by the troops of the line. The bandit then caused the owners of the hut to quit it, and when he saw them out of danger he took his carabine and began firing upon the soldiers, who on their side returned the attack on the hut. When it was riddled with balls, and the bandit had ceased to defend himself, a soldier approached the hut and set fire to it, so great was the fear they entertained of then finding him alive.

These nocturnal interviews having led me to mention Tapuzi, I cannot refrain from dedicating a few lines to this remarkable retreat, where men, when proscribed by the law, live together in a sort of accord and union of a most extraordinary kind.

Tapuzi,* which in the Tagal language, signifies "end of the world," is a little village, situate in the interior of the mountains, nearly twenty-five leagues from Jala-Jala. It was formed there by bandits and men who had escaped from the galleys, who live in liberty, govern themselves, and are altogether, on account of the inaccessible position which they occupy, safe from any pursuit which could be ordered against them by the Spanish government. I had often heard this singular village mentioned, but I had never met anyone who had visited it, or could give me any positive details relative to it. One day, therefore, I resolved to go thither myself. I stated my intention to my lieutenant, who said:

"Master, I shall find there, no doubt, some of my old comrades, and then we shall have nothing to fear."

Three of us set out together, under the pretext of quite a different journey. For two days we walked in the midst of mountains, by paths almost impracticable. The third day we reached a torrent, the bed of which was blocked up by enormous stones. This ravine was the only road by which we could get to Tapuzi; it was the natural and impregnable rampart which defended the village against the attack of the Spanish troops. My lieutenant had just told me:

"Look, master, above your head. None but the inhabitants of Tapuzi know the paths which lead to the top of the mountains. All along the length of the ravine they have placed enormous stones, that they have only to push to throw them

* Tapuzi is situated in the mountains of Limutan. Limutan is a Tagalese word, signifying "altogether forgotten."

down upon those who should come to attack them; a whole army could not penetrate among them, if they wished to give any opposition."

I clearly saw that we were not in a very agreeable position, and against which, if the Tapuzians should consider us as enemies, we could oppose no defence. But we were involved in it, and there was no means of retreating, it was absolutely necessary to go to Tapuzi. We had been already more than an hour in this ravine when an immense block of stone fell down perpendicularly, and broke into pieces only twenty yards before us: it was a warning. We stopped, laid down our arms, and sat down. Perhaps just such another block as what had fallen was hanging over our heads, ready to crush us to pieces. We heard a scream near us. I told my lieutenant to proceed alone towards the direction it came from. In a few minutes he returned, accompanied by two Indians, who, confident in my pacific intentions towards them, came to fetch us, to take us to the village. We proceeded cheerfully on the remainder of the road until we reached the spot where ended the sort of funnel we were walking in. Upon this height there was to be seen a plain, some miles in circumference, surrounded by high mountains. The part that we were in was stopped up by enormous blocks of rocks, lying one on the top of the other. From behind stretched forth an abrupt threatening mountain, without any signs of vegetation—not unlike an ancient European fortress, that some magical power had raised in the midst of the high mountains that commanded it. With one glance I beheld the whole of the site we were crossing, and at the same time reflected upon the great varieties nature presents to our view. We soon reached the long wished-for object of our journey—the village of Tapuzi. It lies at the extreme end of a plain, composed of about sixty thatched huts, similar to those of the Indians. The inhabitants were all at their windows, to witness our arrival. Our guides conducted us to their chief, or *Matanda-sanayon*, a fine old man, from the look of his face about eighty years of age. He bowed affably to us, and addressed himself to me.

"How are you come here—as a friend, or is it curiosity—or do the cruel laws of the Spaniards perhaps compel you to seek refuge among us? If such is the case, you are welcome; you will find us brothers."

"No," I said to him; "we do not come to stay among you. I am your neighbour, and lord of Jala-Jala. I am come to see you, to offer you my friendship, and to ask yours."

At the name Jala-Jala the old man looked quite astonished; he then said to me:

"It is a long time since I heard you spoken of as an agent of the government for pursuing unfortunate men, but I have heard also that you fulfilled your mission with much kindness, and that often you were their protector, so be welcome."

After this first recognition they presented us some mill and some kidney potatoes, and during our repast the old mar conversed freely with me.

"Several years ago," said he to me, "at a period I cannot recollect, some men came to live in Tapuzi. The peace and safety they enjoyed made others imitate their example, who sought like themselves to avoid the punishment of some faults they had committed. We soon saw fathers of families, with their wives and children flock hither; this was the foundation of the small government that you see. Now here almost all is in common; some fields of kidney potatoes or Indian corn, and hunting, suffice for us; he who possesses anything gives to him who has nothing Almost all our clothing is knitted and woven by our wives; the abaca, or vegetable silk, from the forest supplies us the thread that is necessary; we do not know what money is, we do not require any. Here there is no ambition; each one is certain of not suffering from hunger. From time to time strangers come to visit us. If they are willing to submit to our laws, they remain with us; they have a fortnight of probation to go through before they decide. Our laws are lenient and indulgent. We have not forgotten the religion of our forefathers, and God no doubt will forgive me my first faults, on account of my efforts for so many years to promote his worship, and the well-being of my equals."

"But," said I to him, "who is your chief, who are your judges and priests?"

"It is I," said he, "who fulfil all those functions. Formerly they lived like savages here. I was young, robust, and devoted to all my brothers. Their chief had just expired: I was chosen to replace him. I then took care to do nothing but what was just, and conducive to the happiness of those who confided in me. Until then they had devoted but little attention to religion: I wished to put my people in mind that they were born Christians. I appointed one hour every Sunday for us to pray together, and I have invested myself with all the attributes of a minister of the Gospel. I celebrate the marriages, I pour water upon the foreheads of the infants, and I offer consolations to the dying. In my youth, I was a chorister; I remembered the church ceremonies; and if I do not actually possess the necessary attributes for the functions I have given myself, I practise them with faith and love. This is the reason I trust that my good intentions will obtain my forgiveness from Him who is the Sovereign Lord of all."

During the whole time of the old man's conversation I was in continual admiration. I was among people who had the reputation of living in the greatest licentiousness as thieves and robbers. Their character was altogether misunderstood. It was a real, great phalanstery, composed of brothers, almost all worthy of the name. Above all I admired this fine old man, who, with moral principles and simple laws, had governed them for so many years. On the other hand, what an example that was of free men not being able to live without choosing a chief, and bringing one another back to the practice of virtuous actions!

I explained to the old man all my thoughts. I bestowed upon him a thousand praises for his conduct, and assured him that the Archbishop of Manilla would approve all the religious

Church of Pandacan, in the environs of Manilla.

acts he performed with so noble an object. I even offered to intercede with the archbishop in his behalf, that he might send a pastor to assist him. But he replied:

"No, thank you, sir; never speak about us. We should certainly be glad to have a minister of the Gospel here, but soon, under his influence, we should be subjected to the Spanish government. It would be requisite for us to have money to pay our contributions. Ambition would soon creep in amongst us, and from the freedom which we now enjoy, we should gradually sink into a state of slavery, and should no longer be happy. Once more I entreat of you, do not speak of us: give me your word that you will not."

This argument appeared so just to me that I acquiesced to his request. I again gave him all the praise he deserved, and promised never to disturb the peace of the inhabitants of his village under any pretext whatever.

In the evening we received visits from all the inhabitants, particularly from the women and children, who all had an immoderate curiosity to see a white man. None of the Tapuzian women had ever been out of their village, and had scarcely ever lost sight of their huts; it was not, therefore, astonishing that they were so curious.

The next day I went round the plain, and visited the fields of kidney potatoes and Indian corn, the principal nourishment of the inhabitants. The old chief and some elderly people accompanied me. When we reached the spot where, upon the eve, I had already remarked enormous blocks of rock, the old man paused and told me:

"Look yonder, Castilla.* At a time when the Tapuzians

* In the eyes of the natives of Tagal all Europeans are Spaniards.

were without religion, and lived as wild beasts, God punished them. Look at all the part of that mountain quite stripped of vegetation: one night, during a tremendous earthquake, that mountain split in two—one part swallowed up the half of the village that then stood on the place where those enormous rocks are. A few hundred steps further on all would have been destroyed; there would no longer have existed a single person in Tapuzi: but a part on the population was not injured, and came and settled themselves where the village now is. Since then we pray to the Almighty, and live in a manner so as not to deserve so severe a chastisement as that experienced by the wretched victims of that awful night."

The conversation and society of this old man—I might say the King of Tapuzi—was most interesting to me. But I had already been four days absent from Jala-Jula. I ordered my lieutenant to prepare for our departure. We bid most affectionate adieus to our hosts, and set off. In two days I returned home, quite pleased with my journey and the good inhabitants of Tapuzi.

Hunting party at Jala-Jala.

CHAPTER IX.

Suppression of War between two Indian Towns—Flourishing Condition of Jala-Jala—Hospitality to Strangers—Field Sports—Bat and Lizard Shooting—Visit to, and Description of, the Isle of Socolme—Adventure with a Cayman—Cormorants—We Visit Los Banos—Monkey Shooting—Expedition to, and Description of, the Grotto of San-Mateo—Magnificent aspect of the Interior.

I FOUND Anna in great trouble, not only on account of my absence, but because, on the previous evening, information had been received that the inhabitants of the two largest towns in the province had, as it was stated, declared war against each other; the most courageous amongst them, to the number of three or four hundred on each side, had started for the island of Talem. There both parties, in the presence of each other, were upon the point of engaging in a battle; already, while skirmishing, several had been mortally wounded.

This news frightened Anna she knew that I was not a man who would await quietly at home the issue of the battle; she already fancied she saw me, with my ten guards, engaged in the thick of the fight, and perhaps a victim of my devotedness. I comforted her as I had always done, promising to be prudent, and not forget her; but there was not a moment to lose; it was necessary, at all risks, to try to put an end to a conflict that might no doubt cause the death of many men. How could I do so with my ten guards? Dare I pretend to impose my will as law on this vast multitude? Clearly not. To attempt to do it by force would be to sacrifice all: what was to be done? Arm all my Indians—but I had not boats enough to carry them to Talem: in this difficulty I decided upon setting out alone with my lieutenant. We took our arms, and set sail in a canoe, that we steered ourselves; we had scarcely come near the beach within hail of the shore, when some armed Indians called out to us to stand off, otherwise they would fire upon us. Without paying attention to this threat, my lieutenant and I, some minutes later, jumped boldly on shore, and after a few steps we found ourselves in the midst of the combatants.

I went immediately up to the chiefs and addressed them.

"Wretched men," I said to them, "what are you going to do? It is upon you who command that the severity of the law will fall. It is still time: try to deserve your pardon. Order your men to give me up their arms; lay down your own, or else in a few minutes I will place myself at the head of your enemies to fight against you. Obey, if not you will be treated as rebels."

They listened attentively to me; they were half conquered. However, one of them made me this reply:

"And if you take away our arms who will satisfy us that our enemies will not come to attack us?"

"I will," I told them; "I give you my word; and if they do not obey me as you are going to do, I will return to you, I will give you back your arms, and will fight at your head."

These words, said with a tone of authority and command, produced the effect I expected. The chiefs, without uttering a word, laid their arms at my feet. Their example was followed by all the combatants, and, in a moment, a heap of carabines, guns, spears, and cutlasses were laid down before me. I appointed ten among these individuals who had just obeyed me, gave them each a gun, and told them:

"I confide to you the care of these arms. If anyone attempts to take possession of them, fire upon the assailants."

I pretended to take down their names, and went off to the opposite camp, where I found all the combatants on foot, ready to march and fight against their enemies. I stopped them, saying:

"The battle is over—your enemies are disarmed. You, too, must give me up your arms, or else immediately embark in your canoes, and go home. If you do not obey me, I will give back their arms instantly to your opponents, and I will put myself at their head to fight against you. Perform what I command you; I promise you all shall be forgotten."

There was no room for hesitation. The Indians knew that I did not allow much time for reflection, and that my threats and chastisements followed each other closely. Shortly after, they all embarked in their canoes. I remained on the beach alone, with my lieutenant, until I had almost lost sight of this small fleet. I then returned to the other camp, where I was impatiently expected. I announced to the Indians they had no longer any enemies, and that consequently they could go back quietly to their village.

But a few days elapsed, as may be seen, without my having new dangers to encounter. I was accustomed to them: I relied upon my star, and triumphed from all my imprudences. My Indians were blindly submissive to me. I was so certain of their fidelity, that I no longer took against them the precautions which I considered necessary during the first year of my residence at Jala-Jala.

My Anna took part every day more and more in my labours, anxieties, and even in some of my dangers. Would it have been possible not to have loved her with deeper affection, than that which one feels for a companion leading a peaceful and insignificant life? With what gladness she received me after the shortest absence! Joy and satisfaction shone on her face, her caresses were as a balsam that healed all my lassitude, and even the reproaches she addressed me so gently, for the uneasiness I had caused her, fell upon my heart as drops of beatitude.

Jala-Jala was most flourishing; immense fields of rice, sugar-cane, and coffee, had taken the place of woods and forests unproductive in themselves. Rich pasture-grounds were covered with numerous flocks; and a fine Indian village stood in the centre of the labouring-ground. Here, there was everywhere to be seen plenty, activity; and joy smiled on the countenances of all the inhabitants. My own dwelling had become the rendezvous, or resorting-place, of all the travellers arriving at Manilla, and a refuge of convalescence of many patients, who would come and breathe the good and mild air of Jala-Jala, as well as enjoy its pleasures and amusements. Under that roof there was no distinction, no difference; all were equals in our eyes,

Cascade near Jala-Jala.

whether French, Spanish, English, American. No matter to what nation belonged those who landed at Jala-Jala, they were received like brothers, and with all that cordial hospitality to to be found formerly in our colonies. My visitors enjoyed full and active liberty on my little estate; but he who was not desirous of eating alone was obliged to remember the time of meals: during the other hours of the day one and all followed their own inclinations. For instance, naturalists went in pursuit of insects and birds, and made an ample harvest of every species of plants. Persons ailing met with the assiduous care of a physician, as well as with the kind attention and enjoyed the company of a most amiable and well-informed mistress of the house, who had the natural talent of enchanting all those who spent but a short time in her society. They who liked walking might look about for the fine views, and choose their resting-place either in the woods, the mountains, near the cascades or the brooks, or on the beautiful borders of the lake.

But to sportsmen Jala-Jala was really a "promised land;" there they always found a good pack of hounds, Indians to guide them, good stout horses to carry them across the various mountains and plains, where the stag and wild boar were to be met with most plentifully; and were they desirous of less fatiguing exercise, they only had to jump into some of our light canoes, and skim over the blue waters, shooting on their way at the hosts of aquatic birds flying around them in all directions,—they could even land on the various small islands situated between Jala-Jala and the isle of Talem. There they could find a sort of sport utterly unknown in Europe—that is, immense bats, a species of vampire, designated by naturalists by the name of *roussettes*. During six months in the year, at

LA GIRONIERE IN HIS HUNTING DRESS.—*Page* 186.

the period of the eastern monsoon, every tree on these little isles is covered, from the topmost down to the lowest branch, with those huge bats, that supply the place of the foliage which they have entirely destroyed. Muffled up in their vast wings they sleep during the whole day, and in the night-time they start off in large bodies roaming about in search of their prey. But as soon as the western monsoon has succeeded the eastern, they disappear, and repair always to the same place,—the eastern coast of Luzon, where they take shelter; after the monsoon changed, they return to their former quarters.

As soon as our guests would alight upon one of these islands, they opened their fire, and continued it till—frightened by so many explosions and the screams of the wounded, clinging to and hanging from the branches—the bats would fly away in a body—*en masse.* For some time they would whirl and turn round and round like a dense cloud over their abandoned home, imitating, in a most perfect way, those furies we see in certain engravings representing the infernal regions, and then, flying off a short distance, would perch upon the trees in a neighbouring isle. If the sportsmen were not over-fatigued by the slaughter they might then follow them, and set-to again; but they generally found they had made victims enough, and diversified their pleasure by picking up the slain from under the trees. The bat shooting over, our sportsmen would then proceed to a new sport—

"To fresh fields and pastures new;"

that is, in pursuit of and shooting at the iguanas, a large species of lizard, measuring from five to six feet long, which infest the rocks on the borders of the lake. Tired of firing without being obliged to show any skill, our chasseurs would re-embark in their pirogues and row in search of new amusement,—this was, to shoot at the eagles that came hovering over their heads. Here skill was requisite, as well as a prompt, sure glance of the eye, as it is only with ball that these enormous birds of prey can be reached. Our fowlers would then return home, with their boats full of game; and everyone, of course, had his own feats of prowess to relate.

The flesh of the iguana and the bat is savoury and delicate; but as for its taste, that entirely depends upon the imagination, as may here be seen.

After returning from one of these grand shooting excursions to the minor islands, a young American informed me that his friends and he himself were most desirous of tasting the iguana and the bat; so, supposing them all to be of the same mind, I ordered my *maître-d'hôtel* to prepare for dinner a curry of iguana and a ragout of bats. The first dish served round at dinner was the curry, of which they one and all partook with very good appetite; upon which I ventured to say: "You see the flesh of the iguana is most delicate." At these words all my guests turned pale, and they all, by a sudden motion, pushed their plates from before them, not even being able to swallow what their mouths contained. I was therefore obliged to order the removal of the *entrées* of iguana and bats before we could proceed with the repast.

When it was in my power, I would accompany my guests in their excursions, and then the chase was abundant and full of interest, because I ever took care to guide them towards places abounding in game and very picturesque. Sometimes I would take them to the isle of Socolme, a still more curious place indeed than the bat islands. Socolme is a circular lake—

being one league in circumference—in the midst of the great lake of Bay, from which it is separated by a cordon or ribbon of land; or, to express myself better, by a mountain which rises to an elevation of from twelve to fifteen hundred feet; the centre of the mountain at the summit is occupied by the lake of Socolme, and is evidently the crater of an extinct volcano. Both sides are completely covered with large trees of luxuriant growth. It is on the border of the small lake—where the Indians never go, through fear of the caymans—that almost all the aquatic birds of the grand lake resort to lay their eggs. Every tree, white with the guano which they deposit there, is covered with birds'-nests, full of eggs and birds of every size and age.

One day, in company of my brother and Mr. Hamilton Lindsay,* an Englishman, who was as fearless an explorer as ourselves, I started from the plantation, with the intention of having some light canoes carried across the high ground which separates the Socolme lake from the lake of Bay, and of using them on the lake; and, after overcoming many difficulties, we, by the assistance of our Indians, carried out this project.

We were the first tourists that ever ventured to expose our lives on this Socolme lake. The Indians who had come with us refused most decidedly to enter the boats, and exerted all their eloquence to prevent us from going on the water. They spoke to us thus:—

"You are going, for no good purpose, to expose yourselves to very great dangers, against which you have no means of defence, for before you have gone far you will see thousands of

* While this work was in the press, Mr. Hamilton Lindsay, who has already published an account of his "Voyage to the Northern Ports of China," kindly furnished the Publishers with confirmatory proofs of M. de la Gironiere's narrative, see Appendix, No. II.

caymans rising out of the deep water; they will come to attack you, and what can you oppose to those ferocious and invulner able monsters? Your guns and bullets connot wound them. And as for escape by rowing quickly, that is not possible. In their own element they swim much faster than your canoes, and when they come up to you they will turn your boats up-side-down with far more ease than you can drive it along; and then the frightful scene will begin, from which you cannot escape."

There was much good sense in what they said, and there can be no doubt that it was most imprudent of us to embark in a little frail canoe, and to make a trip over a lake inhabited by such numbers of caymans, and especially since it was to be feared that the lake did not supply fish enough to satisfy their voracity; and of course when enraged by hunger they were more to be dreaded.

But we were never deterred by dangers or difficulties; so, taking no account of the prognostics of my prudent Indians, we, while they were delivering their long speeches, had lashed together two canoes for greater security.

We had not proceeded many yards from the bank, when we all experienced feelings of alarm, attributable, no doubt, to the expectation of danger being immediate, as well as to the aspect of the place which presented itself to our view.

We were down in the deepest part of a gulf, surrounded by lofty and precipitous mountains, which were externally covered with very thick vegetation. They, on all sides, presented a barrier, through which it was impossible to pass. The shadows which they cast over the water, at the extreme point of the lake, produced the effect of half darkness, which, in conjunction with the silence prevailing in that dismal solitude, gave it an aspect so dreary and saddening, as to produce in us most painful feelings; each of us as it were, struck with terror, kept his thoughts to himself, and no one spoke.

Our canoes went on, moving farther and farther from the brink from which we had embarked; and it glided easily over the glassy sheet of water, which is never agitated by even the roughest gales, and does not receive the rays of the sun except when that luminary is at the zenith.

The silence in which we were absorbed was suddenly broken by the appearance of a cayman, which raised its hideous head, and opened its enormous jaws, as if about to swallow the canoes, as it darted after us.

The moment was come; the grand drama announced by the Indians was about to be realised, or all our fears would be dissipated without any delay. There was not one instant to be spared, and we had no choice but to try and escape as fast as we could, for the enemy was gaining on us, and it would be madness to await his attack. I was steering, and I exerted myself to the utmost to get away from the danger and to escape to the shore. But the amphibious beast was approaching so fast that he could almost seize us, when Lindsay, running all risks, fired his gun direct at the brute.

The effect produced by the detonation was prodigious, for, as it were by enchantment, it dispelled all our apprehensions. The awful silence was broken in the most striking manner; the cayman was frightened, and sank abruptly to the bottom of the lake; hundreds of echoes resounded from all sides, like the discharges of a rifle corps, and these were repeated to the tops of the mountains, while clouds of cormorants, starting from all the trees around, uttered their screaming and piercing cries, in which they were joined by the Indians, who shouted with joy on seeing from the bank the flight of the hostile beast, of which they are always so much afraid.

All then became tranquil, and we proceeded at our leisure. From time to time a cayman made his appearance; but the explosions caused by our firing soon drove the monsters down into the deepest parts of the lake, more frightened than hurt, for even when we struck them our balls rebounded from their scales without piercing them.

We went close to the large trees, the branches of which were spreading over the water; they were thickly covered with nests, filled with eggs, and so great a quantity of young birds, that we not only captured as many as we wished, but could have filled several boats with them.

The cormorants, alarmed by the explosions we made, whirled over us continually, like an immense cloud, during the time we troubled their gloomy abode, and seemed to "disturb their solitary reign;" but they did not wish to go far from their nests, in which their young broods were crying out for parental care.

After we had rowed round the lake, we came to the spot from which we started, having ended our expedition happily without any accident, and even without having incurred all the dangers that our Indians, who were awaiting our return in order to take our boats once more across the mountain, had wished to make us believe.

Resolved not to finish the excursion without producing some beneficial results for the sake of scientific knowledge, we measured the circumference of the lake, which we found to be about two miles and a half. We were able to take soundings in the deepest parts towards the middle, where we found the depth about three hundred feet; while at some few fathoms from the banks we found it was invariably one hundred and eighty feet. And here the remark may be made, that in no part of the great Lake of Bay has the depth been found to exceed seventy-five feet; from which it may be concluded, as we have previously stated, that the lake of Socolme is formed within the crater of an extinct volcano, its waters having per colated or filtered through from the outer lake of Bay.

From Socolme I took my guests to Los Banos, at the foot of a mountain, several thousand feet high, from which several springs of boiling water flow into the lake, and, mixing with its waters, produce every temperature to be desired in a natural bath. There also, on the hill, we were sure to meet with good and plentiful sport. Wild pigeons and beautiful doves, perched upon majestic trees, "mistrustful of their doom," allowed our sportsmen to approach very near, and they never returned from "the baths" without having "bagged" plenty of them.

Upon our appointed days of relaxation from labour, we would go into the neighbouring woods, and wage war on the monkeys, our harvest's greatest enemies. As soon as a little dog, purposely brought up to this mode of warfare, warned us by his barkings that marauders were in sight, we repaired to the spot, and then the firing was opened. Fright seized hold on the mischievous tribe, every member of which hid itself in its tree, and became as invisible as it possibly could. But the little dog would not leave his post, while we would turn round the tree, and never failed discovering the hidden inmate. We then commence the attack, not ceasing until pug was laid prostrate. After having made several victims, I sent them to be hung up on forks around the sugar-cane fields, as scarecrows to those that had escaped; I, however, always sent the largest one to Father Miguel, our excellent curate, who was very fond of a monkey ragout.

Sometimes I would take my guests to a distance of several days' march, to show them admirable views, cascades, grottoes, or those wonders of vegetation produced by the fertile nature of the Philippines.

One day, Mr. Lindsay, the most intrepid traveller I had ever known, and who had recently accompanied me to the lake of Socolme, proposed to me to go with him to the grotto of San-Mateo, a place that several travellers and myself had visited more than once, but always in so incomplete a manner, that we had only been able to explore a small portion of it. I was too well pleased with the proposal not to accept it with eagerness; but this time I resolved that I would not return from this expedition, as I had from former ones, without having made every possible effort to explore its dimensions and recesses. Lindsay, Dr. Genu, and my brother, participated in my resolution of verifying whether or not there was any semblance of truth in what the Indians related concerning that grotto; or if, as I had so often experienced it myself, their poetic minds did not create what had never existed. Their old Indian traditions attributed to that cavern an immense extent. There, they would say, are to be seen fairy palaces, with which nothing could be compared, and which were the residences of fantastical beings. Determined, then, on seeing with our own eyes all these wonders, we set out for San-Mateo, taking with us an Indian, having with him a crowbar and a couple of pickaxes, to dig us out a way, should we have the chance of prolonging our subterraneous walk beyond the limits which we all already knew. We also took with us a good provision of flambeaus, so necessary to put our project

View at San-Mateo

into execution. We arrived early at San-Mateo, and spent the remaining part of the day in visiting admirable views and situations in the neighbourhood. We also went down into the bed of a torrent that takes its source in the mountains, and passes through the north side of this district; there we saw several Indians, male and female, all busy in washing the sand in search of gold-dust. Their daily produce at this work varies from one to ten francs; this depends on the more or less fortunate vein that perchance they fall on. This trade, together with the tilling of land—to be equalled by no other in fertility—and hewing timber for building, which is to be found most plentifully on the neighbouring mountains, is all the wealth of the inhabitants, who, in most part, live in abundance and prosperity.

At the next day's dawn we were on our way to the grotto, which is about two hours' walk from the village. The road, which is bordered by nature's most beautiful productions in vegetation, traverses the finest rice plantations, and is of most easy access; however, about half-way, it suddenly becomes dangerous and even difficult. Here we leave the cultivated fields, and follow along the banks of the river, which flows in the midst of not very high mountains, and has so many bends, twistings, and meanderings, that, in order to cross it, it is necessary at almost every moment to have recourse to swimming, and then to take the narrow paths leading from its margin. Nothing, until at a very short distance from the grotto, interrupts the monotony of these rural sites and situations. The traveller plods his way through a gorge, or ravine, where upon all sides the view is bounded by rocks, and a long line of verdant vegetation, composed of the shrubs that cover the hills. But through a vast winding, or rather turning, made by the river, the eye is suddenly dazzled by the splendid panorama that seems to develop itself and move on with fairy magnificence. Let the reader imagine that he is standing at the base of two immense mountains, resembling two pyramids in their form, both equally alike and similar in height. The space that intervenes between them allows the eye to plunge into the distance, and to discover there a tableau, a picture, or view, which is impossible to be described. Between the two monster mountains the river has found an issue, and there the traveller beholds it at his feet, precipitating itself like an impetuous torrent in the midst of white marble rocks. The water, both limpid and glossy, seems to play with every object that impedes its course; at one moment it will form a noisy cascade, and then suddenly disappear at the foot of an enormous rock, and soon after appear again, bubbling and foaming, just as if some supernatural strength had worked it from the bowels of the earth. Farther on, and in forming itself into a continuous number of minor cascades, this same river flows, with a vast silvery surface, over a bed of marble, as white and as brilliant as alabaster, and falls upon others of still equal whiteness. Finally, after having passed over all difficulties, all dangers, it flows with much more modesty over a humble bed, where may be seen the reflection of the admirable vegetation its banks are embellished with.

The famous grotto is situated in the mountain on the right side of the river, which the traveller crosses over by jumping from one block of marble to another; and then, after having ascended a steep height of about two hundred yards, he finds himself at the entrance to the grotto, whither I shall conduct the reader step by step.

The entrance, the form of which is almost regular, represents pretty well the portico of a church, with a full arch, adorned with verdant festoons, composed of creeping plants and bind-weeds. When the visitor has once passed under the portico he enters into a large and spacious hall, studded with stalactites of a very yellowish colour, and there a dense crowd of bats, frightened by the light of the torches, fly out with great noise and precipitation. For about a hundred paces, in advancing towards the interior, the vault continues to be very lofty, and the gallery is spacious; but suddenly the former declines immensely, and the latter becomes so narrow that it scarce admits of a passage for one man, who is obliged to crawl on his hands and knees to pass through, and continue in this painful position for about a hundred yards. And now the gallery becomes wide again, and the vault rises several feet high. But here, again, a new difficulty soon presents itself, and which must be overcome; a sort of wall, three or four yards high, must be climbed over, and immediately behind which lies a most dangerous subterraneous place, where two enormous precipices, with open mouths on a level with the ground, seem ready to swallow up the imprudent traveller, who, although he have his torch lighted, would not walk, step by step, and with the greatest precaution, through this gloomy labyrinth. A few stones thrown into these gulfs attest, by the hollow noise produced by their falling to the bottom, that they are several hundred feet deep. Then the gallery, which is still wide and spacious, runs on without presenting anything remarkable till the visitor arrives on the spot where the last researches stopped at. Here it seems to terminate by a sort of rotunda, surrounded by stalactites of divers forms, and which, in one part, represents a real dome supported by columns. This dome looks over a small lake, out of which a murmuring stream flows continually into the precipices already described. It was here that we began our serious investigations, desirous of ascertaining if it were possible to prolong this subterraneous peregrination. We dived several times into the lake without discovering anything favourable to our desires; we then directed our steps to the right, examining all the while, by the light of our torches, the smallest gaps to be seen in the sides of the gallery, when at last, after many unsuccessful attempts, we discovered a hole through which a man's arm could scarcely pass. By introducing a torch into it, how great was our surprise to see within it an immense space, studded with rock-crystal. I need not add that such a discovery inspired us with the greatest desire of more closely examining that which we had but an imperfect view of. We therefore set our Indian to work with his pick-axe, to widen the hole and make a passage for us; his labour went on slowly, he struck his blows gently and cautiously, so as to avoid a falling-in of the rock, which would not only have marred our hopes, but would, besides, have caused a great disaster. The vault of rocks suspended over our heads might bury us all alive, and, as will be seen by the sequel, the precautions we had taken were not fruitless. At the very moment when our hopes were about to be realised, —the aperture being now wide enough to admit of us passing through it—suddenly, and above our heads, we heard a hollow prolonged rustling noise that froze us to death; the vault had been shaken, and we dreaded its falling upon us. For a moment, which seemed to us, however, very long, we were all terrified; the Indian himself was standing as motionless as a statue, with his hands upon the handle of his pick-axe, just in the same position as he was when he gave his last blow. After a moment's solemn silence, when our fright had a little subsided, we began to examine the nature of the danger we had just escaped. Above our heads a long and wide split ran along the vault to a distance of several yards, and, at the place where it stopped, an enormous rock, detached from the dome, had been most providentially impeded in its fall downwards by one of the columns, which, acting as a sort of buttress, kept it suspended over the opening we had just made. Having, after mature examination, ascertained that the column and the rock were pretty solid, like rash men, accustomed to daunt all danger and surmount any sort of obstacle and difficulty, we resolved upon gliding one by one into the dangerous yawning. Dr. Genu, who till then had kept a profound silence, on hearing of our resolution was suddenly seized with such a panic fear that he recovered his voice, imploring and begging of us to take him out of the cavern; and, as if he had been suddenly seized with a sort of vertigo, he told us, with interrupted accents, that he could not breathe—that he felt himself as if he were smothering—that his heart was beating so violently, were he to stay any longer amidst the dangers we were running he was certain of dying from the effects of a rupture of the heart. He offered all he possessed on earth to him who would save his life, and with clasped hands he supplicated our Indians not to forsake him, but to guide him out of the place. We therefore took compassion upon his state of mind, and allowed the Indian to guide him out; but as soon as the latter returned, and having ascertained during his absence that neither the rocky fragment nor the column had stirred, but which had been the momentary cause of our alarm, we put our project into execution, and like serpents, one after the other, we crawled into the dangerous opening, which was scarcely large enough for our passing through. We soon ceased thinking of our past dangers, nor did our present imprudence much pre-occupy our minds, all our attention being entirely absorbed by what presented itself to our ravished eyes. Here we were in the midst of a saloon wearing a most fairy aspect, and, by the light of our torches, the vault, the floor, and the wall were shining and dazzling, as if they had been covered over with the most admirably transparent rock-crystal. Even in some places did the hand of man seem to have presided over the ornamenting of this enchanted palace. Numberless stalactites and stalagmites, as pellucid as the limpid stream that has just been seized by the frost, assumed here and there the most fantastic forms and shapes—they represented brilliant draperies, rows of columns, lustres, and chandeliers. At one end, close to the wall, was to be seen an altar, with steps leading up to it, and which seemed to be in expectation of the priest to celebrate divine service. It would be impossible for my pen to describe everything that transported us with joy, and drew forth our admiration; we really imagined ourselves to be in one of the Arabian Nights' palaces, and the Indians themselves were far from guessing the one-half of the wonders we had just dis covered.

Having left this dazzling palace, we continued our underground ramble, penetrating more and more into the bowels of the earth, following step by step a winding labyrinth, but which for a whole half-league offered nothing remarkable to our view, except now and then the sight of the very great dangers our undauntable curiosity urged us on to. In certain parts the vault no longer presented the aspect of being as solid as stone, earth alone seemed to be its component parts; and here and there, recent proofs of falling-in showed us that still more considerable ones might take place, and cut off from us all means of retreat. Nevertheless we pushed on still, far beyond our present adventurous discovery, and at last arrived at a new, magnificent, and extensive space, all bespangled, like the first, with brilliant stalactites, and in no way inferior to the former in the gorgeous beauty of its details. Here again we gave ourselves up to the most minute examination of the many wonders surrounding us, and which shone like prisms by the light of our torches. We gathered from off the ground several small stalagmites, as large and as round as hazel-nuts, and so like that fruit, when preserved, that some days later, at a ball at Manilla, we presented some of them to the ladies, whose first movement was to put them to their mouth; but soon finding out their mistake, they entreated to be allowed to keep them, to have them, as they said, converted into ear-ring drops

Having fully enjoyed the beautiful and brilliant spectacle presented to our eyes, we now began to feel the effects of hunger and fatigue. We had been walking in this subterraneous domain to the extent of more than three miles, had taken no rest or refreshment since morning, and the day was already far advanced.

I have often experienced that our moral strength decreases in proportion as our physical strength does; and of course we must have been in that state when sinister suppositions took possession of our imaginations. One of our party communicated to us a reflection he had just made—which was, that a falling-in might have taken place between us and the issue from the grotto; or, what appeared still more probable, that the enormous rock, that was suspended and buttressed up by the column, might have fallen down, and thus bar up all passage through the hole we had so rashly made. Had such a misfortune happened to us, what a horrible situation we should have been in! We could hope for no help from without, even from our friend Genu, who, as we had witnessed, had been so upset by fear; so that, rather than suffer the anguish and die the death of the wretch buried alive in a sepulchre, our poignards must have been our last resource.

All these reflections, which we analysed and commented upon, one by one, made us resolve upon returning, and leaving to others, more imprudent than ourselves, if any there be, the care of exploring the space we had still to travel over. We soon got over the ground that separated us from the place we had most to dread. Providence had favoured and protected us—the large fragment of rock, that object of all our fears, was still propped up. One after the other did we squeeze ourselves through the narrow opening, avoiding as much as possible the least friction, till at last we had all passed through. Joyous indeed were we on seeing ourselves out of danger after so perilous an enterprise, and we were already beginning to direct our steps towards the outlet of the cavern, when suddenly a hollow, prolonged noise, and below our feet a rapid trembling excited once more all our fears. But those fears were soon calmed by our Indian, who came running towards us at full speed, brandishing in his hand his pick-axe. The imprudent fellow, unwilling to sacrifice it, had waited till we were some paces distant, and then pulling it to him most forcibly, while all the while he took good care to keep quickly moving away, when thanks to Providence, or to his own nimbleness, he was not crushed to atoms by the fragment of the rock, which, being no longer buttressed up by the column that had been shaken, had fallen to the ground, completely stopping up the issue through which we had passed one after the other: so that no doubt no one, after us, will be able to penetrate into the beautiful part of that grotto which we had just passed through so fortunately. After this last episode we no longer hesitated in returning, and it was with great delight that we beheld once more the great luminary of the world, and found our friend Genu sitting upon a block of marble, reflecting on our long absence, and, at the same time, on our un qualifiable temerity.

Dumont d'Urville.

CHAPTER X.

Dumont d'Urville—Rear-Admiral Laplace: Desertion of Sailors from his Ship—I recover them for him—Origin of the Inhabitants of the Philippine Islands—Their General Disposition—Hospitality and Respect for Old Age—Tagal Marriage Ceremony—Indian Legal Eloquence—Explanation of the Matrimonial Speeches—The Caymans, or Alligators—Instances of their Ferocity—Imprudence and Death of my Shepherd—Method of entrapping the Monster which had devoured him—We Attack and eventually Capture it—Its Dimensions—We Dissect and Examine the Contents of its Stomach—Boa-Constrictors—Their large size—Attack of a Boa-Constrictor on a Wild Boar—We Kill and Skin it—Unsuccessful Attempt to capture a Boa-Constrictor alive—A Man Devoured—Dangerous Venomous Reptiles.

I SHALL perhaps be accused of exaggeration for what I say of the enjoyments and emotions of my existence at Jala-Jala: nevertheless I adhere to the strict truth, and it would be very easy for me to cite the names of many persons in support of the truth of all my narrative. Moreover, the various travellers who have spent some time at my habitation have published, in their works, the tableau or recital of my existence in the midst of my dear Indians, who were all so devoted to me Among other works, I shall cite "The Voyage Round the World," by the unfortunate Dumont d'Urville; and that of Rear-Admiral Laplace, in each of which works will be found a special article dedicated to Jala-Jala.*

Since I have named M. Laplace, I shall here relate a little anecdôte of which he was the hero, and which will show to what a degree my influence was generally considered and looked up to in the province of Lagune.

Several sailors, belonging to the crew of the frigate commanded by M. Laplace, had deserted at Manilla, and, notwithstanding all the searches that the Spanish government had caused to be made, it was found impossible to discover the hiding-place of five of them. M. Laplace coming to pay a few weeks' visit to my little domain, the governor said to him: "If you wish to find out your men you have only to apply to M. Gironiere—no one will discover them if he do not; convey to him my orders to set out immediately in pursuit of them."

On arriving at my habitation M. Laplace communicated to me this order, but I was too independent to think of executing it: my business and occupation had nothing to do with deserters. A few days afterwards a captain, accompanied by about a hundred soldiers, under his orders, arrived at Jala-Jala, to inform M. Laplace that he had scoured the province without being able to obtain the least news of the deserters, whom he had been looking after for the last fortnight; at which news M. Laplace was very much grieved, and coming to me, said: "M. de la Gironiere, I perceive I shall be obliged to sail without the hands that have deserted, if you yourself will not look after

* See Appendix III. and IV.

them. I therefore beg and beseech of you to sacrifice a little of your time, and render me that important service."

This entreaty was no order: it was a prayer, a supplication, that was addressed to me, consequently I took but little time to reply as follows: "Commander, in one hour hence I shall be on my way, and before forty-eight hours are expired you shall have your men here."

"Oh! take care," replied he; "mind, you have to do with more than rough fellows: do not therefore expose your life, and should they perchance make any resistance, give them no quarter, but fire on them."

A few minutes afterwards, accompanied by my faithful lieutenant and one soldier, I crossed over the lake, and went in the direction where I thought that the French sailors had taken refuge. I was soon on their track; and on the second day afterwards I fulfilled the promise I had made Commander Laplace, and delivered up to him his five deserters against whom I had been obliged to employ neither violence nor fire-arms.

I have already had the occasion of speaking about the Tagalocs, and describing their disposition. However, I have not yet entered into the necessary details to make well known a population so submissive to the Spaniards, and whose primitive origin never can be anything but hypothesis—yea, a true problem.

It is probable, and almost incontestible, that the Philippine Islands were primitively peopled by aborigines, a small race of negroes still inhabiting the interior of the forests in pretty large numbers, called Ajetas by the Tagalocs, and Négritos by the Spaniards. Doubtless at a very distant period the Malays invaded the shores, and drove the indigenous population into the interior beyond the mountains; afterwards, whether by accidents on sea, or desirous of availing themselves of the richness of the soil, they were joined by the Chinese, the Japanese, the inhabitants of the archipelago of the South Seas, the Javanese, and even the Indians. It must not, then, be wondered at, that from the mixture proceeding from the union of these various people, all of unequal physiognomy, there have risen the different *nuances*, distinctions and types; upon which, however, is generally depicted Malay physiognomy and cruelty.

The Tagal is well made, rather tall than otherwise. His hair is long, his beard thin, his colour brass-like, yet sometimes inclining to European whiteness; his eye expanded and vivacious, somewhat *á la Chinoise*; nose large; and, true to the Malay race, his cheek bones are high and prominent. He is passionately fond of dancing and music; is, when in love, very loving; cruel towards his enemies; never forgives an act of injustice, and ever avenges it with his poignard, which—like the kris with the Malays—is his favourite weapon. Whenever he has pledged his word in serious business, it is sacred; he gives himself passionately to games of hazard; he is a good husband, a good father; jealous of his wife's honour, but careless of his daughter's; who, despite any little *faux-pas*, meets with no difficulty in getting a husband.

The Tagal is of very sober habits: all he requires is water, a little rice, and salt-fish. In his estimation an aged man is an object of great veneration; and where there exists a family of them in all periods of life, the youngest is naturally most subservient to the eldest.

The Tagal, like the Arab, is hospitably inclined, without any sentiment of egotism, and certainly without any other idea than that of relieving suffering humanity: so that when a stranger appears before an Indian hut at meal-time, were the

A Tagal Indian Dwelling.

poor Indian only to have what was strictly necessary for his family, it is his greatest pleasure to invite and press the stranger to take a place at his humble board, and partake of his family cheer. When an old man, whose days are dwindling to the shortest span, can work no longer, he is sure to find a refuge, an asylum, a home, at a neighbour's, where he is looked upon as one of the family. There he may remain till he is called to "that bourne from whence no traveller returns."

Amongst the Tagals the marriage ceremony is somewhat peculiar. It is preceded by two other ceremonies, the first of which is called *Tain manoc*, Tagal words, signifying or meaning "the cock looking after his hen." Therefore, when once a young man has informed his father and mother that he has a predeliction for a young Indian girl, his

Young Tagal Indian and his Betrothed.

parents pay a visit to the young girl's parents upon some fine evening, and after some very ordinary chat the mamma of the young man offers a piaster to the mamma of the young lady. Should the future mother-in-law accept, the young lover is admitted, and then his future mother-in-law is sure to go and spend the very same piaster in betel and cocoa-wine. During the greater portion of the night the whole company assembled upon the occasion chews betel, drinks cocoa-wine, and discusses upon all other subjects but marriage. The young men never make their appearance till the piaster has been accepted, because in that case they look upon it as being the first and most essential step towards their marriage.

On the next day the young man pays a visit to the mother, father, and other relatives of his affianced bride. There he is received as one of the family; he sleeps there, he lodges there, takes a part in all the labours, and most particularly in those labours depending upon the young maid's superintendence. He now undertakes a service or task that lasts, more or less, two, three, or four years, during which time he must look well to himself; for if anything be found out against him he is discarded, and never more can pretend to the hand of her he would espouse.

The Spaniards did their best to suppress this custom, on account of the inconveniencies it entailed. Very oftèn the father of a young girl, in order to keep in his service a man who cost him nothing, keeps on this state of servitude indefinitely, and sometimes dismisses him who has served him for two or three years, and takes another under the same title of *prétendant*, or lover. But it also frequently happens that if the two lovers grow impatient for the celebration of the marriage ceremony—for "hope deferred maketh the heart sick,"—some day or other the girl takes the young man by the hair, and presenting him to the curate of the village, tells him she has just run away with her lover, therefore they must be married. The wedding ceremony then takes place without the consent of the parents. But were the young man to carry off the young girl, he would be severely punished, and she restored to her family.

If all things have passed off in good order, if the lover has undergone two or three years of voluntary slavery, and if his future relations be quite satisfied with his conduct and temper, then comes the day of the second ceremony, called *Tajin-bojol*, "the young man desirous of tying the union knot."

This second ceremony is a grand festival-day. The relations and friends of both families are all assembled at the bride's house, and divided into two camps, each of which discusses the interests of the young couple; but each family has an advocate, who alone has the right to speak in favour of his client. The relations have no right to speak; they only make, in a low tone of voice, to their advocate, the observations they think fit.

The Indian woman never brings a marriage portion with her. When she takes a husband unto herself she possesses nothing; the young man alone brings the portion, and this is why the young girl's advocate speaks first, and asks for it, in order to settle the basis of the treaty.

I will here set before my readers the speeches of two advocates in a ceremony of this kind, at which I had the curiosity to be present. In order not to wound the susceptibility of the parties, the advocates never speak but in allegorical terms, and at the ceremony which I honoured with my presence the advocate of the young Indian girl thus began:—

"A young man and a young girl were joined together in the holy bands of wedlock; they possesed nothing—nay, they had not even a shelter. For several years the young woman was very badly off. At last her misfortunes came to an end, and one day she found herself in a fine large cottage that was her own. She became the mother of a pretty little babe, a girl, and on the day of her confinement there appeared unto her an angel, who said to her:—'Bear in mind thy marriage, and the time of penury thou didst go through. The child that has just been born unto thee will I take under my protection. When she will have grown up and be a fine lass, give her but to him who will build her up a temple, where there will be ten columns, each composed of ten stones. If thou dost not execute these my orders thy daughter will be as miserable as thou hast been thyself.'"

After this short speech, the adverse advocate replied:—"Once upon a time there lived a queen, whose kingdom lay on the sea-side. Amongst the laws of her realm there was one which she followed with the greatest rigour. Every ship arriving in her states' harbour could, according to that law, cast anchor but at one hundred fathoms deep, and he who violated the said law was put to death without pity or remorse. Now it came to pass one day that a brave captain of a ship was surprised by a dreadful tempest, and after many fruitless endeavours to save his vessel, he was obliged to put into the queen's harbour, and cast anchor there, although his cable was only eighty fathoms long, for he preferred death on the scaffold to the loss of his ship and crew. The enraged queen commanded him to her audit chamber. He obeyed, and throwing himself at her feet, told her that necessity alone had compelled him to infringe upon the laws, and that, having but eighty fathoms long, he could not possibly cast out a hundred, so he besought her most graciously to pardon him."

And here ended his speech, but the other advocate took it up, and thus went on:—

"The queen, moved to pity by the prayer of the suppliant captain, and his inability to cast his anchor one hundred fathoms deep, instantly pardoned him, and well did she devise."

On hearing these last words joy shone upon every countenance, and the musicians began playing on the guitar. The bride and bridegroom, who had been waiting in an adjoining chamber, now made their appearance. The young man took from off his neck his rosary, or string of beads, put it round the young girl's neck, and took back hers in lieu of the one he had given her. The night was spent in dancing and merriment, and the marriage ceremony—just as Christian-like as our own—was arranged to take place in a week.

I shall now, just as I heard it myself, give the explanation of the advocates' speeches, which I did not entirely understand. The bride's mother had married without a wedding portion on her husband's side, so she had gone through very adverse and pinching circumstances. The temple that the angel had told her to demand for her daughter was, a house; and the ten columns, composed of ten stones each, signified that with the house a sum of one hundred piasters would be requisite—that is, twenty pounds sterling.

The speech of the young man's advocate explained that he would give the house, as he said nothing about it; but, being worth only eighty piasters, he threw himself at the feet of the parents of his betrothed, that the twenty piasters which he was minus, might offer no obstacle to his marriage. The pardon accorded by the queen signified the grace shown to the young man, who was accepted with his eighty piasters only.

The servitude which precedes matrimony, and of which I have spoken, was practised long before the conquest of these isles by the Spaniards. This would seem to prove the origin I attribute to the Tagalocs, whom I believe to be descended from the Malays, and these latter, being all Mussulmans, would naturally have preserved some of the ancient patriarchal customs.

Believing that I have sufficiently described the Indians and their habits, I will now introduce to my readers two species of monsters that I have often had occasion to observe, and even to combat—the one a denizen of forests, the boa constrictor; the other of lakes and rivers, the cayman or alligator. At the period at which I first occupied my habitation, and began to colonise the village of Jala-Jala, caymans abounded on that side of the lake. From my windows I daily saw them sporting in the water, and waylaying and snapping at the dogs that ventured too near the brink. One day, a female servant of my wife's, having been so imprudent as to bathe at the edge of the lake, was surprised by one of them, a monster of enormous size. One of my guards came up at the moment she was being carried off; he fired his musket at the brute, and hit it under the fore-leg, or arm-pit, which is the only vulnerable part. But the wound was insufficient to check the cayman's progress, and it disappeared with its prey. Nevertheless, this little bullet hole was the cause of its death; and here it is to be observed, that the slightest wound received by the cayman is incurable. The shrimps which abound in the lake get into the orifice, gradually their number increases, until at last they penetrate deep into the solid flesh, and into the very interior of the body. This is what happened to the one which devoured my wife's maid. A month after the frightful occurrence the cayman was found dead upon the bank, five or six leagues from my house. Some Indians brought back to me the unfortunate woman's earrings, which they had found in the monster's stomach.

Upon another occasion, a Chinese was riding onwards in advance of me. We reached a river, and I let him go on alone, in order to ascertain whether the river was very deep or not. Suddenly, three or four caymans which lay in waiting under the water, threw themselves upon him; horse and rider disappeared, and for some minutes afterwards the water was tinged with blood.

I was curious to obtain a near view of one of these voracious animals, and, at the time when they frequented the vicinity of my house, I made several attempts to accomplish my wishes. One night I baited a huge hook, secured by a chain and strong cord, with an entire sheep. Next morning, sheep and chain had disappeared. I lay in wait for the creatures with my gun, but the bullets rebounded, half flattened upon their scales, without doing the slightest injury. One evening that a large dog of mine had died, belonging to a race peculiar to the Philippines, and exceeding in size any of the canine species of Europe, I had his carcass dragged to the shore of the lake, and hid myself in a little thicket, with my gun ready cocked, in the event of any cayman presenting itself to carry off the bait. Presently I fell asleep; when I awoke, the dog had disappeared, the cayman, luckily for me, not mistaking his prey.

In the course of a few years' time, these monsters had disappeared from the environs of Jala-Jala; but one morning, when out with my shepherds, at some leagues' distance from my house, we came to a river, which could only be crossed by swimming. One of my people said to me:

"Master, the water is deep here, and we are in the courses where the caymans abound; an accident soon happens, let us try further up the river, and pass over in a shallower spot."

We were about to follow this advice, when another man, more rash than his comrades, said: "I'm not afraid of caymans!" and spurred his horse into the stream. He had scarcely got half-way across, when we perceived a monstrous cayman rise and advance to meet him. We uttered a warning shout, the Indian himself perceived the danger, threw himself from his horse, and swam for the bank with all his strength. He had already reached it, but imprudently stopped behind the trunk of a tree that had been felled by the force of the current, and where he had the water up to his knees. Believing himself secure, he drew his cutlass, and watched the movements of the cayman, which, meanwhile, had reached the horse just as, the Indian quitted the animal. Rearing his enormous head out of the water, the monster threw himself upon the steed and seized him by the saddle. The horse made a violent effort, the girths broke, and thus enabled him to reach the shore. Soon, however, finding that his prey had escaped, the cayman dropped the saddle, and made towards the Indian. We perceived this movement, and quickly cried out: "Run, run, or the cayman will have you!" The Indian, however, would not stir, but calmly waited, cutlass in hand. The monster advanced towards him; the Indian struck him a blow on the head, which took no more effect than a flip of the fingers would have on the horns of a bull. The cayman made a spring, seized him by one of his thighs, and for more than a minute we beheld my poor shepherd—his body erect above the surface of the water, his hands joined, his eyes turned to heaven, in the attitude of a man imploring Divine mercy—dragged back again into the lake. The drama was over: the cayman's stomach was his tomb. During these agonizing moments, we all remained silent, but no sooner had my poor shepherd disappeared than we all swore to avenge him.

I caused to be made three nets of strong cords, each of of which nets was large enough to form a complete barrier across the river. I also had a hut built, and put an Indian to live in it, whose duty was to keep constant watch, and to let me know as soon as the cayman returned to the river. He watched in vain, for upwards of two months, but at the end of that time he came and told me that the monster had seized a horse, and had dragged it into the river to devour at leisure. I immediately repaired to the spot, accompanied by my guards, and by my priest, who positively would see a cayman hunt, and by an American friend of mine, Mr. Russell,* who was then staying with me. I had the nets spread at intervals, so that the cayman could not escape back into the lake. This operation was not effected without some acts of imprudence; thus, for instance, when the nets were arranged, an Indian dived to make sure that they were at the bottom, and that our enemy could not escape by passing below them. But it might very well have happened that the cayman was in the interval between the nets, and so have gobbled up my Indian. Fortunately everything passed off as we wished. When all was ready, I launched three pirogues, strongly fastened together, side by side, with some Indians in the centre, armed with lances, and with long bamboos, with which they could touch the bottom. At last, all measures having been taken to attain my end, without risk of accident, my indians began to explore the river with their long bamboos.

An animal so formidable in size as the one we were in search of, could not hide himself very easily, and soon we beheld him on the surface of the river, lashing the water with his long tail, snapping and clattering with his jaws, and endeavouring to get at those who disturbed him in his retreat. A universal shout of joy greeted his appearance; the Indians in the pirogues hurled their lances at him, whilst we, upon either shore of the lake, fired a volley. The bullets rebounded from the monster's scales, which they were unable to penetrate; the keener lances made their way between the scales,

* Of the house of Russell and Sturges, a good and true friend, the recollection of whom, often present to my mind, will never be effaced.

and entered into the cayman's body some eight or ten inches. Thereupon he disappeared, swimming with incredible rapidity, and reached the first net. The resistance it opposed turned him back; he re-ascended the river, and again appeared on the top of the water. This violent movement, broke the staves of the lances which the Indians had stuck into him, and the iron alone remained in the wounds. Each time that he appeared the firing recommenced, and fresh lances were plunged into his enormous body. Perceiving, however, how ineffectual fire arms were to pierce his cuirass of invulnerable scales, I excited him by my shouts and gestures, and when he came to the edge of the water, opening his enormous jaws all ready to devour me, I approached the muzzle of my gun to within a few inches, and fired both barrels, in the hope that the bullets would find something softer than scales in the interior of that formidable cavern, and that they would penetrate to his brain. All was futile. The jaws closed with a terrible noise, seizing only the fire and smoke that issued from my gun, and the balls flattened against his bones without injuring them. The animal, which had now become furious, made inconceivable efforts to seize one of his enemies; his strength seemed to increase, rather than to diminish, whilst our resources were nearly exhausted. Almost all our lances were sticking in his body, and our ammunition drew to an end. The fight had lasted more than six hours, without any result that could make us hope for its speedy termination, when an Indian struck the cayman, whilst at the bottom of the water, with a lance of unusual strength and size. Another Indian, at his comrade's request, struck two vigorous blows with a mace upon the butt-end of the lance; the iron entered deep into the animal's body, and immediately, with a movement as swift as lightning, ne darted towards the nets and disappeared. The lance pole, detached from the iron head, returned to the surface of the water; for some minutes we waited in vain for the monster's re-appearance; we thought that his last effort had enabled him to reach the lake, and that our chase would result fruitlessly.

Attacking the Cayman.

We hauled in the first net, a large hole in which convinced us that our supposition was correct. The second net was in the same condition as the first. Disheartened by our failure, we were hauling in the third, when we felt a strong resistance. Several of the Indians began to drag it towards the bank, and presently, to our great joy, we saw the cayman upon the surface of the water. He was expiring. We threw over him several lassos of strong cords, and when he was well secured, we drew him to land. It was no easy matter to haul him up on the bank; the strength of forty Indians hardly sufficed. When at last we had got him completely out of the water, and had him before our eyes, we stood stupified with astonishment, for it was a very different thing to see his body thus and to see him swimming, when he was fighting against us Mr. Russell, a very competent person, was charged with his measurements. From the extremity of his nostrils to the tip of his tail, he was found to be twenty-seven feet long, and his circumference was eleven feet, measured under the arm-pits. His belly was much more voluminous, but we thought it unnecessary to measure him there, judging that the horse upon which he had breakfasted must considerably have increased his bulk.

This process at an end, we took counsel as to what we should do with the dead cayman. Every one gave his opinion. My wish was to convey it bodily to my residence, but that was impossible; it would have required a vessel of five or six tons burthen, and we could not procure such a craft. One man wanted the skin, the Indians begged for the flesh, to dry it, and use it as a specific against asthma. They affirm, that any asthmatic person who nourishes himself for a certain time with this flesh, is infallibly cured. Somebody else desired to have the fat, as an antidote to rheumatic pains; and, finally, my worthy priest demanded that the stomach should be opened, in order to ascertain how many Christians the monster had devoured. Every time, he said, that a cayman eats a Christian he swallows a large pebble; thus, the number of pebbles we should find in him would positively indicate the number of the faithful to whom his enormous stomach had afforded sepul ture. To satisfy everybody, I sent for an axe wherewith, to cut off the head, which I reserved for myself, abandoning the rest of the carcass to all who had taken part in the capture. It was no easy matter to decapitate the monster. The axe buried itself in the flesh to half-way up the handle without reaching the bones; at last, after many efforts, we succeeded in getting the head off. Then we opened the stomach, and took out of it, by fragments, the horse which had been devoured by the monster that morning. The cayman does not masticate, he snaps off a huge lump with his teeth, and swallows it entire. Thus we found the whole of the horse, divided only into seven or eight pieces. Then we came to about a hundred and fifty pounds' weight of pebbles, varying from the size of a fist to that of a walnut. When my priest saw this great quantity of stones:

"It is a mere tale," he could not help saying; "it is impossible that this animal could have devoured so great a number of Chrstians."

It was eight o'clock at night when we had finished the cut ting up. I left the body to our assistants, and had the head placed in a boat to convey it to my house. I very much desired to preserve this monstrous trophy as nearly as possible in the state in which it then was, but that would have required a great quantity of arsenical soap, and I was out of that chemical. So I made up my mind to dissect it, and preserve the skeleton. I weighed it before detaching the ligaments; its weight was four hundred and fifty pounds; its length, from the nose to the first vertebræ, five feet six inches.

I found all my bullets, which had become flattened against the bones of the jaws and palate as they would have done against a plate of iron. The lance thrust which had slain the cayman was a chance—a sort of miracle. When the Indian struck with his mace upon the but-end of the pole, the iron pierced through the nape, into the vertebral column, and penetrated the spinal marrow, the only vulnerable part.

When this formidable head was well prepared, and the bones dried and whitened, I had the pleasure of presenting it to my friend Russell, who has since deposited it in the museum at Boston, United States.

The other monster, of which I have promised a description, is the boa-constrictor. The species is common in the Philippines, but it is rare to meet with a specimen of very large dimensions. It is possible, nay probable, that centuries of time are necessary for this reptile to attain its largest size; and to such an age, the various accidents to which animals are exposed, rarely suffer it to attain. Full-sized boas are consequently to be met with only in the gloomiest, most remote, and most solitary forests.

I have seen many boas of ordinary size, such as are found in our European collections. There were some, indeed, that inhabited my house, and one night I found one, two yards long, in possession of my bed. Several times, when passing through the woods with my Indians, I heard the piercing cries of a wild boar. On approaching the spot whence they proceeded, we almost invariably found a wild boar, about whose body a boa had twisted its folds, and was gradually hoisting him up into the tree round which it had coiled itself.

When the wild boar had reached a certain height, the snake pressed him against a tree with a force that crushed his bones and stified him. Then the boa let its prey fall, descended the tree, and prepared to swallow it. This last

A WILD BOAR ATTACKED BY A BOA CONSTRICTOR.—*Page* 222.

operation was much too lengthy for us to await its end. To simplify matters, I sent a ball into the boa's head. My Indians took the flesh to dry it for food, and the skin to make dagger sheaths of. It is unnecessary to say that the wild boar was not forgotten, although it was a prey that had cost us but little trouble to secure. One day an Indian surprised one of these reptiles asleep, after it had swallowed an enormous deer. Its size was so great, that a buffalo waggon would have been necessary to transport it to the village. The Indian cut it in pieces, and contented himself with as much as he could carry off. Having been informed of this, I sent after the remains, and my people brought me a piece about eight feet long, and so large in circumference that the skin, when dried, enveloped the tallest man like a cloak. I presented it to my friend Hamilton Lindsay.

I had not yet seen any of these largest sized serpents alive, when, one afternoon, crossing the mountains with two of my shepherds, our attention was drawn to the constant barking of my dogs, which seemed to be assailing some animal that stood upon its defence. We at first thought that it was a buffalo that they had roused from its lair, and approached the spot with due caution. My dogs were dispersed along the brink of a deep ravine, in which was an enormous boa constrictor. The monster raised his head to a height of five or six feet, directing it from one edge to the other of the ravine, and menacing his assailants with his forked tongue; but the dogs, more active than he was, easily avoided his attacks. My first impulse was to shoot him; but then it occurred to me to take him alive, and to send him to France. Assuredly he would have been the most monstrous boa that had ever been seen there. To carry my design into execution we manufactured

Attacking the Boa-Constrictor.

nooses of cane, strong enough to resist the efforts of the most powerful wild buffalo. With great precaution we succeeded in passing one of our nooses round the boa's neck; then we tied him tightly to a tree, in such a manner as to keep his head at its usual height—about six feet from the ground. This done, we crossed to the other side of the ravine, and threw another noose over him, which we secured like the first. When he felt himself thus fixed at both ends, he coiled and writhed, and grappled several little trees which grew within his reach along the edge of the ravine. Unluckily for him everything yielded to his efforts; he tore up the young trees by the roots, broke off the branches, and dislodged enormous stones, round which he sought in vain to obtain the hold or point of resistance he needed. The nooses were strong, and withstood his almost furious efforts.

To convey an animal like this, several buffaloes and a whole system of cordage were necessary. Night approached; confident in our nooses, we left the place, proposing to return next morning and complete the capture; but we reckoned without our host. In the night the boa changed his tactics, got his body round some huge blocks of basalt, and finally succeeded in breaking his bonds and getting clear off. When I had assured myself that our prey had escaped us, and that all search for the reptile in the neighbourhood would be futile, my disappointment was very great, for I much doubted if a like opportunity would ever present itself. It is only on rare occasions that accidents are caused by these enormous reptiles. I once knew of a man becoming their victim. It happened thus:—

This man having committed some offence, ran away, and sought refuge in a cavern. His father, who alone knew the place of his concealment, visited him occasionally to supply him with food. One day he found, in place of his son, an enormous boa sleeping. He killed it, and found his son in its stomach. The poor wretch had been surprised in the night, crushed to death, and swallowed. The curate of the village, who had gone in quest of the body to give it burial, and who saw the remains of the boa, described them to me as being of an almost incredible size. Unfortunately this circumstance happened at a considerable distance from my habitation, and I was only made acquainted with the particulars when it was too late to verify them myself: but still there is nothing surprising that a boa which can swallow a deer should as easily swallow a man. Several other feats of a similar nature were related to me by the Indians. They told me of their comrades, who, roaming about the woods, had been seized by boas, crushed against trees, and afterwards devoured, but I was always on my guard against Indian tales, and I am only able to verify positively the instance, I have just cited, which was related to me by the curate of the village, as well as by many other witnesses. Still there would be nothing surprising that a similar accident should occur more than once.

The boa is one of the serpents the least to be feared among those infesting the Philippines. Of an exceedingly venomous description is one which the Indians call *dajon-palay*, (rice leaf). Burning with a red-hot ember is the only antidote to its bite; if that be not promptly resorted to, horrible sufferings are followed by certain death. The *alin-morani* is another kind, eight or ten feet long, and, if anything, more dangerous still than the "rice leaf," inasmuch as its bite is deeper, and more difficult to cauterise. I was never bitten by any of these reptiles, despite the slight precaution I observed in wandering about the woods, by night as well as by day.

Twice only I endangered myself: the first time was by treading upon a dajon-palay; I was warned by a movement under my foot. I pressed hard with that leg, and saw the snake's little head stretching out to bite me on the ankle; fortunately my foot was on him at so short a distance from his head that he could not get at me. I drew my dagger, and cut off his head. On another occasion, I noticed two eagles rising and falling like arrows amongst the bushes, always at the same place. Curious to see what kind of anima. they were attacking, I approached the place; but no sooner had I done so, than an enormous alin-morani, furious with the wounds the eagles had inflicted on him, advanced to meet me. I retreated; he coiled himself up, gave a spring, and almost caught me on the face. By an instantaneous movement, I made a spring backwards, and avoided him; but I took care not to turn my back and run, for then I should have been lost. The serpent returned to the charge, bounding towards me; I again avoided him, and was trying, but in vain, to reach him with my dagger, when an Indian, who perceived me from a distance, ran up, armed with a stout switch, and rid me of him.

Rice Stacking in the Philippines.

CHAPTER XI.

The Prosperity and Happiness of my Life at Jala-Jala—Destructiveness of the Locusts—Agriculture in the Philippines—My Herds of Oxen, Buffaloes, and Horses—My Wife presents me with a Daughter, who Dies—The Admiration of the Indian Women for my Wife—Birth of my Son—Continued Prosperity—Death of my brother Henry—My Friendship with Malvilain—His Marriage with my eldest Sister—His Premature Death—I take my Wife to Manilla—Melancholy Adieus—We Return to Jala-Jala—Death of my Wife—My friend Vidie—I determine to Return to France.

NEVER was life more actively spent, or more crowded with emotions, than the time I passed at Jala-Jala, but it suited my tastes and my character, and I enjoyed as perfect happi ness as one can look for when far away from one's home and country. My Anna was to me an angel of goodness; my Indians were happy, peace and plenty smiled upon their families; my fields were covered with abundant corps, and my pasturages with numerous herds. It was not, however, without great difficulty and much toil that I accomplished my aim; how often did I find all my courage and all my philosophy necessary to face, without despair, reverses which it was impossible for me to avoid? How often did I behold hurricanes and inundations destroy the fine harvest that I had protected with so much labour against the buffaloes, the wild boars, the monkeys, and even against an insect more destructive still than all the other pests which I have just mentioned—the locust, one of the plagues of Egypt, apparently transported into this province, and which almost regularly, every seven years, leave the isles of the south in clouds, and fall upon Luzon, bringing desolation, and often famine. It is indeed necessary to have witnessed this desolation to be able to form any idea of it. When the locusts arrive, a fire-coloured cloud is perceived in the horizon, formed of countless myriads of these destructive insects. They fly rapidly, often covering, in a closely packed body, a space of two or three leagues in diameter, and occupy from five to six consecutive hours in passing over head. If they perceive a fine green field they pounce down upon it, and in a few minutes all verdure has disappeared, the ground is stripped completely bare; they then continue their flight elsewhere, bearing on their wings destruction and famine. At evening it is in the forests, upon the trees, that they take shelter. They hang in such dense masses upon the ends of the boughs that they break down even the stoutest limbs from the trees. During the night,

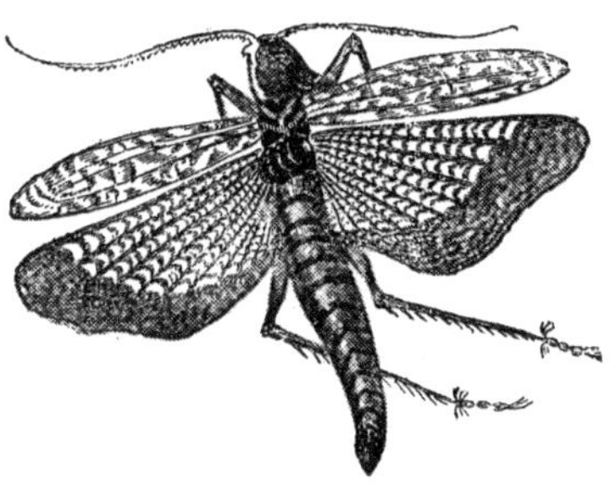

The Locust.

from the spot where they are reposing, there issues a continual croaking, and so loud a noise, that one scarcely believes it to be produced by so small an insect. The following morning they leave at day-break, and the trees upon which they have reposed are left stripped and broken, as though the lightning had swept the forest in every direction; they pursue their course elsewhere to commit fresh ravages. At certain periods they remain on vast plains or on fertile mountains; where, elongating the extremity of their bodies in the form of a gimblet, they pierce the earth to the depth of an inch and upwards to deposit their eggs. The operation of laying being completed, they leave the ground pierced like a sieve, and disappear, for their existence has now reached its termination. Three weeks afterwards, however, the eggs open, and myriads of young locusts swarm the earth. On the spot where they are born, whatever will serve them for food is quickly consumed. As soon as they have acquired sufficient strength they abandon their birth-place, destroy all kinds of vegetation that comes in their way, and direct their course to the cultivated fields, which they desolate until the period when their wings appear. They then take flight in order to devas tate more distant plantations.

As may be seen, agriculture in the Philippines presents many difficulties, but it also yields results that may be looked for in vain in any other country. During the years which are exempt from the calamities I have described the earth is covered with riches; every kind of colonial produce is raised in extraordinary abundance, frequently in the proportion of eighty to one, and on many plantations two crops of the same species are harvested in one year. The rich and extensive pasturages offer great facilities for raising a large number of cattle, which absolutely cost nothing but the trifling wages paid by the proprietor to a few shepherds.

Upon my property I possessed three herds—one of three thousand head of oxen, another of eight hundred buffaloes, and the other of six hundred horses. At that period of the year when the rice was harvested, the shepherds explored the mountains, and drove these animals to a vast plain at a short distance from my dwelling. This plain was covered by these three species of domesticated animals, and presented, especially to the proprietor, an admirable sight. At night they were herded in large cattle-folds, near the village, and on the following day a selection was made of the oxen that were fit for slaughter, of the horses that were old enough for breaking-in, of the buffaloes that were strong enough to be employed in working. The herds were then re-driven to the plain, there to remain until night. This operation lasted during a fortnight, after which time the animals were set at liberty until the same period of the following year. When at liberty the herd divided itself into bands, and thus roamed about the mountains and the valleys they had previously quitted, the only trouble caused to the shepherds being an occasional ramble about the spots where the animals tranquilly grazed.

Around me all was prosperity. My Indians were also happy, and entertained towards me a respect and obedience bordering on idolatry. My brother gave me every assistance in my labours, and when near my beloved Anna I forgot all the toils and the contrarieties I had experienced. About this time a new source of hope sprung up, which augmented the happiness I enjoyed with her, and made her dearer to me than ever. During several months the health of my wife had changed: she then found all the symptoms of pregnancy. We had been married twelve years, and she had never yet shown any signs of maternity. I was so persuaded that we should never have children that the derangement of her health was causing me serious uneasiness, when one morning as I was going to my work she said to me: "I don't feel well to-day, and I wish you to remain with me:" Two hours afterwards, to my great surprise, she gave premature birth to a little girl, whose arrival no one expected. The infant was born before the due time, and lived only one hour, just sufficient to receive baptism, which I administered to her. This was the second human being that had expired in the house of Jala-Jala; but she was also the first that had there first drawn the breath of life. The regret which we all experienced from the loss was softened by the certainty that my dear Anna might again become a mother, under more favourable circumstances. Her health was speedily re-established, and she was again gay and beautiful as ever indeed she appeared so handsome, that often Indian women came from a long distance for the sole purpose of looking at her They would remain for half-an-hour gazing at her, and after wards returned to their villages, where they gave birth to creatures little resembling the model which they had taken such pains to observe, with a confidence approaching to simplicity.

Eventually Anna exhibited new signs of maternity; her pregnancy went through the usual course, and her health was not much affected. In due time she presented me with a little boy, weakly and delicate, but full of life. Our joy was at the highest, for we possessed that which we had so long wished for, and that which alone was in my opinion wanting.

My Indians were delighted with the birth, and for several days there was a round of rejoicings at Jala-Jala; and my Anna, although confined to bed, was obliged to receive visits, at first from all the women and maidens of the village, and afterwards from all the Indians who were fathers of families Each brought some little present for the newly born, and the cleverest man of them was commissioned to express a compliment in the name of all ; which comprised their best wishes for the happiness of the mother and child, and full assurances of the satisfaction they felt in thinking that they would one day be ruled over by the son of the master from whom they had experienced so much kindness, and who had conferred upon them such benefits. Their gratitude was sincere.

The news of the accouchement of my wife brought a very numerous party of friends and relations to my house, where they waited for the baptism, which took place in my drawing-room. Anna, then almost thoroughly well, was present on the occasion: my son was named Henry, after his uncle. At this time I was happy; Oh, so truly happy! for my wishes were nearly gratified. There was but one not so—and that was to see again my aged mother and my sisters; but I hoped that the time was not far distant when I should realise the project of revisiting my native country. My farming speculation was most prosperous: my receipts were every year on the increase; my fields were covered with the richest crops of sugar-canes, to the cultivation of which, and of rice, I had joined that of coffee. My brother had taken upon himself the management of a very large plantation, which promised the most brilliant results; and appeared likely to secure the premium which the Spanish government had promised to give to the proprietor of a plantation of eighty thousand feet of coffee in product. But, alas! the period of my happiness had passed away, and what pain and what grief was I not doomed to suffer before I again saw my native country.

My brother—my poor Henry—committed some imprudences, and was suddenly attacked with an intermittent fever, which in a few days carried him off.

My Anna and I shed abundance of tears, for we both loved Henry with the warmest affection. For several years we had lived together; he participated in all our labours, our troubles, and our pleasures. He was the only relative I had in the Philippines. He had left France, where he had filled an honourable position, with the sole object of coming to see me, and of aiding me in the great task which I had undertaken. His amiable qualities and his excellent heart had endeared him to us: his loss was irreparable, and the thought that I had no longer a brother added poignancy to my bitter grief. Prudent, the youngest, had died at Madagascar; Robert, the next to me, died at La Planche, near Nantes, in the little dwelling where we spent our childhood; and my poor Henry at Jala-Jala. I erected a simple tomb for him near the door of the church, and for several months Jala-Jala was a place of grief and mourning.

We had scarcely begun, not indeed to console ourselves, but rather to bear with resignation the loss we had experienced, when a new dispensation of fate came to strike me to the earth.

On my arrival in the Philippines, and while I resided at Cavitè, I formed a close connection with Malvilain, a native of St. Malo, and mate of a ship from that port. During several years which he spent at Cavite our friendship was most intimate. A day seldom passed that we did not see each other, and two days never, for we were much attached. Our two ships were at anchor in the port, not far one from the other. One day as I was walking on deck, waiting for a boat to take me on board Malvilain's ship, I saw his crew at work in regulating one of the masts, when a rope suddenly snapped, and the mast fell with a frightful crash on the deck, in the midst of the men, amongst whom Malvilain was standing. From the deck of my own ship I beheld all that passed on that of my friend, who I thought was killed or wounded. My feelings were worked to the highest pitch of anguish and alarm; I could not control myself; I jumped into the water and swam to his ship, where I had the pleasure of finding him uninjured, although considerably stunned by the danger from which he had escaped. Wet as I was from my sea-bath I caught him in my arms, and pressed him to my heart; and then hastened to afford relief to some of the crew, who had not been so fortunate to escape without injury as he had been.

Another time I was the cause of serious alarm to Malvilain. One day, a mass of black and thick clouds was gathered close over the point of Cavite, and a frightful—that is, a tropical—

storm burst. The claps of thunder followed each other from minute to minute, and before each clap the lightning, in long serpent-like lines of fire, darted from the clouds, and drove on to the point of Cavite, where it tore up the ground of the little plain situate at the extremity, and near which the ships were moored. Notwithstanding the storm I was going to see Malvilain, and was almost in the act of placing my foot on the deck of his vessel, when the lightning fell into the sea so near to me that I lost my breath. Instantly I felt an acute pain in the back, as if a burning torch had been laid between my shoulders. The pain was so violent, that the moment I recovered myself I uttered a sharp scream. Malvilain, who was within a few paces of me, felt very sensibly the electric shock which had struck me, and, on hearing my cry, imagined that I was dangerously hurt. He rushed towards me and held me in his arms until I was able to give every assurance of my recovery. The electric fluid had grazed me, but without causing any positive injury.

I have related these two slight anecdotes to show the intimacy that subsisted between us, and how I afterwards suffered in my dearest affections.

My existence has to this day, when I write these lines, been filled with such extraordinary facts, that I have been naturally led to believe that the destiny of man is regulated by an order of things which must infallibly be accomplished. This idea has had great influence over me, and taught me to endure all the evils which have afflicted me. Was it, then, my destiny which bound me to Malvilain, and bound him to me in the same manner? I have no doubt of it.

Some days before the terrible scourge of the cholera broke out in the Philippines, Malvilain's ship set sail for France.

With hearts oppressed with grief we separated, after promising each that we should meet again; but, alas! fate had ordained it otherwise. Malvilain returned home, went to Nantes to take the command of a ship, and there became acquainted with my eldest sister, and married her. This news, which reached me while I resided in Manilla, gave me the greatest satisfaction, for if I had had to choose a husband for my dear sister Emilie, this marriage was the only one to satisfy the wishes I had formed for the happiness of both.

After his marriage Malvilain continued to sail from the port of Nantes. His noble disposition and his accurate knowledge of his duties caused him to be highly esteemed by the leading merchants. His affairs were in a state sufficiently good as not to require him to expose himself longer to the dangers of the sea, and he was on his last voyage, when, at the Mauritius, he was attacked by an illness, which carried him off, leaving my sister inconsolable, and with three very young girls to lament him.

This fresh and irreparable loss, the news of which had then reached me, added to my grief for the sad death of my poor brother. Every calamity seemed to oppress me. After some years of happiness I saw, by little and little, disappear from this world, the persons on whom I had concentrated my dearest affections; but, alas! I had not even then reached the term of my sorrows, for other and most bitter sufferings were still to be passed through.

I saw with pleasure my boy was enjoying the best health, and that he was daily increasing in strength; and yet I was far from being happy, and to the melancholy caused by the losses I had experienced was added another most fearful alarm. My beloved Anna had never thoroughly recovered after her accouchement, and day by day her health was growing weaker. She did not seem aware of her state. Her happiness at being a mother was so great that she did not think of her own condition.

I had gathered in my sugar-cane crop, which was most abundant, and my plantations were finished, when, wishing to procure some amusement for my wife, I proposed to go and spend some time at the house of her sister Josephine, for whom she entertained the warmest affection. She, with great pleasure, agreed to do so. We set out with our dear little Henry and his nurse, and took up our quarters at the house of my brother-in-law, Don Julian Calderon, then residing in a pretty country-house on the banks of the river Pasig, half a league from Manilla.

Of the three sisters of my wife, Josephine was the one for whom I had the most affection: I loved her as I did my own sister. The day of our arrival was one of rejoicing. All our friends at Manilla came to see us, and Anna was so pleased in seeing our little Henry admired that her health seemed to have improved considerably; but this apparent amelioration lasted but a few days, and soon, to my grief, I saw that she was growing worse than ever. I sent for the only medical man in Manilla in whom I had confidence, my friend Genu. He came frequently to see her, and after six weeks of constant attention, he advised me to take her back to my residence near the lake, where persons attacked with the same malady as my dear Anna had often recovered. As she herself wished to return, I appointed a day for our departure. A commodious boat, with good rowers, was ready for us on the Pasig, at the end of my brother in-law's garden; and a numerous assemblage of our friends accompanied us to the water's edge. The moment of

View on the River Pasig.

separation was one of most melancholy feelings to us all. The countenance of each seemed to ask: "Shall we meet again?" My sister-in-law Josephine, in a flood of tears, threw herself into Anna's arms. I had great difficulty in separating them ; but we were obliged to set out. I took my wife into the boat, and then those two sisters, who had always maintained towards each other the most tender love, addressed with their voices their last adieus, while promising not to be long separated, and that they would see each other very soon.

Those painful adieus and the sufferings of my wife caused the trip, which we had often previously made with the greatest gaiety, to be melancholy and silent. On our arrival, I did not look on Jala-Jala with the usual feelings of satisfaction. I had my poor patient placed in bed, and did not quit her room, hoping by my continual care to afford her some relief in her sufferings. But, alas! from day to day the malady made fearful progress. I was in despair. I wrote to Josephine, and sent a boat to Manilla for her to come and take care of her sister, who was most anxious to see her. The boat returned without her; but a letter from kind-hearted Josephine informed me that she was herself dangerously ill, and confined to her room, and could not even leave her bed; that she was very sorry for it, but I might assure Anna that they would soon be re-united, never again to be separated.

Fifty days—longer to me than a century—had scarcely elapsed since our return to Jala-Jala than all my hopes vanished. Death was approaching with rapid strides, and the fatal moment was at hand when I was to be separated from her whom I loved with such intensity. She preserved her senses to the last, and saw my profound melancholy, and my features altered by grief; and finding her last hour was near, she called me to her, and said: "Adieu, my beloved Paul, adieu. Console thyself—we shall meet again in Heaven! Preserve thyself for the sake of our dear boy. When I shall be no more, return home to thy own country, to see thy aged mother. Never marry again, except in France, if thy mother requires thee to do so. Do not marry in the Philippines, for thou wilt never find a companion here to love thee as I have loved." These words were the last which this good and gentle angel spoke. The most sacred ties, the tenderest and purest union, were then severed—my Anna was no more! I held her lifeless body clasped in my arms, as if I hoped by my caresses to recall her to life; but, alas! her destiny was decided!

It required absolute force to tear me from the precious remains which I pressed against my heart, and to draw me into a neighbouring room, where my son was. While I pressed him convulsively to my breast, I wished to weep; but my eyes were tearless, and I was insensible to the caresses even of my poor child.

The strongest constitution cannot resist the fatigue of fifty days of constant watching and uneasiness; and the state of annihilation in which I was, both physically and morally, after despair had taken the place of the glimmering hope which sustained us to the last moment, was such that I fell into a state of insensibility, which ended in a profound sleep. I awoke on the following day with my son in my arms. But how frightful was my state on awaking. All that was horrible in my position presented itself to my imagination. Alas! she was no more; my adorable companion, that beloved angel and consolatrix, who had, on my account, abandoned all—parents, friends, and the pleasures of a capital—to shut herself up with me in a deserted wilderness, where she was exposed to a thousand dangers, and had but me to support her. She was no more; and fatal destiny had torn her from me, to sink me for ever in desolation and grief.

The funeral took place on the following day, and was attended by every inhabitant of Jala-Jala. Her body was deposited near the altar in the humble church which I had caused to be erected, and before which altar she had so often poured forth prayers for my happiness.

For a long time mourning and consternation reigned in Jala-Jala. All my Indians showed the deepest sympathy for the loss which they had suffered. Anna was, during her life, beloved even to idolatry, and after her death she was most sincerely lamented.

For several days I continued in a thorough depression,

unable to attend to anything, except to the cares which my son, then my only remaining consolation, required. Three weeks elapsed before I quitted the room in which my poor wife had expired. I then received a note from Josephine, in which she stated that her illness had grown worse. The note ended with these words: "Come, my dear Paul; come to me: we shall weep together. I feel that your presence will afford some consolation."

I did not hesitate to comply with the request of dear Josephine, for whom I entertained an affection as if for my own sister. My presence might prove a solace to her, and I myself felt that it would prove to me a great consolation to see a person who had so sincerely loved my Anna. The hope of being useful to her re-animated my courage a little. I left my house under the care of Prosper Vidie, an excellent friend, who during the last days of my wife's life had not quitted me, and departed, accompanied by my son.

After the first emotion which Josephine and I felt on meeting, and when we both had shed abundant tears, I examined her state. It required a strong effort on my part to conceal from her my anxiety, on finding her labouring under a most serious malady, and which gave me grounds for fearing that a fresh misfortune was not far distant. Alas! my forebodings were correct; for eight days afterwards poor Josephine expired in my arms, after the most poignant sufferings. What abundant sources of woe in so short a space of time! It required a constitution strong as mine was to bear up against such a number of sorrows, and not to fail under the burthen.

When I had paid the last duties to my sister-in-law I went back to Jala-Jala. To me everything was burthensome. I was obliged to betake myself to my forests and to my mountains, in order to recover a little calmness. Some months passed over before I could attend to my affairs; but the last wishes of my poor wife required to be fulfilled, and I was to quit the Philippines and return to my country. I commenced preparations for the purpose. I made over my establishment to my friend Vidie, who was, as I considered, the person best adapted for carrying out my plans, and for treating my poor Indians well. He requested me to stop a little time with him, and to show him the secrets of my little government. I consented, and the more willingly, as those few months would serve to render my son stronger, and better able to support the fatigues of a long voyage. I therefore remained at Jala-Jala; but life had become painful to me, and without an object, so that it was positively a trouble. There was nothing to distract me—nothing to remove the most painful thoughts from me. The pretty spots of Jala-Jala, over which I had often looked with the greatest pleasure, had become altogether indifferent to me. I sought out the most melancholy and silent places. I often went to the banks of a rivulet, concealed in the midst of high mountains, and shaded by lofty trees. This spot was perhaps known to no other person; and probably no human being had ever previously been seated in it. There I gave free vent to my bitter recollections—my wife, my brothers, my sister-in-law, engrossed my imagination. When the thought of my son drove away these sombre reveries, I returned slowly to my house, where I found the poor child, who, by his caresses, seemed to try to find some way to cause a change in my grief; but they seemed only to recall the time when Anna always came to welcome me home, and when, clasping me in her arms, she caused me to forget all the toil and trouble I met with when absent from her. Alas! that blissful time had flown away, and was never to return; and in losing my companion I lost every happiness.

My friend Vidie tried every means in his power to rouse me. He spoke to me often of France, of my mother, and of the consolation I should feel on presenting my son to her. The love of my country, and the thought of finding there those affections of which I stood so much in need, was a soft balm, which lulled for a while the sufferings that were constantly vibrating in the bottom of my heart.

My Indians were deeply afflicted on learning the resolution I had taken of quitting them. They showed their trouble by saying to me, every time they addressed me! "Oh, master: what will become of us when we shall not see you again?" I quieted them as well as I could, by assuring them that Vidie would exert himself for their welfare; that when my son should be grown up, I would come back with him and then never leave them. They answered me with their prayers: "May God grant it, master! But what a long time we shall have to pass without seeing you! However, we shall not forget you"

Ajetas Indians.

CHAPTER XII.

My friend Adolphe Barrot visits me at Jala-Jala—The Bamboo Cane—The Cocoa-Nut Tree—The Banana—Majestic Forests of Gigantic Trees—The Leeches—A Tropical Storm in a Forest—An Indian Bridge—"Bernard the Hermit"—We arrive at Binangon-de-Lampon—The Ajetas—Veneration of the Ajetas for their Dead—Poison used by the Ajetas—I carry away a Skeleton—We Embark on the Pacific in an old Canoe, reaeh Maoban, and ultimately arrive at Jala-Jala.

AT this epoch of my recollections, in the midst of my melancholy and of my troubles, I formed an intimate and enduring friendship with a compatriot, a good and excellent man, for whom I always preserve the attachment first formed in a foreign country, several thousand leagues from home. I now speak of Adolphe Barrot, who was sent as consul-general to Manilla. He came with several friends to spend some days at Jala-Jala. Being unwilling that he should suffer any unpleasantness from the state of my feelings, I endeavoured to render his stay at Jala-Jala as agreeable as in my power. I arranged several hunting and shooting parties, and excursions through the mountains and on the lake. For his sake I resumed my old mode of life, such as I had been used to before I was overwhelmed by misfortune.

The days which I thus spent in company with Adolphe Barrot aroused within me my former taste for exercise, and my ruling passion for adventure. My friend Vidie—always with the intention of exciting me to action—pressed me very much to go and visit a certain class of the natives which I had often expressed a wish to examine. My affairs being almost regulated; my son being placed under his care, and that of his nurse, and of a housekeeper in whom I had every confidence; I was induced, by this feeling of security, and by the instances of my friend, to proceed to visit the district of the Ajetas, or Black-men, who were a wild race, altogether in a state of nature. They were the aborigines of the Philippines, and had for a long time been masters of Luzon At a time not very far distant, when the Spaniards conquered the country, the Ajetas levied a kind of black-mail from the Tagalese villages situated on the banks of the lake of Bay. At a fixed period they quitted their forests, entered the villages, and forced the inhabitants to give them a certain quantity of rice and maize; and if the Tagalese refused or were unable to pay these contributions, they cut off a number of heads, which they carried away as trophies for their barbarian festivities. After the conquest of the Philippines by the Spaniards, the latter took upon themselves the defence of the Tagalese, and the Ajetas, terrified by their fire-arms, remained in the forests, and did not re-appear among the Indians.

The same race is found in various parts of the Malay country; and the people of New Zealand—the Paponins—resemble them very much in form and colour.

My intention was to pass some days amongst those wild savages, and our preparations were speedily made. I chose two of my best Indians to accompany me. It is not requisite to state that my lieutenant was one of the party, for he was always with me in all my perilous expeditions.

We took each of us a small haversack, containing rice for three or four days, some dried venison, a good provision of powder, ball, and shot for game, some coloured handkerchiefs, and a considerable quantity of cigars for our own use, and to insure a welcome amongst the Ajetas. Each of us carried a good double-barreled gun and his poignard. Our clothes were those which we wore in all our expeditions,—on our heads the common salacote, a shirt of raw silk, the pantaloon turned up to above the knee; the feet and legs remained uncovered. With these simple preparations we set out on a trip of some weeks, during which, and from the second day of our starting, we could expect no shelter but the trees of the forest, and no food but the game we shot, and the edible parts of the palm tree.

I took special care not to forget the *vade mecum* which I always took with me, whenever I made these excursions for any number of days—I mean paper and a pencil, with which I made notes, to aid my recollections, and enable me afterwards to write down in a journal the remarks I made during my travels. Every preparation being made, we one morning started from Jala-Jala. We traversed the peninsula formed by my settlement, and embarked on the other side in a small canoe, which took us to the bottom of the lake to the north-east of my habitation. We passed the night in the large village of Siniloan, and at an early hour the following day resumed our march. This first day's journey was one of toil and suffering: we were then beginning the rainy season, and the heavy storms had swelled the rivers. We marched for some time along the banks of a torrent, which rushed down from the mountains, and which we were obliged to swim through fifteen times during the day. In the evening we came to the foot of the mountains where begin the forests of gigantic trees, which cover almost all the centre of the island of Luzon. There we made our first halt, lighted our fires, and prepared our beds and our supper. I think that I have already described our beds, which use and fatigue always rendered agreeable to us, when no accident occured to disturb our repose. But I have said nothing of the simple composition of our meals, nor of our manner of preparing them. Our rice and palms required to be cooked, an operation which might seem rather embarrassing, for we had with us no large kitchen articles: we sometimes wanted a fire-box and tinder. But the bamboo supplied all these. The bamboo is one of the three tropical plants which Nature, in her beneficence and care, seems to have given to man to supply most of his wants. And here I cannot forbear dedicating a few lines to the description of those three products of the tropics, viz: the bamboo, the cocoa-nut tree, and the banana-plant.

The bamboo belongs to the gramineous family; it grows in thick groves, in the woods, on the river banks, and wherever it finds a humid soil. In the Philippines there are counted wenty-five or thirty kinds, different in form and thickness. There are some of the diameter of the human body, and hollow in the interior: this kind serves especially for the construction of huts, and for making vessels to transport and to keep water. The filaments are used for making baskets, hats, and all kinds of basket-work, cords, and cables of great solidity.

Another bamboo, of smaller dimensions, and hollow within, which is covered with varnish, almost as hard as steel, is employed in building Indian houses. Cut to a point it is extremely sharp, and is used for many purposes. The Indians make lances of it, and arrows, and fleams for bleeding horses, and lancets for opening abcesses, and for taking thorns or other things out of the flesh.

A third kind, much more solid, and as thick as one's arm, and not hollow within, is used in such parts of the buildings as require sold timber, and especially in the roofing.

A fourth kind, much smaller, and also without being hollow, serves to make the fences that surround enclosed fields when tilled. The other kinds are not so much employed, but still they are found to be useful.

To preserve the plants, and to render them very productive, the shoots are cut at ten feet from the ground. These shoots look like the tubes of an organ, and are surrounded with branches and thorns. At the beginning of the rainy season there grows from each of those groves a quantity of thick bamboos, resembling large asparagus, which shoot up as it were by enchantment. In the space of a month they become from fifty to sixty feet long, and after a short time they acquire all the solidity necessary for the various works to which they are destined.

The cocoa-nut tree belongs to the palm family: it requires to grow seven years before it bears fruit; but after this period, and for a whole century, it yields continually the same product—that is, every month about twenty large nuts. This produce never fails, and on the same tree may be seen continually flowers and fruits of all sizes. The cocoa nut affords, as everyone knows, nutritious food, and when pressed yields a quantity of oil. The shell of the nut serves to make vases, and the filamentary parts are spun into ropes and cables for ships, and even into coarse clothing. The leaves are used to make baskets and brooms, and for thatching the huts.

The Cocoa-Nut.

A liquor is also taken from the cocoa-nut tree, called cocoa-wine; it is a most stupifying drink, of which the Indians make great use at their festivities. To produce the cocoa-wine, large groves of the cocoa-trees are laid out, from which merely the sap or juice is expected, but nothing in the shape of fruit. These trees have long bamboos laid at their tops from one to another, on which the Indians pass over every morning, bearing large vessels, in which they collect the liquid. It is a laborious and dangerous employment,—a real promenade in the air, at the height of from sixty to eighty feet from the ground. It is from the bud which ought to produce the flower that the liquid is drawn of which the spirit is afterwards made. As soon as the bud is about to burst, the Indian employed in collecting the liquid ties it very tight, a few inches from its point, and then cuts across the point beyond the tying

From this cutting, or from the pores which are left uncovered, a saccharine liquid flows, which is sweetish and agreeable to the palate before it has fermented. After it has passed the fermentation it is carried to the still, and submitted to the process of distillation, it then becomes the alcoholic liquor known in the country as cocoa-wine.

Besides these uses, the cocoa-nut shell, when burned, gives the fine black colour which the Indians make use of to dye their straw hats.

The banana is an herbaceous plant, without any woody matter: the trunk of each is formed of leaves placed one above the other. This trunk rises from twelve to fifteen feet from the ground, and then spreads out into long broad leaves, not less than five or six feet each. From the middle of these leaves the flower rises, and also the spike (*régime*). By this word is to be understood a hundred of large bananas growing from the same stalk, forming together a long branch, that turns towards the sun.

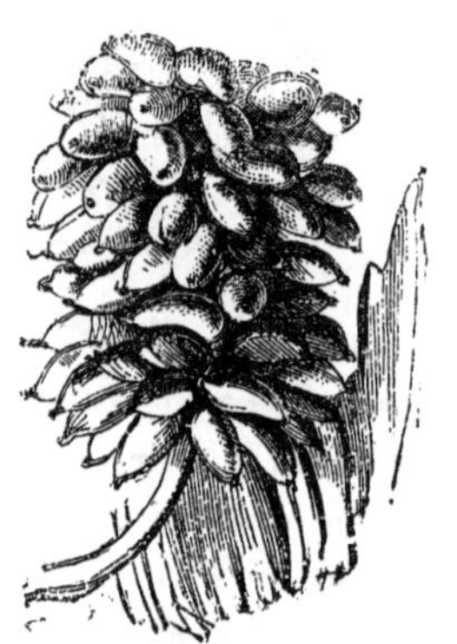

The Banana.

Before the fruit has reached its full ripeness, the spike is cut, and becomes fit for use. The part of the plant which is in the earth is a kind of large root, from which proceed successively thirty shoots, and each shoot ought not to have more than one spike, or bunch; it is then cut fronting the sun, and as all the shoots rising from the same trunk are of different ages, there are fruits to be found in all the stages of growth; so that every month or fortnight, and at all seasons, a spike or two may be gathered from the same plant. There is also a species of banana the fruit of which is not good to eat, but from which raw silk is formed, called abaca, which is used to make clothes, and all kinds of cordage. This filament is found in the trunk of the plant, which, as I have said, consists of leaves placed one over another, which, after being separated into long strips, and left for some hours in the sun, is then placed on an iron blade, not sharp, and then dragged with force over it. The parenchyme of the plant is taken off by the iron blade, and the filaments then separate. Nothing is now wanting but to expose them for some time to the sun's rays; after which they are brought to market.

I observe that I have left my journey aside to describe three tropical plants, which afford a sufficiency for all the wants of man. Those plants are well-known; yet there may be some persons ignorant of the utility, and of the various services which they render to the inhabitants of the tropics. My readers will from them be naturally led to reflect how the inhabitants of the torrid zone are favoured by nature, in comparison with those of our frigid climate.

We were at the foot of the mountains, preparing to pass the night. Our labour was always divided one got the beds ready, another the fire, a third the cookery. He who had to prepare the fire collects a quantity of dry wood and of brambles. Under this heap of firewood he puts about twelve pounds of elemi gum, which is common in the Philippines, where it is found in quantities at the foot of the large trees from which it flows naturally. He then takes a piece of bamboo, half a-yard long, which he splits to its length, tears with poignard so as to make very thin shavings, which he rubs together while rolling them between his hands, and then puts them into the hollow part of the other piece, and lays it down on the ground, and then with the sharp side of the piece from which he had taken the shavings, he rubs strongly the piece lying on the ground, as if he wished to saw it across. In a short time the bamboo containing the shavings is cut through and on fire. The flame rising from the shavings, when blown lightly upon, quickly sets the elemi gum in a blaze, and in an instant there is a fire sufficient to roast an ox.

He who had to manage the cooking cut two or three pieces of the large bamboo, and put in each whatever he wished to cook—usually rice or some part of the palm tree—he added some water, stopped the ends of the bamboo with leaves, and laid it in the middle of the fire. This bamboo was speedily burned on the outside, but the interior was moistened by the water, and the food within was as well boiled as in any earthen vessels. For plates we had the large palm leaves. Our meals, as may be observed, were Spartan enough, even during the days while our provision of rice and dried venison lasted. But when game was found, and that a stag or a buffalo fell to our lot, we fed like epicures. We drank pure water whenever a spring or a rivulet tempted us, but if we were at a loss we cut long pieces of the liana, called "the traveller's drink," from which flowed a clear and limpid draught, preferable perhaps to any which we might have procured from a better source.

It was evident I was not travelling like a nabob; and it would have been impossible to take more baggage. How could any one, with large provisions and a pompous retinue move in the midst of mountains covered with forests literally along untouched by human feet, and forced, in order to get through them, at every instant to swim across torrents, and having no other guide than the sun, or the blowing of the breeze There was no choice but to travel in the Indian style, as I did, or to remain at home.

The first night we spent in the open air passed quietly; our strength was restored, and we were recruited for the journey. At an early hour we were up, and, after a frugal breakfast, we resumed our march. For more than two hours we climbed up a mountain covered with heavy timber, the ascent was rough and fatiguing, at last we reached the top, quite exhausted, where there was a vast flat, which it would take us some days to traverse. It was there, on this flat, that I beheld the most majestic, the finest virgin forest that existed in the world. It consists of gigantic trees, grown up as straight as a rush, and to a prodigious height. Their tops, where alone their branches grow, are laced into one another, so as to form a vault impenetrable to the rays of the sun. Under this vault, and among those fine trees, prolific nature has given birth to a crowd of climbing plants of a most remarkable description. The rattan and the flexible liana mount up to the topmost branches, and re-descending to the earth, take fresh root, receive new sustenance, and then remount anew, and at various distances they join themselves to the friendly trunks of their supporting columns, and thus they form very often most beautiful decorations. Varieties of the pandanus are to be seen, of which the leaves, in bunches, start from the ground, forming beautiful sheaves. Enormous ferns were to be met with, real trees in shape, and up which we clambered often, to cut the top branches, for their delicious perfume and which serve as food nearly the same as the palms. But, in the midst of this extraordinary vegetation nature is gloomy and

LA GIRONIERE AND HIS INDIANS TRAVERSING A NATIVE FOREST.—*Page 254.*

silent; not a sound is to be heard, unless perhaps the wind that shakes the tops of the trees, or from time to time the distant noise of a torrent, which, falling precipitately, cascades from the heights of the mountains to their base. The ground is moist, as it never receives the sun's rays: the little lakes and the rivers, that never flow unless when swollen by the storms, present to the eye water black and stagnant, on which the reflection of the fine clear blue sky is never to be seen.

The sole inhabitants of these melancholy though majestic solitudes are deer, buffaloes and wild boars, which being hidden in their lairs and dens in the daytime, come out at night in search of food. Birds are seldom seen, and the monkeys so common in the Philippines, shun the solitude of these immense forests. One kind of insect is met with in great abundance, and it plagues the traveller to the utmost; they are the small leeches, which are found on all the mountains of the Philippines that are covered with forests. They lie close to the ground in the grass, or on the leaves of the trees, and dart like grasshoppers on their prey, to which they fasten. Travellers are therefore always provided with little knives, cut from the bamboo, to loosen the hold of the insects, after which they rub the wound with a little chewed tobacco. But soon another leech, attracted by the flowing blood, takes the place of the one which was removed, and constant care is necessary to avoid being victimised by those little insects, of which the voracity far exceeds that of our common leeches.

Our way lay through these singular creations of nature, and I was engaged in looking at and examining the curiosities around me, while my Indians were seeking some kind of game—deer, buffalo, or wild boar—to replace our stock of rice and venison, which was exhausted. We were at length reduced to the palms as our only resource; but the palms, though pleasing to the palate, are not sufficiently nutritive to recruit the strength of poor travellers, when, suffering under extreme fatigue, and after a laborious march, they find no lodging but the moist ground, and no shelter but the vault of the sky.

Fruit of the Palm Tree.

We directed our course as near as possible towards the eastern coast, which is bathed by the Pacific ocean. We knew that it was in that direction the Ajetas commenced their settlement. We wished also to pass through the large Tagalese village, Binangonan de Lampon, which is to be found, isolated and hidden, at the foot of the eastern mountains, in the midst of the savages. We had already spent several nights in the forest, and without experiencing any great inconvenience. The fires which we lighted every evening warmed us, and saved us from the myriads of terrible leeches, which otherwise would certainly have devoured us. We imagined that we were within one day's march of the sea-shore, where we expected to take some time for rest, when, of a sudden, a burst of thunder at a distance gave us reason to apprehend a storm. Nevertheless, we continued our journey; but in a short time the growling of the thunder approached so near as to leave no doubt that the hurricane would burst over us. We stopped, lighted our fires, cooked our evening's repast, and placed some of the palm leaves on poles by the side of a slope to save us from the heavy rain

We had not finished all our preparations when the storm broke. If we had not had the glimmering glare of our firebrands we should have been in profound obscurity, although it was not yet night. We all three, with pieces of palm branches in our hands, crouched under the slight shelter which we had improvised, and there awaited the full force of the storm. The thunder-claps were redoubled; the rain began with violence to batter the trees, and then to assail us like a torrent. Our fires were speedily extinguished; we found ourselves in the deepest darkness, interrupted only by the lightning, which from time to time rushed, serpent-like, through the trees of the forest, scattering a dazzling light, to leave us the moment after in profound obscurity. Around us the din was horrible; the thunder was continuous, the echoes of the mountains repeating from distance to distance its sound, sometimes deadened, and sometimes with awful grandeur. The wind, which blew with violence, shattered the uppermost parts of the trees, breaking off large branches, which fell with a crash to the ground. Some trunks were uprooted, and, while falling, tore down the boughs of the neighbouring trees. The rain was incessant, and in the intervals between the thunder we could hear the awful roar of the waters of a torrent which rushed madly past the base of the mound where we had taken refuge. Amidst all this frightful commotion, mournful and dismal sounds were heard, like the howls of a large dog which had lost its master: they were the cries of the deer in their distress, seeking for a place of shelter. Nature seemed to be in convulsions, and to have declared war in every element. The loose thatch under which we had taken refuge was soon penetrated, and we were completely deluged. We soon quitted this miserable hole, preferring to move our stiffened and almost deadened limbs, covered with the fearful little leeches, which terrible infliction deprived us of the strength so necessary in our awful position.

I avow that at this moment I sincerely repented my fatal curiosity, for which I paid so dearly. I could compare this frightful night only to the one I had passed in the bamboos, when I was wrecked on the lake. In appearance there was not such pressing danger, for we could not be swallowed up by the waves; but there were large trees, under which we were obliged to stop, and one of which might be uprooted and fall upon us; a bough torn off by the wind might crush us; and the lightning, equally terrific in its reports and its effects, might strike us at any moment. One thing was especially painful, and that was the cold, and the difficulty of moving our frozen and almost paralysed limbs. We awaited with impatience the cessation of the storm; but it was not until after three hours of mortal agony that the thunder gradually ceased. The wind fell; the rain subsided; and for some time we heard nothing but the large drops which dripped from the trees, and the dread sound of the torrents. Calm was restored; the sky became pure and starry: but we were deprived of that view which gives hope to the traveller, for the forest presented only a dome of green, impenetrable to the sight.

Exhausted as we were by our exposure to the elements and our exertions, we were so overpowered by nature's great renovator sleep, that, notwithstanding our clothes were saturated with the rain, we were able to pass the remainder of the night in tranquillity. At break of day the forest, which a few hours previously had been the scene of the terrors which I have described, was again tranquil and silent. When we quitted our lair we were frightful to look at; we were covered with leeches, and the marks of blood on our faces rendered us hideous. On looking at my two poor Indians I could not avoid laughing aloud; they also looked at me, but their re spect for me prevented their laughing. I was no doubt equally punished, and my white skin must have served to show well the ravages of these creatures. We were, indeed, knocked up; we could scarcely move, so weak had we become. However, act we must, and promptly,—to light a fire quickly, in order to warm us; to cook some of the palm stalks; to cross, by swimming, a torrent which, with a terrible noise, was rushing on below us; and to reach, during the day, the shores of the Pacific ocean. If we delayed to start it might not be possible to pass through the torrents,—we had left several behind us,—we might find ourselves in the impossibility of going either backward or forward, and perhaps be obliged to remain several days waiting for the waters to subside before we could proceed. Besides, other storms might arise, frequent as they are at this season, and we should have to remain for several weeks in a desert spot without resources, and where the first night passed under such a bad roof was no recommendation. There was no time to be lost. From a large heap of palm leaves, where we had placed and covered up our haversacks in order to preserve them from the wet, we drew them out safe; our precautions had fortunately been successful, they were quite dry. We made a large fire, thanks to the elemi gum, which burns with such ease. Our feelings were delightful when the heat entered our frames, dried our dripping garments, re-animated our courage, and gave us some strength. But, to enjoy that satisfaction fully, one should have acquired it at the same cost as I had. I very much doubt that any European would like to participate in the scenes of that night simply for the enjoyments of the following day.

Our scanty cookery was soon ready, and expeditiously dispatched, and we moved off in quick time.

My Indians were uneasy, as they feared they would not be able to pass through the torrent which was heard at a distance, consequently they marched quicker than I did. On reaching the bank I found them in a consternation. "Oh, master!" said my faithful Alila, "it is not possible to pass; so we must spend some days here." I cast my eyes on the torrent, which was rolling between steep rocks, in a yellow, muddy stream: it had all the appearance of a cascade, and was carrying down the trunks of trees and branches broken off during the storm. My Indians had already come to a decision, and were arranging a spot for a fit bivouac; but I did not wish to give up all hopes of success so speedily, and set about examining with care the means of overcoming the difficulty.

The torrent was not more than a hundred yards in breadth and a good swimmer could with ease get over in a few minutes. But it was necessary, on the opposite side, to arrive at a spot which was not too steep, and where one could find safe footing, and out of the torrent; otherwise the risk would be run of being drawn down, no one could tell whither.

From the bank on which we were it was easy to jump into the water, but on the other side, for a hundred yards down the stream, there was but one spot where the rocks were interrupted. A small stream joined there the one we wished to cross. After I had carefully calculated by sight the length of the passage, I considered myself strong enough to attempt it. I was a better swimmer than my Indians; and I was certain if I was once on the other side, that they would follow. I told them that I was going to cross over the torrent.

But one reflection caused me to hesitate. How could I preserve our haversacks, and save our precious provision of powder? How keep our guns from injury? It would not be possible to think of carrying those articles on my back through a torrent so rapid, and in which, beyond doubt,. I should be under water more than once before I gained the other side.

The Indians, being fertile in expedients, speedily extricated me from this difficulty: they cut several rattans, and joined the ends together, so as to form a considerable length. One of them climbed a tree which leant over the torrent, and there fastened one end of the rattan length, while I took the other end to carry it over to the other bank. All our arrangements being effected I plunged into the water, and without much difficulty gained the opposite side, having the end of the rattan with me, which I fastened to a tree on the steep bank I had gained, allowing a slight inclination of the line towards me, yet raised sufficiently over the water to allow the articles which we were anxious to pass over to slide along without touching the water. Our newly constructed bridge was wonderfully successful. The articles came across quite safe and dry; and my Indians, by its aid, quickly joined me. We congratulated each other on our fortunate passage, and the more so, as we expected before sunset to reach the Pacific ocean. Of the woods we had had enough: and we now looked for the sun, which for several days had been obscured by clouds; the leeches caused us considerable suffering, and weakened us very much, and our miserable diet was not sufficient to recruit our exhausted frames. Moreover we did not doubt that, on reaching the sea, we should be amply recompensed for all the privations we had endured. In fine, with renewed hopes we found our courage revive, and soon forgot the fatal night of the storm

I walked nearly as quick as my Indians, who, like me, hastened to get clear of the insupportable humidity in which we had existed for several days.

Two hours after we had passed the torrent a dull and distant sound struck our ears. At first we supposed it to be a fresh storm; but soon we knew, from its regularity, that it was nothing less than the murmur of the Pacific ocean, and the sound of the waves which come from afar to break themselves on the eastern shore of Luzon. This certainty caused me a most pleasing emotion. In a few hours I should again see the blue sky, warm myself in the generous rays of the sun, and find a boundless horizon. I should also get rid of the fearful leeches, and should soon salute Nature, animated in creation, in exchange for the solitudes from which we had just emerged.

We were now on the declivity of the mountains, the descent of which was gentle and our march easy. The sound of the waves increased by degrees. Near three o'clock in the afternoon we perceived through the trees that the sun was clear; and an instant afterwards we beheld the sea, and a magnificent beach, covered with fine glittering sand. The first movement of all three was to strip off our clothes and to plunge into the waves; and while we thus enjoyed a salutary bath, we amused ourselves in collecting off the rocks a quantity of shell-fish, which enabled us to make the most hearty meal we had eaten since we started from home.

Having thus satisfied our hunger, our thoughts were directed to taking rest, of which we stood in great need; but it was no longer on knotty and rough pieces of timber, that we were going to repose,—it was on the soft sand, which the shore offered to us, warmed as it was by the last rays of the setting sun.

It was almost night when we stretched ourselves on this bed, which to us was preferable to one of down. Our sacks served as pillows; we laid our guns, which were properly primed, close by our sides, and after a few minutes were buried in a profound sleep. I know not how long I had enjoyed this invigorating balm when I was awakened by the painful feeling of something crawling over me. I felt the prickings of sharp claws, which fastened in my skin, and occasionally caused me great pain. Similar sensations had awakened my two Indians. We collected the embers which were still ignited, and were able to see the new kind of enemies which assailed us. They were the crabs called "Bernard the Hermit,"* and in such quantities that the ground was crawling with them, of all sizes and of all ages. We swept the sand on which we laid down, hoping to drive them away, and to have some sleep; but the troublesome—or rather, the famishing hermits—returned to the charge, and left us neither peace or quiet. We were busy in resisting their attacks, when suddenly, on the edge of the forest, we perceived a light, which came towards us. We seized our guns, and awaited its approach in profound silence and without any movement. We then saw a man and woman coming out of the wood, each having a torch in their hands. We knew them to be Ajetas, who were coming, no doubt, to catch fish on the beach. When they reached within a few steps from us, they stood for an instant motionless and gazed at us with fixed attention. We three were seated, watching them, and trying to guess their intentions. One of them put his hand to his shoulder, as if to take his bow; and I instantly cocked my

* Bernard the Hermit is a crab, which lodges in the abandoned shell of the molluscæ, and comes at night in search of food, which it finds on the sea beach.

gun. The noise caused by the movement of the gun-lock was sufficient to frighten them: they threw down their light, and scampered off like two wild beasts, in the highest alarm, to hide themselves in the forest.

Their appearance was enough to prove that we were in a place frequented by the Ajetas. The two savages whom we had seen were perhaps gone to inform their friends, who might come in great numbers and let fly at us their poisoned arrows. This dread, and the incessant attacks of Bernard the Hermit, caused us to spend the remainder of the night near a large fire.

As soon as day broke we made an excellent breakfast, thanks to the abundance of shell-fish, of which we could take whatever quantity we liked, and then set out again. Our way lay sometimes along the shore, and at other times through the woods. The journey was very fatiguing, but without any incident worthy of notice. It was after night-fall when we arrived at the village of Binangonan de Lampon. This village, inhabited by Tagalocs, is thrown, like an oasis of men, somewhat civilised, in the midst of forests and savage people, and who had no direct communication with the other districts which are governed by the Spaniards.

My name was known to the inhabitants of Binangonan de Lampon, consequently we were received with open arms, and all the heads of the village disputed with each other for the honour of having me as a guest. I gave the preference to him who had first invited me, and in his dwelling I experienced the kindest hospitality. I had scarcely entered when the mistress of the house herself wished to wash my feet, and to show me all those attentions which proved to me the pleasure they felt that I had given them this preference.

Inhabitants of Binangonan de Lampon

During supper, while I was enjoying the good food which was before me, the small house in which I was seated became filled with young girls, who gazed at me with a curiosity which was really comic. When I had finished my meal the con versation with my host began to weary me, and I stretched myself on a mat, which on that occasion I regarded as an excellent substitute for a feather-bed.

I spent three days with the kind Tagalocs, who received and treated me like a prince. On the fourth day I bade them adieu, and we shaped our course to the northward, in the midst of mountains covered with thick forests, and which, like those that we had quitted, showed no path for the traveller, except some tracks or openings through which wild animals passed. We proceeded with great caution, for we found ourselves in the district peopled by Ajetas. At night we concealed our fire, and each of us in turn kept watch, for what we dreaded most was a surprise.

One morning, while marching in silence, we heard before us a number of shrill voices, resembling rather the cries of birds than human sounds. We kept strict watch, and shaded ourselves as much as possible by the aid of the trees and of the brushwood. Suddenly we perceived before us, at a very little distance, forty savages of both sexes, and of all ages; they absolutely seemed to be mere brutes; they were on the bank of a river, and close to a large fire. We advanced some steps presenting the but-end of our guns. The moment they saw us they set up a shrill cry, and were about to take to flight; but I made signs, and showed the packet of cigars which we wished to give them. Fortunately I had learned at Binangonan the way by which I was to approach them. As soon as they understood us they ranged themselves in a line, like men about to be reviewed; that was the signal that we might come near them. We approached with the cigars in our hands, and at one end of the line I began to distribute my presents. It was highly important to make friends of them, and, according to their custom, to give to each an equal share. My distribution being finished, our alliance was cemented, and peace concluded: the savages and we had nothing to dread from each other. They all began smoking. A stag had been suspended to a tree; their chief cut three large pieces from it with a bamboo knife, which he threw into the glowing fire, and a moment afterwards drew it out again and handed it round, a piece being given to each of us. The outside of this steak was burned, and a little spotted with cinders, but the inside was raw and full of blood ; however it was necessary not to show any repugnance, and to make a cannibal feast, otherwise my hosts would have been affronted, and I was anxious to live with them for some days on a good understanding. I therefore eat my portion of the stag, which, after all, was not bad : my Indians did as I had done. Good relations were thus established between us, and treachery was not then to be expected.

I now found myself in the midst of a tribe of men whom I had come from Jala-Jala to see, and I set about examining them at my ease, and for as long as I wished. We fixed our bivouac some steps from theirs, as if we wished to form part of the family of our new friends. I could not address them but by signs, and I had the greatest difficulty in making them understand me, but on the day after my arrival I had an interpreter. A woman came to me with a child, to which she wished to give a name ; she had been reared amongst the Tagalocs; she had spoken that language, of which she remembered a little, and could give, although with much difficulty, all the information I desired which was to me of interest.

The creatures with whom I had thus formed a connection for a few days, and as I saw them, seemed rather to be a large family of monkeys than human beings. Their voices very much resembled the shrill cries of those animals, and in their gestures they were exactly like them. The only difference I could see was that they knew how to handle a bow and a lance, and to make a fire. To describe them properly I shall give a sketch of their forms and physiognomies.

The Ajeta, or little negro, is as black as ebony, like the

Africans; his greatest height is four feet and a-half; his hair is woolly, and as he takes no trouble about cutting it, and knows not how to arrange it, it forms around his head a sort of crown, which gives him an odd aspect, and, at a distance makes him appear as if surrounded with a kind of halo; his eye is yellowish, but lively and brilliant, like that of an eagle. The necessity of living by the chase, and of pursuing his prey, produces the effect on this organ of giving to it the most extraordinary vivacity. The features of the Ajetas have something of the African black, but the lips are not so prominent; while young their forms are pretty; but their lives being spent in the woods, sleeping always in the open air without shelter, eating much one day and often having nothing—long fastings, followed by repasts swallowed with the voracity of wild beasts—gave them a protruding stomach, and made their extremities lank and shrivelled. They never wear any clothing, unless a belt of the rind of a tree, fromeight to ten inches in breadth, which they tie round their waist; their arms are composed of a bamboo lance, a bow of the palm tree, and poisoned arrows. Their food consists of roots, of fruits, and of the products of the chase; the flesh they eat nearly raw; and they live in tribes composed of from fifty to sixty individuals. During the day, the old men, the infirm, and the children, remain near a large fire, while the others are engaged in hunting; when they have a sufficiency of food to last for some days, they remain round their fire, and sleep pell-mell among the cinders.

It is extremely curious to see collected together fifty or sixty of these brutes of every age, and each more or less deformed; the old women especially are hideous, their decrepid limbs, their big bellies and their extraordinary heads of hair, give them all the looks of furies, or of old witches.

I had scarcely arrived than women with very young children came in crowds to me. In order to satisfy them I caressed their babes: but that was not what they wanted, and, notwithstanding their gestures and their words, I could not make out their wishes. On the following day, the woman whom I have already mentioned as having lived for some time among the Tagalocs, arrived from a neighbouring tribe, accompanied by ten other women, each of whom had an infant in her arms. She explained what I was not able to comprehend on the previous day, and said: "We have amongst us very few words for conversation: all our children take at their birth the name of the place where they are born. There is great confusion, then, and we have brought them to you that you may give them names."

As soon as I understood this explanation, I wished to celebrate the ceremony with all the pomp that the circumstances and the place allowed. I went to a small rivulet, and there, as I knew the formula for applying the baptismal water, I took my two Indians as sponsors, and during several days baptised about fifty of these poor children. Each mother who brought her infant was accompanied by two persons of her own family. I pronounced the sacramental words, and poured water on the head of the child, and then announced aloud the name I had given to the child. Therefore, as they have no means of perpetuating their recollections, from the time that I pronounced the name,—Francis, for instance,—the mother and her accompanying witnesses repeated it very often, until they learned to say it correctly, and commit it to memory. Then they went away, and were constantly repeating the name, which they were anxious to retain.

The first day the ceremony was rather long; but the second day the number lessened, and I was allowed to pursue my examination of the character of my hosts. I had retained the woman who spoke Tagaloc, and in the long conversations which I held with her, she initiated me thoroughly in all their customs and usages.

The Ajetas have no religion; they do not adore any star. It seems, however, that they have transmitted to, or received from, the Tinguianes, the practice of adoring, during one day, a rock or a trunk of any tree on which they find any resemblance whatever of an animal; they then abandon it, and think no more of an idol until they meet with a strange form, which, for a short time, constitutes the object of their frivolous worship. They have a strong veneration for the dead; and during several years it is their practice to visit their graves, and there to leave a little tobacco or betel. The bow and arrows which once belonged to the deceased are hung up over his grave on the day of his interment; and every night, according to the belief of his surviving comrades, he rises up out of his grave, and goes to hunt in the forest.

Interments take place without any ceremony. The dead body is laid at full length in a grave, which is covered up with earth. But whenever one of the Ajetas is dangerously ill, and his recovery despaired of, or that he has been even slightly wounded by a poisoned arrow, his friends place him seated in a deep hole, with the arms crossed over his breast, and thus inter him while living.

I thought of speaking to my interpreter on religion, and asked her if she did not believe in a Supreme Being—an all-powerful Divinity, on whom all nature—even we ourselves—depend in all things; and who had created the firmament, and who was looking on at our acts. She looked at me with a smile, and said: "When I was young, amongst your brothers, I remember that they spoke to me of a master, who, as they said, had Heaven for his dwelling-place; but all that was lies; for see"—(she here took up a small stone and threw it into the air, saying, in a very serious tone)—"how can a king, as you say, remain in the sky any more than that stone?" What answer could I give to such reasoning? I left religion aside, to put to her other questions.

I have already stated that the Ajetas did not often wait for the death of a person to put him into the ground. As soon as the last honours are rendered to a deceased, it is requisite, conformably to their usages, to take revenge for his death. The hunters of the tribe to which he belonged set out, with their lances and their arrows, to kill the first living creature which should appear before their eyes—be it man, stag, wild boar, or buffalo. From the moment they start in search of a victim, they take care, in every part of the forest through which they pass, to break the young shoots of the arbustus shrub, by pointing its tops in the direction which they are following. This is done to give a caution to their friends, and other passers-by, to avoid those places in which they are searching for a victim, for if one of themselves fell into their hands, he would, without fail, be taken as the expiatory victim.

They are faithful in marriage, and have but one wife. When a young man has made his choice, his friends or his parents make a demand for the young girl; a refusal is never given. A day is chosen; and on the morning of that day the young girl is sent into the forest, where she hides herself or not, just as she pleases, and according as she wishes to be married to the young man who has asked her. An hour after her departure, the young man is sent to find out his bride. If he has the good luck to find her, and to bring her back to her parents before sunset, the marriage is concluded, and she becomes his wife without fail; but if, on the contrary, he returns to the camp without her, he is not allowed to renew his addresses.

Among the Ajetas old age is highly respected. It is always one of the oldest men who governs the assembled body. All the savages of this race live, as I have stated, in large families of from sixty to eighty persons. They ramble about through the forests, without having any fixed spot for their abode; and they change their encampment according to the greater or less quantity of game which they find in various places.

While thus living in a state of nature altogether primitive, these savages have no instrument of music, and their language imitating, as I have stated, the cries of monkeys, has very few sounds, which are extremely difficult for a stranger to pronounce, how much soever may be his eagerness to study them. They are excellent hunters, and make a wonderful use of the bow. The young negroes, however little, of each sex, while their parents are out hunting, amuse themselves on the banks of the rivulets with their small bows. If by chance they see any fish in the translucent stream they let fly an arrow at it, and it is seldom that they miss their aim.

All the weapons of the Ajetas are poisoned; a simple arrow could not cause a wound so severe as to stop a strong animal, such as a deer, in its course; but if the dart has been smeared with the poison known to them, the smallest puncture of it produces in the wounded animal an inextinguishable thirst, and death ensues upon satisfying it. The hunters then cut out the flesh around the wound, and use the remainder as food, without any danger; but if they neglect this precaution, the meat becomes so exceedingly bitter that even the Ajetas them selves cannot eat it.

Never having given credit to the famous *boab* of Java, I made experiments at Sumatra on the sort of poison of which the Malays make use to poison their weapons. I discovered that it was simply a strong solution of arsenic in citron juice, with which they coated their arms several times. I tried to find the poison used by the Ajetas. They led me to the foot of a large tree, and tore off a piece of its bark, and told me that that was the poison they used. I chewed some of it before them; it was insupportably bitter, but otherwise not injurious in its natural state. But the Ajetas make a preparation of it, the secret of which they refused to impart to me. When their poison is made up as a paste, they give to their arms a thin coating of it, about an eighth of an inch in thickness.

The Ajetas in their movements are active and supple to an incredible degree; they climb up the highest trees like monkeys, by seizing the trunk with both hands, and using the soles of their feet. They run like a deer in the pursuit of the wild animals: this is their favourite occupation. It is a very curious sight to see these savages set out on a hunting excursion; men, women, and children move together, very much like a troop of ourang-outangs when going on a plundering party. They have always with them one or two little dogs, of a very special breed, which they employ in tracking out their prey whenever it is wounded.

I enjoyed quite at my ease the hospitality exercised towards me by these primitive men. I saw amongst them, and with my own eyes, all that I was desirous of knowing. The painful life which I had led since my departure from home, without any shelter but the trees, and eating nothing but what the savages provided, began to tire me exceedingly: I resolved to return to Jala-Jala. Having previously noticed several graves at a short distance from our bivouac, an idea struck me of carrying away a skeleton of one of the savages, which would, in my judgment, be a curiosity to present to the Jardin des Plantes or to the Museum of Anatomy at Paris. The undertaking was one of great danger, on account of the veneration of the Ajetas for their dead. They might surprise us while violating their graves, and then no quarter was to be expected. I was, however, so much accustomed to overcome whatever opposed my will, that the danger did not deter me from acting upon my resolution. I communicated my intentions to my Indians, who did not oppose my project.

Some few days afterwards we packed up our baggage, and took farewell of our hosts. We shaped our course towards the Indian cemetery. In the first graves which we opened we found the bones decayed in part, and I could only procure two skulls, which were not worth the danger to which they exposed us. However, we continued our researches, and towards the close of the day discovered the remains of a woman, who, from the position of the body in the grave, must have been buried before her death. The bones were still covered with skin; but the body was dry, and almost like a mummy. This was a fit subject. We had taken the body out of the grave, and were beginning to pack it up piece by piece into a sack, when we heard small shrill cries at a distance. The Ajetas were coming upon us, and there was no time to be lost. We seized our prize and started off as quick as possible. We had not got a hundred yards, when we heard the arrows whistling about our ears. The Ajetas, perched on the tops of the trees, waited for us and attacked us, without our having any means of defence. Fortunately night came to our aid; their arrows, usually so sure, were badly directed, and did not touch us. While escaping we fired a gun to frighten them, and were soon able to leave them far behind, without having received any other injury than the alarm, and a sufficient notice of the danger to be encountered in disturbing the repose of their dead. On emerging from the wood, some drops of blood caused me to remark a slight scratch on the forefinger of my right hand; I attributed this to the hurry of my flight, and did not trouble myself much about it, was my practice with trifles, but continued my march towards the sea-shore.

We still retained the skeleton, which we laid on the sandy beach, as well as our haversacks and guns, and sat down to rest after the fatigue of the journey. My companions then began to make reflections on our position, and my lieutenant, inspired by his affection for me, and his sense of the danger we were exposed to, addressed me in the following strain:

"Oh, master! what have we done, and what is to become of us? To-morrow morning the enraged Ajetas will come to attack us for the execrable booty which we have carried off from them at the risk of our lives. If they would attack in the open ground, with our guns we might defend ourselves; but what can one do against those animals, perched here and there like monkeys in the top branches of the trees of their forest? Those places are for them so many fortresses, from which they will to-morrow shower down upon us those darts, which, alas! never fail to do mischief. Luckily it was night when they attacked us just now, for otherwise we at this hour should have a lance through each of our bodies, and then they would have cut off our heads to serve as trophies for a superb fête. Your head, master, would first have been laid on the ground, and the brutes would have danced round it, and, as our leader, you would have been a target of honour for them to practise upon.

"And now, master, all that which would have occurred to us if the night had not favoured our escape is but deferred, for, alas! we cannot remain continually on this beach, although it is the only spot where we can protect ourselves against these black rascals. We must go to our homes, and this we cannot do without passing through the woods inhabited by these abominable creatures, who made us eat raw meat, and seasoned only with cinders. Well, master, before you undertook this excursion, you ought to have recollected all that happened to us among the Tinguians and the Igorrots."

I listened calmly to this touching lamentation of my lieutenant, who was perfectly right in all he said; but when he finished I sought to rouse his courage, and replied:

"What! my brave Alila! are you afraid? I thought the Tic-balan, and the evil spirits could alone affect your courage. Do you want to make me think that men like yourself, without any arms but bad arrows, are enough to make you quake? Come, enough of this cowardice; to-morrow we shall have daylight, and we shall see what is to be done. In the meantime let us search for shell-fish, for I am very hungry, notwithstanding the alarm into which you are trying to throw me."

This little sermon gave courage to Alila, who immediately set about making a fire, and then, by the aid of lighted bamboos, he and his comrade went to the rocks to find out the shell-fish.

Alila was nevertheless quite right, and I myself could not disguise the fact, that good luck alone could extricate us from the critical position in which we were placed by my fault, in having thought of my country, and in wishing to ornament the Museum of Paris with a skeleton of an Ajetas.*

From disposition and habit I was not a man to alarm myself with any danger which was not immediate; yet I avow that the last words I had said to Alila:—"To-morrow we shall have daylight, and we shall see what is to be done:"—came back to my mind, and for a short time occupied my thoughts.

My Indians brought back a large quantity of shell-fish, sufficient for our supper, and Alila ran up quite breathless, saying:

"Master, I have made a discovery! A hundred steps from this I have found a canoe, which the sea has cast upon the beach; it is large enough to hold us three. We can make use of it to get to Binangonan, and there we shall be safe from the poisoned arrows of those dogs the Ajetas."

This discovery was either that Providence had come to our aid, or it was a complication of dangers greater than those reserved to us on land on awaking in the morning.

I went instantly to the spot where Alila had made his important discovery, and having disencumbered the canoe from the sand with which it was partly covered, I soon became certain that, with some bamboos, and by stopping a few cracks, it would be staunch enough to take us over the Pacific ocean, away from the Ajetas.

"Well," said I to Alila, "you see I was right, and you must admit the hand of Providence is here. Is it not evident

* The skeleton is now in the Musée Anatomique of Paris.

that this fine boat, built, perhaps, several thousand leagues from this, has arrived express from the Polynesian islands to carry us away from the claws of the savages."

"True, master, true; it is our luck. To-morrow they will finely be taken in on not finding us here; but let us set to work, for we have much to do before this fine boat, as you call it, will be in a fit state for going through the water."

We immediately made a large fire on the shore, and went into the woods to cut down bamboos and rattans; then we set to work to stop the holes, which decreased fast enough under our handy-work upon the abandoned canoe.

Persons who have never travelled amongst the savages cannot imagine how, without having been instructed in the arts, and without nails, one could stop up the fissures in such a boat, and put it in a state fit for sea. Yet the means were very simple; our poignards, bamboos, and rattans supplied everything; by scraping a bamboo we obtained from it something like tow, which we put into the chinks, so that the water could not enter. If it was necessary to stop any breach a few inches in width, we took from the bamboo a little plank, somewhat larger than the opening we wished to close, and then with the point of the poignard we pierced it all round with little holes, to match those which were made in the same manner in the boat itself. Afterwards, with long strings of the rattan, which we split up and made fine, we sewed the little plank to the boat, just as one would a piece of cloth on a coat; we covered the sewing with the elemi gum, and were sure the water could not pass through. The rattan served instead of hemp, and supplied all our necessities on the occasion.

We worked with ardour at this our new and only means of safety. Once caulked, we placed in it two large bamboos as beams, for without those beams we could not have sailed for ten minutes without being upset. Another bamboo served as our mast; the large sack of matting that contained our skeleton was transformed into a sail. At last, before the night was far advanced, every preparation was finished. The wind was favourable, and we hastened to try our boat, and to struggle with new difficulties.

We placed in the canoe our arms and the skeleton, the cause of our new troubles; we then pushed the boat over the sand and got it afloat. It took us a good half-hour to get clear of the breakers. We were every moment in danger of being swamped by the large waves, which rolled on, dashing against the rocks that bound the shore. At last, after we had overcome a thousand difficulties and dangers, we reached the open sea, and the regular wave—a real movable mountain—lifted up, without any sudden shock, our frail boat almost to the skies, and then in the same quiet manner let it sink into an abyss, from which it was again raised to the top of a liquid mountain. These large waves, which follow each other usually from interval to interval very regularly, cause no danger to a good pilot, who takes the precaution of turning the prow of his boat so as to meet them. But woe to him if he forgets himself, and makes a false manœuvre, he is then sure to be upset and wrecked. Being used to the management of canoes, and, more confident in my own vigilance when at sea than in that of my Indians, I took the helm. The wind was favourable; we set up our little sail, and went very fast, although every moment I was obliged to turn the prow to the heavy waves. We were already a sufficient distance from the shore not to fear, if the wind changed, that we should be driven in among the breakers. Everything led us to expect a safe voyage, when unfortunately my poor Indians were taken ill. They had never sailed before except on the lakes of fresh water, and were now attacked with sea-sickness. This was vexatious to me, for I knew from experience that a person so attacked for the first time is altogether incapable of rendering any service, and even of protecting himself against the smallest danger that threatens him. I had no one to aid me in managing the boat, and was obliged to rely on my own exertions. I told him who held the sheet of the sail to hand it to me, and I twisted it round my foot, for both my hands were engaged in holding the paddle which was our helm. My Indians, like two inanimate bodies, lay at the bottom of the boat.

When I reflect on my position,—on the ocean, in a frail boat; having only for helps two individuals who could not move, two skulls, and a skeleton of an Ajetas,—I cannot help thinking that the reader may imagine that I have concocted a story for his amusement. However, I relate facts exactly as they occurred, and I leave all at liberty to believe as they please.

I was, as it were, alone in my frail boat, struggling continually with the large waves, which obliged me every moment to deviate from the course. I longed for daylight, for I hoped to be able to discern the beach of Binangonan de Lampon, as a place of refuge, where I should find the frank hospitality and the valuable assistance of my old friends.

At last the long-wished-for sun arose above the horizon and I saw that we were about three leagues from the coast. I had gone far too much out to sea, and had passed Binangonan a long way. It was not possible to steer back, the wind would not allow it; so I decided on pursuing the same course, and on doing my best to reach, before night, Maoban, a large Tagaloc village, situate on the coast of Luzon, and which is separated by a small ridge of mountains from the lake of Bay. The first rays of the sun and a little calm restored my Indians to a state of being able to render me some service. We passed the day without eating or drinking, and we had the regret of seeing that we had not attained our purpose. Our position was most distressing: a storm might rise, the wind might blow with force, and our only resource then would be to throw ourselves into the breakers, and to reach the shore as well as we could. But luckily nothing of the kind took place; and about midnight we knew, from meeting a small island, that we were in front of the village of Maoban. I steered to it, and in a short time we arrived in a calm quiet bay, near a sandy shore. The fatigue and want of food had thoroughly exhausted my strength. I had no sooner landed than I threw myself on the ground, and fell into a deep sleep, which lasted until day. When I awoke I found the sun's rays were shining full upon me: it was near seven o'clock. On any other occasion I should have been ashamed of my laziness, but could I feel dissatisfied with myself for sleeping soundly after thirty-six hours' fasting, and spent in such extraordinary exertions. During my sleep one of my Indians went into the village in search of provisions, and I found excellent rice and salt fish near me. We made a delicious and splendid breakfast. My Indians, on behalf of the inhabitants, asked me to go to the village, and spend the day, but I was too eager to reach home. I knew by walking quickly we could get through the mountains, and arrive at night on the banks of the lake, within a few hours' journey from my house. I determined to start without any delay. We took our things out of the boat; the little sail retook its former shape, as a sack, to hold the skulls and the skeleton, the cause of all the disasters to which we had been exposed, and, with re-united strength, and abundant provisions for the day, we began to mount the high hills which separate the gulf of Maoban from the lake of Bay. The journey was laborious and painful. At seven o'clock we embarked on the lake, and towards mid-night we reached Jala-Jala, where I very speedily forgot all the toil and trouble of my long and dangerous journey, while pressing my son in my arms and covering him with paternal kisses.

My excellent friend Vidie, to whom I sold my house and establishment, gave me letters which he had received from Manilla, and from them I learned that my presence was desired there on affairs of importance. I resolved to start on the following day.

View of Manilla from the Environs.

CHAPTER XIII.

I Determine not again to Separate from my Son—I take him to Manilla—The Effects of the Wound I received among the Ajetas—My Recovery—Kindness of the Spanish and other Inhabitants of Manilla—Illness of my Son—I return with him to Jala-Jala—Sorrowful Remembrances—The Death of my poor Boy—His Interment—My frantic Grief and Despair—I Determine to Quit the Philippines—I am Called to Manilla by Madame Dolorès Seneris—My Final Departure from Jala-Jala—I Arrive at Manilla, where I resume Practice as a Surgeon—I Embark for France—Discontent—My Travels through Europe—I Marry again—Death of my Mother and my Second Wife—Conclusion.

HAVING now concluded my last trip into the interior of the Philippines, I was desirous of not separating myself again from my son, the only being that remained to me of all those whom I had loved so tenderly. I took him with me to Manilla; but I did not altogether bid farewell to Jala-Jala, yet I had almost the intention of never going back to it.

The journey was as agreeable as my melancholy recollections

would permit. I experienced such pleasure in holding my boy in my arms, and in receiving his gentle caresses, that I occasionally forgot every sorrow.

I arrived at Manilla, and took up my quarters in the environs, at the abode of Baptiste Vidie, brother of the friend whom I had left at Jala-Jala.

After my escape from the Ajetas, I had noticed a small wound on the forefinger of my right hand, which I attributed to having been accidentally scratched by a branch or a thorn, while we were endeavouring to make our escape with such precipitation from the arrows which the savages let fly at us. The first night I spent at Manilla, I felt in the place where the wound was such extreme pain that I fell down twice totally senseless. The agony increased every instant, and became so violent that I could no longer doubt that it was caused by the poison of an arrow, shot at me by the Ajetas. I sent for one of my *confrères*, and after a most careful examination, he made a large incision, which did not, however, afford me any relief: the hand, on the contrary, festered up. By little and little the inflammation extended itself up my arm, and I was soon in an alarming state.

In short, after suffering during a whole month, and after the most cruel incertitude, it seemed that the poison had passed into my breast. I could not sleep for an instant; and, in spite of me, dead and painful cries came forth from my breast, which was on fire. My eyes were veiled—I could not see; a burning sweat covered my face; my blood was on fire, and did not circulate in my veins; my life seemed about to become extinct. The medical men declared that I could not pass through the night. According to the usages of the country, I was told that I ought to regulate my affairs for death. I asked that the consul-general of France, my excellent friend Adolphe Barrot, should be sent for.

Adolphe I knew to be a man of true heart and affection, and to him I recommended my poor boy. He promised to take care of him as if he were his own son, to take him to France, and to give him over to my family.

Lastly a good Dominican friar came, and with him I had several long conferences, and after he had dispensed to me the consolations of his ministry, he gave me extreme unction. Everything was done according to the customary form, and nothing was wanting but my death.

However, amidst all these preparations, I alone was not so eager; and, although in excessive anguish, I preserved my presence of mind, and declared I should not die. Was it courage? Was it great confidence in my strength and robust health, which made me believe in my recovery? Was it a presentiment, or was it an inward voice which told me: "The doctors are wrong, and how great will be their surprise to-morrow on finding me better?" In short, I did not wish to die; for, according to my system, my will ought to stop the order of nature, and to make me survive all imaginable pain.

The following day I was better: the doctors found my pulse regular, and without any intermitting symptom. Some days afterwards the poison passed out to my skin: my whole body was covered with a miliary eruption, and thenceforth I was safe. My recovery was very gradual, and for more than a year I felt acute pains in my breast.

During the course of my illness I received the kindest attention from my fellow-countrymen, and in general from all the Spanish inhabitants of Manilla; and here I ought to state, to the praise of the latter class, that during twenty years spent in the Philippines, I always found amongst those with whom I had dealings, a great nobleness of soul and a devotedness free from egotism. I shall never forget the kindnesses I received from this noble race, for which I entertain feelings of the warmest gratitude. To me, every Spaniard is a brother; and to him I shall always be happy to prove that his countrymen have not conferred obligations on an ungrateful character. I hope the reader will pardon me for having quitted my subject for a short time to fulfil the duty of gratitude; but are they not my recollections which I am detailing? *

* Gratitude here requires that I should name some of those to whom I am specially indebted for marks of affection and kindness. It would be indeed ungrateful on my part to forget them, and I beg them to accept this proof of my recollections.

The Governors of the Philippines to whom I owe these remembrances are :—Generals Martinès, Ricafort, Torres Enrile, Camba, and Salazar; in the various administrations of the colony, the Judges (Oidores) Don Inigo Asaola, Otin-i Doazo, Don Matias Mier, Don Jacobo Varela, administrator-general of the liquors; Don José de la Fuente, commissary of the engineers, who rendered me innumerable kindnesses; Colonel Don Thomas de Murieta, corregidor of Tondoc; the colonel of engineers, Don Mariano Goicochea; the Colonel-Commandant Lante Romana; the Governor of the province, Don José Atienza; the brothers Ramos, sons of the judge; all the family Calderon; that of Seneris; Don Balthazar Mier, Don José Ascaraga; and lastly my friend, Don Domingo Roxas, whose son, Don Mariano Roxas, after having received a solid and brilliant education at Manilla, came to travel in Europe. He has acquired the most extensive information in the sciences and arts, and when he shall have returned to the Philippine Islands, he will most worthily replace his dignified father, whom a premature death has snatched away from the industry, the agriculture, and the advancement of his country. If gratitude has induced me to mention here the Spaniards from whom I experienced many acts of kindness, the same feeling compels me to allude to an English gentleman to whom I was indebted for one of those important services which are never to be forgotten. I allude to Mr. Thomas Dent, with whom I have frequently conversed upon our hunting parties at Jala-Jala, in which he was occasionally one of the principal actors.

The wish to undertake, together with my boy, the voyage which would restore me to my country; the hope of seeing my kind good mother, my sisters, and all the friends whom I had left behind, reconciled me somewhat to existence, and made me experience a little happiness. I was awaiting with impatience the time for embarking; but, alas! my mission was not yet terminated in the Philippines, and a new catastrophe, quickly opened afresh all my sorrows.

I was scarcely recovered, when my dear boy—my sole delight the last beloved being that remained to me on this earth, so fruitful in joys, and still so destructive of them—my poor Henry fell suddenly ill, and his disease made the most rapid progress. My friends immediately foreboded that a great misfortune would befall me. I alone did not know the state in which my child really was. I loved him with such an ardent passion, that I believed it impossible that Providence would deprive me of him. My medical attendant, or rather my friend, Genu, advised me to take him to Jala-Jala, where his native air and the country, as he said, would without doubt promote his recovery. I liked the advice, for so many persons had recovered their health at Jala-Jala that I hoped for my child a similar good result. I set out with him and his governess; the voyage was one of sadness, for I saw my poor boy continually suffering, without being able to afford him any relief.

On our arrival Vidie came to receive us, and in a few moments I occupied, with my Henry, the room which brought to my remembrance two very sorrowful losses—the death of my little daughter and that of my beloved Anna. It was, moreover, in that very room my Henry was born,—a cruel association of the happiest moments of my existence with that when I was bewailing the state of my beloved boy. Nevertheless, I did not altogether despair, for I had hopes in my art and experience. I seated myself by his bedside, and did not leave him for a moment. I slept close to him, and I passed every day in administering the medicine and all the comforts in my power, but without any good result, or any relief for his sufferings. I lost all hope, and on the ninth day after our arrival the dear boy expired in my arms.

It is not possible for me to give an account of my feelings on this last trial. My heart was broken, my head on fire! I became mad, and never did despair take such a hold on me. I listened to nothing but my sorrow; and force became necessary to tear from my arms the mortal remains of my child.

On the following day he was laid close to his mother, and another tomb was erected in the church of Jala-Jala.

In vain did my friend Vidie endeavour to afford me consolation, or to change the current of my affliction. Several times he tried to remove me from the fatal room, which I now looked upon as a scene of misfortunes, but he could not succeed. I hoped at the time—and I also thought that I too had a right—to die there, where my wife and my son had breathed their last sighs. My tears refused to flow, and even words failed me to express the full extent of my grief. An ardent fever, which devoured me, was far too slow for the eagerness of my wishes. In a moment of bewilderment, I was near committing the greatest act of cowardice which man can perpetrate against his Creator. I double-locked the door; I seized the poignard which I had so often used to protect my life, and pointed it against myself. I was already choosing the spot in which I should strike, in order by one blow to terminate my miserable existence. My arm, strengthened by delirium, was about to smite my breast, when one sudden thought came to prevent me from consummating the crime which has no pardon—although the crime of despair. My mother, my poor mother, whom I had so much loved, my good mother presented herself to my mind, and said to me: "Thou wouldst abandon me—I shall see thee no more!" I recollected then the words of Anna: "Go, and see thy mother again!" This thought changed my resolution completely. I threw the poniard aside with horror, and fell on my bed quite exhausted. My eyes, which during many days had been dry and burning, were once again overflowing with tears, which removed the heavy weight from my lacerated heart.

The force of mind of which I stood so much in need was awakened again within me: I no longer thought of death, but of fulfilling my rigorous destiny. Calmed and relieved already by the abundant flow of tears, I gave myself wholly up to the idea of embracing my mother and my sisters. Then I wished to add the following pages to my journal. My head was not thoroughly right. I shall translate what I then wrote in Spanish, which was my adopted and familiar language, in preference even to French, which I had scarcely spoken during twenty years:—

"How have I strength to take this pen? My poor boy!—my son!—my beloved Henry!—is no more: his soul has flown to his Creator! Oh, God! pardon this complaint in my distress. What have I done to be thus cruelly afflicted? My boy!—my dear son!—my only hope!—my last happiness!—I shall never again see thee! Formerly I was happy; I had my good Anna and my dear child; but cruel fate soon tore my companion from me. My trouble was indeed great, and my affliction was profound; but thou wast still with me, Oh, my child! and all my affections were concentrated in thee. With thy caresses thou didst dry my tears; thy smile was like that of thy mother, and thy beautiful features reminded me of her, and in thee I found her again. But to-day, alas! I have lost you both. What a void! Oh, God! what a solitude! Oh! I ought to die in this room which is the depository of all my misfortunes. Here I bewailed my poor brother; here I closed the eyes of my daughter; here, also, Anna, when dying, bade me, bathed in tears, her last adieus; and here at last, thou, my son, they tore thee from my arms, to lay thee near the ashes of thy mother.

"So many afflictions and so many troubles for one man! Oh, God of goodness and mercy, will you not restore to me my poor child? Alas! I scarcely feel that I am mistaken: but He will pity my bewilderment—he who has been beloved and who has seen carried off, one by one, all the elements of his happiness. As for me, an isolated being, and henceforward useless on this earth, it matters little where I shall sink under the weight of my afflictions. If it was not from the hope of seeing my mother and sisters, I should terminate my wretched existence, my grave should be with you—you all!—whom I loved so much. I should remain near you, and during the rest of my miserable existence I should every day visit your tombs! But no; a sacred duty obliges me to leave you, and to separate for ever from you. Cruel! Oh, cruel indeed will be the hour when I shall depart from you. And thou my beloved, my good, excellent wife, my Anna, thy last words shall be accomplished. I will set out, but regret and grief accompany me during the voyage; my heart and my memory will remain at Jala Jala. Oh! land bedewed with my sweat, with my blood, and with my tears! when fate brought me to thy shores thou wast covered with dismal forests which this day have given place to rich harvests: among thy inhabitants order, abundance, and prosperity have taken the place of debauchery and misery. My efforts were crowned with full success; all was prosperity around me. Alas! I was too happy! But while misfortune strikes me down and overwhelms me, it will have stricken me alone, my work will outlive me. You will be happy, Oh, my friends! and if I myself have been so in contributing to your welfare, let a thought sometimes awaken your feelings towards him to whom you often gave the name of 'Father;' and if you preserve gratitude towards him, Oh, take a religious care of the tombs, trebly dear to him, which he now intrusts to you."

My readers will pardon this melancholy and long lamentation; they will understand it if they examine with care my position. Separated from my country by five thousand five hundred leagues, the stroke of fate which laid all my cherished hopes in the dust was the more acutely felt as it was unexpected. I had no relatives in the Philippines; in France alone I might yet find some affections; and, at the moment of quitting Jala-Jala for ever, the idea of parting with my Indians—attached, devoted, as they were to me—was an additional grief to the many which overpowered me. Thus I could not resolve to acquaint them beforehand of this separation. I remained in my room, without quitting it even at meal times. My friend Vidie did everything possible to prepare me for these adieus, and to console me. He pressed me to start speedily for Manilla, and to make arrangements for my departure; but an irresistible force retained me at Jala-Jala. I was weak; my heart was so crushed by sorrows that I had no courage to adopt any resolutions. I put it off from day to day, and from day to day I was more undecided. An unexpected occasion was necessary in order to conquer my apathy; it was requisite also to triumph over me by sentiments of gratitude—sentiments which I could never resist.

On this occasion the motive which decided my departure was furnished by Providence. I had a friend in Manilla, a lady of angelic goodness, gentleness, and devotedness. United from the period of my arrival in the most intimate manner with all her family, I had known her as a child, and afterwards married to a highly honourable man, of whom when she was subsequently bereaved, I afforded her all the consolations which the sincerest friendship could offer. She was a witness of the happiness which I enjoyed with my dear Anna, and, hearing that I was unhappy, she did not hesitate to undertake a long journey, and in her turn to come and take a part in my troubles. The excellent Dolorès Seneris arrived one morning at Jala-Jala; she threw herself into my arms, and for some moments tears alone were the interpreters of our thoughts. When we recovered from our first emotions, she told me that she had come to take me away, and she herself made the preparations for my departure. I was too grateful for this proof of the friendship of the good Dolorès not to acquiesce in her wishes, and it was decided that on the following day I should quit Jala-Jala for ever.

The report was soon spread among my Indians. They all came to bid me farewell: they wept, and they said to me:

"Oh, master, do not deprive us of all hope of seeing you again. Go, and receive consolation from your mother, and then return to your children." That day was filled with most distressing feelings.

The day following was Sunday. I went to say adieu to the remains of those whom I had loved even in their tombs.

I heard for the last time the divine service in the modest little church which I had erected, and in which for a long time, surrounded by my dearest friends, I was happy to assemble, on the same day of the week, the small congregation of Jala-Jala.

After the service I proceeded to the beach, where the boat was waiting, which was to take me to Manilla. There—surrounded by my Indians, the good parish priest, Padre Miguel, and my friend Vidie—I bade adieu to them all for the last time. Dolorès and I got into the boat, which was scarcely pushed off from the shore when every arm was stretched out towards me, and everyone exclaimed :—"May your voyage be happy, master! And, oh! return soon!"

One of the oldest Indians made a sign for silence, and then in a loud voice uttered these solemn words :—"Brothers, let us weep and pray, for the sun is obscured to us; the star which is going has shed light on our best days, and now for the future, being deprived of that light, we cannot tell how long will last the night in which we are plunged by the misfortune of his departure."

This exhortation of the old Indian were the last words that reached us: the boat moved away as I, for the last time, fixed my eyes on the beloved land which I was never again to behold.

We reached Manilla late: it was one of those enchanting nights, which I have described in the happy period of my voyages. Dolorès insisted that I should not lodge in any house but hers. Before she set out her careful friendship had provided for everything. I was surrounded by all those little attentions of which woman alone has the secret, and which she knows how to confer with such grace on him who is the object for whom they are designed.

My windows looked on the pretty river Pasig. I there passed whole days in looking at the graceful Indian canoes gliding over the water, and receiving the visits of my friends, who came with eagerness to endeavour to divert my thoughts, and to afford sources of pleasing conversation.

When I was alone I sought to dispel my melancholy by thinking of my voyage; on the happiness I should experience on seeing again my poor mother and sisters, a brother-in-law whom I did not know, and nieces born during my absence.

The obligation of returning the visits I received, and the re-establishment of my health, allowed me at length to enter into affairs connected with my departure.

My friend Adolphe Barrot, consul-general of France, was every day in expectation of intelligence from his government, with orders for his return home. He proposed to me to wait for him, so that we might make the voyage together. I accepted the proposal with pleasure, and we decided amongst ourselves that, for our return, we should take the route of India, of the Red Sea, and of Egypt.

While I stayed at Manilla I did not wish to be idle. The Spaniards reminded me that at a former epoch I had carried on the art of medicine, and with great success. I soon had patients from all quarters of the island, and I resumed my old profession, and gave advice. But what difference between *this* time and that of my *début*. Then I was young, full of strength and of hope; then I indulged in the illusions usual to youth; a long future of happiness presented itself to my imagination. Now, overwhelmed by the weight of troubles and of the laborious works I had executed, there was only one wish to excite me, and that was, to see France again; and yet my recollections took me continually back to Jala-Jala. Poor little corner of the globe, which I civilised! where my best years were spent in a life of labour, of emotions, of happiness, and of bitterness! Poor Indians! who loved me so much! I was never to see you again! We were soon to be separated by the immensity of the ocean.

Reflections and recollections beyond number thus occupied my mind. But, alas! it is vain to struggle against one's destiny; and Providence, in its impenetrable views, was reserving me for rude trials and fresh misfortunes.

Having again become a doctor at Manilla, where I had such difficulty at my commencement, I visited patients from morning until night. To Dolorès and to her sister Trinidad I was indebted for the most touching and most delicate attentions, calculated to heal the wounds which were still bleeding in the bottom of my heart. I frequently saw the two sisters of my poor wife, Joaquina and Mariquita, as well as my young niece, the daughter of excellent Josephine, for whom I had entertained so warm a friendship, and who so soon followed my darling Anna to the grave. By little and little I was forming new ties of affection, which I was soon to break, and never afterwards to renew. I could not forget Jala-Jala, and my recollections never quitted that place where were deposited the remains of those whom of all the world I had most loved. My eager wishes induced me to hope that my work of colonisation should continue, and that my friend Vidie should find some compensation for the rough task he had undertaken. At this period, even while I remained in Manilla, a great misfortune was nearly the cause of throwing Jala-Jala back into its former state of barbarism. The bandits, who always respected the place while I was in possession of it, came one night to attack it, and made themselves masters of the house in which

Vidie had shut himself up, and defended until he was forced to escape out of a window, and to run and hide in the woods, leaving his daughter, then very young, to the care of an Indian nurse. The bandits pillaged and shattered everything in the house; wounded his daughter by a sabre-cut, of which to this day she bears the marks; and then went off with the plunder they had made. But Jala-Jala had become too important a point to be neglected; and the Spanish government sent troops to it, to protect Vidie, and to maintain order.

At last, Adolphe Barrot received from the French government the long awaited instructions to return home; all my preparations were made for setting out. It was in 1839: twenty years had passed over since I left my country, which I was now about to return to with satisfaction. For a long time I had received no news from my mother, and the pleasure which I anticipated from seeing her was troubled by the dread of having new sorrows to experience on my arrival. My mother was then very old; her life had been passed in long tribulations, and in complete sacrifice of self. The numerous moral troubles which she had gone through must have affected her state of health. Besides, I had been so unfortunate: fate seemed to have so roughly treated all my affections, that I could not refrain from thinking that I should never again see her for whom I abandoned my much loved country. The day for sailing came; yet it was not without a heartfelt grief that I tore myself away from my friends, and bade adieu to the Philippines.

Here ought to terminate the account which I proposed: yet I cannot refrain from dedicating a few lines to my return to my native land.

On board various vessels I passed the coasts of India, the Persian Gulf, and the Red Sea.

After having often admired the grand works of nature, I felt a strong desire to see the gigantic works executed by the hand of man.

I went to Thebes, and there visited in detail its palaces, its tombs, and its monolithes. I descended the Nile, stopping at every place which contained any monuments worthy of my curiosity. I ascended one of the Pyramids. I passed several days in Cairo, and set out for Alexandria, where I embarked anew, to pass over the small space of sea which separated me from Europe.

I have sometimes wished to compare the grandest of human productions with the works of the Creator; the comparison is by no means favourable to the former, for all those useless ornaments are nothing but lasting proofs of pride, and of the fanaticism of a few men, who were obeyed by a people in slavery. I also saw all that remained of the traces of destruction committed by two of the greatest conquerors of the world: the first was but a haughty despot, causing cohorts of slaves to act as he pleased, and carrying the sword and destruction amongst peaceful people, to profane their tombs, to follow up useless conquests,—history afterwards shows him dying of an orgie; and the other, alas! was enchained to a rock.

From the summit of one of the Pyramids, in religious abstraction, I had contemplated the majestic Nile, which glides serpent-like through a vast plain, bordered by the Desert and arid mountains. Looking, then, below me, I could with difficulty descry some of my travelling companions, who were gazing at the Sphynx, and who appeared like little spots on the sand. And I then exclaimed: "It is not these useless monuments that we ought to admire, but rather this magnificent river, which, in obedience to the laws of all-powerful wisdom, overflows every year, at a fixed period, its limits, and spreads itself, like a vast sea, to water and to vivify these immense plains, which are afterwards covered with rich harvests. If this immutable and beneficent order of nature did not endure, all these fertile districts would be but a desert waste, where no living creature could exist."

These reflections took their origin, without doubt, from my having spent almost all my life amidst those grand creations of Nature, from which man continually derives sentiments that elevate him to the Supreme Being. I had studied that Nature —in all her details, her beneficence, and her magnificence—too attentively to allow the productions of man's genius to make upon me the impression which I thought might be expected, when I first formed a wish to see the monuments of Egypt; and, while sailing for Europe, I already anticipated the feeling, that a short sojourn in the midst of civilisation would cause me to regret my ancient freedom, my mountains, and my solitudes in the Philippine Islands.

On arrival at Malta I was for eighteen days locked up in Fort Manuel, and then passed the quarantine. I there received news of my family. My mother and sisters wrote to me that they were in the enjoyment of excellent health, and were awaiting with impatience my coming to them. After the quarantine was over, I stopped nearly a week in the city, while waiting for a steamer that was going to France. I embraced the opportunity of seeing every curiosity in the island. I then resumed my voyage to my native land, and the following week I recognised the arid rocks of Provence and France, from which I had been absent for twenty years.

In a few days I reached Nantes, where for some time I enjoyed, in every respect, all the happiness which one feels when with those beloved beings from whom one had been long severed, and who formed the last living ties of affection for an unhappy being who had been severely tried by a capricious destiny. But the want of excitement in which I lived soon became irksome; my life had been too active, so that the sudden transition could not fail to prove injurious to my health, and the idea of submitting during the remainder of my existence to a life sterile and monotonous became intolerable. Not knowing how to employ myself, I resolved to travel through Europe, and to study the civilised world, which was then so strange to me. I travelled through France, England, Belgium, Spain, and Italy, and returned to my family, without being able to discover anything that could induce me to forget my Indians, Jala-Jala, and my solitary excursions in the virgin forests. The society of men reared in extreme civilisation could not efface from my memory my past modest life. Notwithstanding all my efforts, I retained in my heart a fund of sadness, which it was not possible to conceal. My kind-hearted mother, who with deep regret observed my repugnance to establish myself in any part of the country, and who entertained fears, perhaps well-founded ones, that I should yet endeavour to go back to the Philippines, used every means to prevent me. She spoke to me of marriage; and in all her letters repeated that she should not be happy until I agreed to enter into the ties of a new union: she said my name would otherwise become extinct, and, as her last consolation, she asked me to allow her to choose a companion for me.

The wish to satisfy her, and also the remembrance of Anna's last words: "Return to thy country, and marry one of thy countrywomen," decided my resolution.

I soon made choice of one, who would have fully rendered a man happy who had not too frequently before him the remembrance of a previous union. Nevertheless, I was as happy as I could be. My new wife possessed every quality necessary for my happiness. By her I became father of two children, and I began to bless the determination which my mother had contributed so much to make me adopt; but, alas! happiness was never for me lasting; the cup of bitterness was not yet exhausted, and I had still to shed many tears.

In the cemetery of Vertoux, a modest tomb for thee, poor mother! is erected, between that of a husband and a son; and soon after another grave was opened at Neuilly. In profound affliction I had the following lines engraved on the latter:

"Veille, du haut des cieux, sur ta triste famille;
Conserve-moi ton fils et revis dans ta fille."*

* "From Heaven's height look down and see
The sorrows of thy family;
Preserve for me thy only boy,
And in thy daughter give me joy."

STATISTICS OF THE PHILIPPINE ISLANDS.

The Philippines are a large group of islands in the North Pacific Ocean, and were discovered by Magellan in 1521; they were afterwards taken possession of by the Spaniards, in the reign of Philip II., from whom they take their name. The islands are said to be eleven hundred in number, but some hundreds of them are very small, and all are nominally subject to the Spanish government at Manilla.

In order to give the reader an idea of their riches, and the vast resources they can furnish to Spain, I shall here give some details of the division of the country into provinces, with the number of towns contained in each, of the population, and of the various branches of industry exercised by the Indians, and, finally, a description of the principal agricultural products.

Division of all the Philippines into Provinces and Market-town Districts, and their Population, according to the Census taken in 1833.

Provinces.	*Number of Towns.*	*Population.*
Tondo	30	285,030
Bulacan	19	187,735
Panpanga	26	182,360
Bataan	10	38,920
Zambales	15	39,510
Pangasinan	31	215,635
Ilocos (South)	23	206,085
Ilocos (North)	14	190,160
Islas Batanes	3	800
Cagayan	34	107,600
Nueva Ecija	15	23,285
Laguna	33	135,810
Batangas	13	196,695
Cavite	10	83,010
	Carried forward	1,892,635

Provinces.	*Number of Towns.*	*Population.*
	Brought forward	1,892,635
Tayabas	16	77,315
Camarinco (North)	11	25,035
Camarinco (South)	27	187,315
Albai	38	139,595
Zamboanga ...	2	10,000
Misamis	23	35,180
Caraga	30	32,510
Leite	31	91,275
Samar	28	92,730
Zebou	38	203,555
Isla de Negros ...	23	60,980
Ilaila	31	232,055
Antique	11	78,250
Capis	22	115,440
Calamianes ...	12	20,730
Mindoro	8	41,190
		3,345,790

In this number—3,345,790—of inhabitants, which constitute all the population under the Spanish Government, are comprised from 25,000 to 30,000 Chinese. Exclusive of this population there exist unknown numbers of Indians, who, to avoid the payment of taxes, have found means to escape from the census; and also the wild savages in the interior of the island of Luzon, whose number there is no means of knowing.

Mechanical and Agricultural Products.

The Philippines yield every colonial product that man can desire. There are abundant crops of rice, coffee, sugar, indigo, tobacco, cotton, cacao, abaca, or vegetable silk, pepper, gums, cocoa-nuts, dye-woods, timber of all descriptions for furniture and for buildings, rattans of various kinds, and all the agreeable fruits of the tropics. On the shores are found nacre, or mother of pearl, magnificent pearls, birds'-nests, shells of every description, an incredible quantity of excellent fish, and the *trèpang*, or *balaté,* a sea-worm, or animal substance, found on the shores of the Philippine Islands, resembling a large pudding. The Chinese are very fond of it, and mix it with fowl and vegetables.

The inhabitants practise various kinds of industry; they weave matting of extraordinary fineness and of the brightest colours, straw hats, cigar cases, and baskets; they manufacture cloth and tissues of every sort from cotton, silk, and abaca; they, from filaments taken from the leaves of the *etuana,* make cambric of a texture much finer than that of France; and they also manufacture coarse strong cloth for sails, &c., and ropes and cables of all dimensions; they tan and dress leather and skins to perfection; they manufacture coarse earthenware, and forge and polish arms of various kinds; they build ships of heavy tonnage, and also light and neat boats; and at Manilla they frame and finish-off beautiful carriages; they are also very clever workers in gold, silver, and copper; and the Indian women are specially expert in needlework, and in all kinds of embroidery.

I.

Of the Soil of the Island of Luzon, and the Sources of its Fertility.

The island of Luzon is the largest of the Philippines, and extends from north to south for the length of about six degrees. It is divided throughout its whole extent by a chain of mountains, which in general owe their formation to volcanic eruptions. Traces are found throughout of the great convulsions produced by subterraneous fires, and in proof of this theory I shall make some observations which demonstrate it.

In the middle of the lake of Bonbon, in the province of Batangas, the volcano of Taal is always in combustion; and, although during many years there has been no eruption, enormous clouds of smoke are continually ascending from its vast crater. From this mountain to that of Mainit (signifying "hot"), a distance of about five or six leagues, there is subterraneous communication, for this latter mountain is always threatening great eruptions, and at its summit there are various chinks, occasionally emitting a thick smoke, and sometimes flames. At its base, in the part bathed by the waters of the lake of Bay, which is distant from ten to twelve leagues from the lake of Bonbon, there are numbers of thermal springs, that burst forth at the temprature of boiling water. All these springs, the waters of which discharge themselves into the lake, emit a great quantity of vapour, so that, from a distance, one might imagine the lake to be always boiling.

At about from three to four miles in the lake of Bay the little island of Socolme is to be seen; it is formed of a circular cordon of land, elevated above the water from twelve to fifteen hundred feet, and in the middle of this cordon is the little lake of the same name, which is evidently nothing but an extinct crater, into which the water has penetrated.

In the provinces of Laguna and Batangas there is the high mountain called Maijai, one of the loftiest in Luzon, which is beyond doubt an ancient crater; on the summit a little lake is found, the depth of which cannot be measured. At some period the lava that then flowed from the summit towards the base, in the neighbourhood of the town of Nacarlan, covered up immense cavities, which are now recognisable by the sonorous noise of the ground for a great extent; and sometimes it happens that, in consequence of an inundation or an earthquake, this volcanic crust is in some places broken, and exposes to the view enormous caverns, which the Indians call "the mouths of hell."

Finally, in the district about the town of San Pablo, which is situated on the mountains, are found great numbers of little circular lakes and immense heaps of rotten stones, basalt, and different descriptions of lava, which show that all these lakes are nothing else than the craters of old volcanoes. Altogether the soil to the southward, in the province of Albai, is completely volcanic, and the frequent eruptions of the volcano bearing that name may, as the natives say, be attributed to the same cause as the earthquakes so often felt in the island of Luzon.

Over almost the whole of these mountains, where fire has thus played so conspicuous a part, there is a great depth of vegetable earth, and they are covered with a most splendid vegetation. Their declivities nourish immense forests and fine pastures in which grow gigantic trees—palm trees, rattans, and lianas of a thousand kinds, or gramineous plants of various sorts, particularly the wild sugar cane, which rises to the height of from nine to twelve feet from the ground; in their interior are rich mines of copper, gold, iron, and coal.

There are two distinct and strongly marked seasons in the island of

Luzon, namely, the rainy or the wintry season, and the dry or summer season. For six months of the year—that is from, June to December—the wind blows from the south-west to the north-east, and then the declivities of the mountains and all the western side of the island are in the season of the rains; in the six other months, the wind changes, and blows from the north-east to the south-west, when all the eastern parts of the island have the season of winter.

During the rainy season, the incessant fall of rain on the mountains causes the rivers, both large and small, to overflow and to become torrents, that rush down upon the plains, covering them with water, and depositing the broken earth and slime which they have gathered in their course.

In the dry season, water is supplied for irrigation from reservoirs, which are carefully filled during the rains. From these causes it follows that, without any manuring, and with scarcely any improvement from human industry, the soil of the Philippines is as fertile as any in the world; so that, without great labour, the cultivator has most abundant harvests.

The different products—of the cultivation of which I shall now give a description—are rice, wheat, a vast variety of leguminous vegetables, indigo, tobacco, vegetable silk, coffee, cacao, cotton, pepper, bamboos—which grow almost without any culture—and, lastly, the cocoa-nut tree.

II.

Rice.

There are more than thirty kinds of rice cultivated in the Philippines, all quite distinct in taste, in form, in colour, and in the weight of the grain. These are divided into two classes—first, the mountain rice; and second, the aquatic rice. They are cultivated differently, although the mountain rice may be treated in the same manner as the aquatic crop.

Culture of Mountain Rice.

The mountain rice is cultivated in high lands, not exposed to the danger of inundation during the rains. The following are the names of the different descriptions:—Pinursegui, Lanlan-Sanglay, Quinarayon, Pinurutung, Quinamalig-Pinulut, Mangasarag-Puti, Binuriri, Pinagocpoc, Quinandanpula, Quinandanputi, Mangusa, Bolivon, Dinumero, Quinabibao, Binoliti, Quiriquiri, Binulut-Cabayo, Dinulang, Macapilaypusa, Tinuma, Mangoles.

In the western part of the island of Luzon, as soon as the first rains fall, towards the end of May or the beginning of June, the cultivator prepares the ground, by giving it two ploughings and two harrowings. The plough represented by Fig. 1, p. 334, is the one employed for this purpose. The harrow is triangular, and like the one used in France.

The lands being well prepared and well tilled, the rice is sown broadcast, and, after about a month, it is well hoed and weeded, which is usually sufficient for the removal of all the noxious weeds that have sprung up among the plants.

If the crop be of the kind called Pinursegui, which is one of the earliest, the rice may be gathered in about three months or three months and a-half after it is sown; if it be one of the other kinds, it is necessary, in order that the grain should come to full maturity, to wait for at least five months, after which the rice is cut down with a hook (see Fig. 3, p. 335), put in small sheaves, of which large cocks are made, to wait for several fine days, in order to separate the grain from the straw. This operation is performed by means of buffaloes, which are kept moving round in a large area, or thrashing-floor, on which the rice is spread; or else on bamboo trellises, raised perhaps ten feet from the ground, on which an Indian tramples with his feet over the rice sheaves as they are handed up to him, and the grain falls through the interstices of the trellis work.

Mountain rice is sometimes sown without any ploughing.

Culture of Rice for Clearing-Grounds.

After the trees or brushwood which had covered the land are cut down, they are burned, and then rice is sown, by making, with a stick or dibble, a hole, into which are thrown three or four grains of rice; or perhaps the rice is sown broadcast, and then, for about a month, a herd of buffaloes is kept on the ground, so that they, by trampling, sink the seed into the earth. In this kind of tillage, from the abundance of grass and weeds, several hoeings and weedings become necessary; but the labour is amply repaid by an abundant crop, which generally yields a hundred-fold and upwards.

In the small fields the ears are cut singly, in order afterwards to dry them in the sun. This mode of gathering the crop is troublesome and tedious, but it has this advantage over the process of collecting in heaps, that a great deal of the grain is saved from the voracious birds.

All the other kinds of mountain rice are sown in the same manner as that called Pinursegui, but this last has the advantage of being fit for harvesting in twelve or fourteen weeks, while the others require twenty weeks.

Culture of Aquatic Rice.

There are ten kinds of aquatic rice :—Macabunutdila, Macon, Macan, Soulucay, Macon-Sulug, Macon-Muriti, Macon-Susoy, Macay-Bucave, Malaquit-Puti, and Malaquit-Pula.

They are all cultivated in a similar manner in China and Lombardy.

The two last kinds, Malaquit-Puti and Malaquit-Pula, do not serve for every-day food; the one grain is a dead white, while the other is pervaded by a fine violet colour. They are both used in general for delicacies, and to make a kind of paste, a substitute for starch.

All these kinds of rice are first raised in seed-beds, from which they are transplanted into lands properly prepared for them. For a superficies of 40,000 yards it takes about 750 lbs. of seed.

Seed-Beds.

When the first rains fall in June, the ground is prepared for the seed. It is first covered with from six to eight inches of water, and then it is well ploughed, and the comb-harrow is passed over it (see Fig. 4, p. 335) until it is reduced into liquid mud; it is then left to let the water drain off. The seed is then cast over it; but, previous to being sown, the seed is generally steeped in water for twenty-four hours, in order to promote its vegetation. When the ground is entirely covered with seed, a board of about a yard and a-half or two yards in breadth is passed over the whole surface, for the purpose of sinking the grains in the mud, and of covering them.

For five or six days it is not useful to irrigate them; but if, when the plants have risen some inches above ground, the drought is very great, it will be necessary to supply them with water, taking always great care never to cover the young leaves, for under water they would all perish.

Transplanting.

Forty or forty-five days after the seed has been put into the earth, the rice plants are fit to be transplanted; the land in which they are to be fixed is divided into large squares, and surrounded by little raised paths, which serve to confine the water with which it must be completely covered; it is then again ploughed, and, as has been done for the seed sowing, by means of the comb-harrow it is reduced into a state of liquid mud, and on the following day the water is let off, and the plants are got ready to be placed in it.

It is usual to have men to take up the plants, and women to fix them in the earth. Two men are enough for this work; one of them pulls the plants, and the other removes them to the planting-ground, which is never far off, and distributes them to the women planting there. The man who is occupied with pulling the plants has before him a little table, fixed in the earth by a stake, and a large quantity of small bamboo strings, which he carries fastened to his waist, as gardeners in France carry rushes when they are pruning trees. He pulls up the plants without much precaution, and, laying them on the table, cuts off the long roots and the leaves, and makes them into little bundles of the thickness of his arm, and lays them in a kind of sliding car, drawn by buffaloes, which the other Indian leads to the planting-ground, and throws the bundles about in all directions on the prepared land, only separating them so that the women planters may take them up by stretching out their arms, without having to quit the lines that they are following in the planting.

All the women planting are up to the calf of the leg in the mud; they follow each one a line, and, moving backwards, take up the little bundles which are thrown behind them, undo the tying, separate the plants from each other, and then, with their thumbs, stick the plants, one by one, into the mud, at a distance of from four to six inches from each other. They are so used to this practice of planting as to do it with the greatest rapidity, and with such perfectly regularity that one would be almost tempted to believe that they had a measure to guide them in their exact observance of the distances.

When the planting is finished, and although the sun is burning hot, the rice field is not watered for eight or ten days, but as soon as the plants shoot up their green leaves, if there have not any rains fallen, they are irrigated, and the land is covered with two or three inches of water, and, in proportion to the growth of the plants, the water is increased.

These lands are seldom weeded, but careful cultivators do not neglect every opportunity of removing the large noxious weeds which might damage the rice.

When the rice has come to its full height—that is, from forty to fifty inches there is no longer any necessity for irrigation; on the contrary, it would be rather injurious at the time when the plant is in flower.

Sometimes, when the land is exceedingly fertile, the plants grow to the height of European wheat, and then they would have become all stalk; to prevent this, and to force them to produce grain instead of straw, an Indian takes a long pole and, stretching it over the, plants, stamps on the middle of it, and thereby lays all the plants level on the earth, so that they seem as if flattened by violent winds.

Four months after the transplanting—that is, about five months and a-half after the sowing—the rice is fully ripe and fit for being harvested. It is then cut with the sickle, by both men and women, and in proportion as the bundles of sheaves are large and many, they are gathered to a high spot, and made into cocks or ricks, to wait for the general carrying home.

In some parts of the island of Luzon the first crop of rice is followed by a second planting of an early or precocious kind—that is, the mountain rice, called Pinursegui; but then the sowing of the seed is effected beforehand, and in a quite different manner from that of which I have given a description.

Three weeks or a month previous to gathering the first crop off the ground, the Indians place on the ponds and rivers little bamboo rafts, which they cover over with a deep layer of straw, and on the straw they make seed-beds; the grain sprouts, and the roots weave themselves in through the straw, and so reach the surface of the water, in order thence to draw nourishment. When the first crop is taken off the ground and the field has received a ploughing, and has been prepared for the second planting, the seedlings are taken off the rafts by rolling up the straw—in the same manner as a mat is rolled up—and carried to the place then ready, and there the young plants are pulled, one by one, out of the straw, their long roots and leaves are cut off, and they are stuck in the earth. By this means in less than three months a second crop is obtained, which is by no means as abundant, it is true, as the first one, but which, notwithstanding, amply indemnifies the tiller for his toil.

The Indian native of the Philippines has studied every way of procuring his natural food, and he makes use of every means that the fertile soil of his country offers, to gain that object. For that purpose he employs another mode to obtain, almost without labour, abundant crops.

There is a kind of rice which is essentially an aquatic plant—the Macon-Sulug—and it yields abundantly, although continually bathed by water. In some parts of the island there are marshes and lakes of very little depth, and the Indians prepare for them seed-beds of this kind of rice, which has the property of shooting forth very long leaves. These seed-beds are prepared in the same manner as those of the other aquatic rice, and after six weeks' growth the plants are pulled up, and their roots shortened, but care is taken to preserve the leaves entire in all their length. The plants are then put on board the lightest boats, which are rowed by Indians into the shallow parts of the lake, where the men's arms can reach the bottom; the plants are there stuck in the mud, and the leaves are allowed to swim on the surface. The plants soon become strong, and shoot up stalks—as if they were growing on earth—at the surface of the water. If by any accident the water is increased in the lake, the rice stalks shoot up in proportion to that increase, so that it can swim over the water, for it would perish where it wholly submerged.

Four months after the transplanting, the crop is gathered in by the little boats, in which the Indians go from one part of the lake to another where any rice has been planted.

All these kinds of aquatic rice yield most abundantly; the poorest crop may be estimated at twenty-five, and the good at from sixty to eighty-fold. There is, however, one scourge, which every seven or eight years, deprives the cultivator of the benefit of his labours and toils—I mean the locusts, which coming suddenly, like a dark cloud, alight on a field covered with luxuriant vegetation, and then suddenly ruin it, even to the very roots. Great droughts also destroy the rice fields of the mountains; and it is for these reasons that the Indian says with such sincerity: "Give us sunshine, give us water, and keep away the locusts, then our crops are safe."

III.

INDIGO.

Culture and Crops.

In various parts of the Philippines, and especially at Luzon, indigo is cultivated with success, yet this cultivation is that which runs most risks. Bad weather for a few days, and strong gales, often ruin all the crop. Sometimes, also, myriads of caterpillars devour all the leaves in a few hours, and if any are left they are scarcely sufficient to defray the expense of the manufacturing process. But, if the season be favourable, if no accidents take place, and if that process is carried on with judgment, the high price of the indigo always indemnifies the grower.

The cultivation begins immediately after the cold season, and before the great heats, and when there is no apprehension of the heavy rains: the land is got ready by two or three ploughings and harrowings, and when it is sufficiently tilled the seed is sown broad-cast. The plant shows itself over ground on the third or fourth day, and continues to shoot up while it finds any moisture, but if there be a drought it remains stationary during the time of its duration. As soon as the first rains fall, at the commencement of the south-west monsoon, on this side of the island, its growth is rapid and strong. But with it grow also the bad weeds, which it is necessary to eradicate by two or three careful hoeings.

Two months and a-half after the first rains the plants have acquired their full size, and they are known to be fit for pulling when the leaves are thick, covered with a whitish velvety down, and are easily broken by the slightest pressure. They are usually thoroughly mature at the end of July—that is, in the middle of the rainy season; but then, every preparation is made for their being properly handled, so that there will not be any blunder in the matter, and that the plants may not have time to cast off any portion of their leaves, which would occur if there was any delay.

The preparations, which are more or less considerable according to the importance of the crop, consist in several batteries. Each of these batteries is composed of two large vats, from three yards to nearly three yards and a half in diameter, and three yards in depth, one of which is designed for the fermentation process, and the other for the beating or churning one. This last vat is a little smaller than the former. They are both placed on the brow of a rivulet, or of a river, in order to have the facility of obtaining water. The vat for fermentation ought to be placed on a spot somewhat higher than the other, so that, by means of cocks or spiggots, which are placed longitudinally, all the water contained in that vat may be easily removed into the churning one. There are also one or two buckets, placed at one end of long poles, with weights at the other end, which poles are placed across a wooden fork of two strong pieces, and raised some yards above the fermentation vat. This apparatus resembles very much in construction those which are to be seen along the banks of the Nile, and in Spain, and other parts of the south of Europe. Two long bamboos, having fastened at one end a small board, from five to six inches in length, and from two to three inches in breadth, are what may be called the beating or churning dashes. Lastly, there is a small vat under a shed, a little distance from the batteries, where there are articles for straining, made of coarse cotton cloth, and a small press for squeezing those articles, and large hurdles for drying the indigo.

Every arrangement being thus made, the gathering-in is begun. On the first day, enough plants are cut down to allow the cutters to be always one day in advance of the vats. The plant is cut level to the earth with a kind of cutlass, which the Indian wears by his side, and is called *bolo*. If the after-season continues favourable, the plant sprouts afresh, and sometimes produces two or three crops in the same year.

Each battery is managed by two Indians, one fills the vat with the plants, and the other supplies the vat with water, and the two together beat or churn the produce. At a very early hour in the morning the fermentation vat is filled to the brim with plants, and they are kept down by pieces of wood, which are fastened in ledges or grooves on the inside of the vat : without this precaution the vat would overflow. When it is full of plants and water, fermentation takes place in from twenty to twenty-four hours, according to the heat of the temperature. When the fermentation has reached its greatest height, which is generally the next morning, the plants are removed out of the vat, and care is taken that no water is removed with them, for which purpose they are well shaken. When nothing remains but the liquor, which is then of an emerald colour, the Indian puts a certain quantity of quick lime in a bucket of water, which he very carefully pours it into the fermentation vat. The Indian then takes one of the beating or churning dashes, and plunges to it the bottom of the vat, where he moves it about, so that the lime is circulated throughout the whole. He soon knows if he has put enough by the colour, which suddenly changes its shade; from an emerald green it becomes a deep green, and the liquor appears to contain a number of little clots or globules, which are nothing but the indigo in a state of solution. The quantity of lime necessary for the operation cannot be calculated, but a man of experience can give a good guess. Upon this quantity entirely depends the quality of the product which is wished for, as well as the shade of colour required.

After the lime has been mixed with the liquor it is left at rest for some minutes, during which all the particles not belonging to the indigo sink to the bottom of the vat, but the indigo remains suspended in the water. After a few minutes all the cocks and spiggots, over one another on the side of the vat, are gradually opened, and the liquor flows into the beating or churning vat.

The fermentation vat is then cleared of the deposit from the lime, and every other thing remaining at the bottom, and is immediately filled with fresh plants for a new fermentation.

During the afternoon the beating or churning takes place. The two Indians take their dashes, and with all their force stir the liquor up from the bottom to the top, in order that the matter which forms the indigo may come into contact with the air, which renders it insoluble in the water. When the whole has acquired a fine blue colour the process is finished. Three or four hours afterwards, all the indigo contained in the liquor deposits itself at the bottom of the vat, and then the cocks and spiggots, one above the other, are opened, to let the water flow off, and which does not then contain any colouring matter whatever.

Each of these operations produces, on an average, about sixteen pounds of indigo. Every six days, when from two hundred and fifty to three hundred pounds are collected, they are taken out of the vat, and removed to a much smaller vat, placed near the drainers. The product is left for some time, and all the water is drawn off by a syphon. At length, when there is no more to be drawn off, the indigo appears to be a sort of mud, it is put into the drainers, where it finishes the dripping. It is then put into the press, and from thence it is taken out in a state resembling a coarse cake, and is divided by a brass wire into small squares, which are placed in the drying places. A month's time is often required for it to become thoroughly dry, but this depends on the state of the atmosphere. When the indigo is perfectly dry it is put into cases, and sent to the market for sale.

This mode of making indigo is practised throughout the Philippines. Nevertheless, some of the great growers of the plant have adopted a change in a part of the process, of which I was the introducer, and which has diminished very considerably the expense of the workmanship. This alteration consists in substituting for the fermentation vats a large bason, built of mason-work, and so arranged as to receive naturally the water required for its use. In the course of an hour, from a distance of from fifty to sixty yards, on a flat spot below the level of this bason, the number of vats necessary for receiving all its contents are filled. This bason, of which the brink is on a level with the ground, facilitates the process very much, and makes a great saving in the working-men ; for first, it can be filled with water without that water being drawn by the Indians, and the labour is avoided of taking the plants up a height of from four to five yards. The Indian who is carrying the plants to the fermentation vat comes with a little car, without wheels, to the brink of the reservoir, and then, without any difficulty, discharges his load into the reservoir. The vats for beating or churning are placed fifty or sixty yards off on the same line. The first communicates with the reservoir by bamboos, split in two, and forming a kind of channel, and each vat communicates with the others by the same means. The liquor passes from the reservoir to the first vat, and during its passage comes into contact with the air, and when the first vat is filled the surplusage is sent on to the others, and so on, to the last of all. All this movement of the liquor serves a real beating, and saves two-thirds of the workmen necessary for the fermentation.

IV.

Tobacco.

Next to the cultivation of rice that of tobacco is, in a pecuniary point of view, the most important, although all the product is obliged to be given up to the monopolising government which is the sole purchaser, and which, in its great establishment at Binondoc, employs continually from 15,000 to 20,000 workmen and workwomen in manufacturing cigars for the consumption of the country and for exportation. They are sent all over India, where they are as much prized as are the Havanna cigars in Europe.

In the island of Luzon, the greatest quantity of tobacco is cultivated in the provinces of Nueva Ecija and Cagavan. The mode of cultivation does not differ in any great respect from that followed in other parts of the world. It consists in making great seed-beds, from which the plants are removed out into ground that is well tilled by several ploughings and harrowings. The young plants are set at intervals of a yard, in regular lines, which are separated by a distance of a yard and a half from each other.

During the first two months after the trasplanting it is indispensably necessary to give four ploughings to the ground between the rows of the plants, and, every fifteen days to handpick, or even better, to root out with the mattock, all the weeds which cannot be touched by the plough.

These four ploughings ought to be done in such a manner as to leave alternately a furrow in the middle of each line, and on the sides, and consequently, at the last ploughing, the earth covers the plants up to their first leaves, and there remains a trench in the middle of the rows for letting off the water. As soon as each plant has gained a proper height, its head is lopped off to force the sap to turn into the leaves, and, in a few weeks afterwards, it is fit for being gathered.

Mode of Gathering in the Crop.

This crop consits in tearing off all the leaves from the trunk, and in separating them into three classes, according to their size, and afterwards in making them into bunches of fifty or a hundred, and in passing through them, near the foot, a little bamboo cane, as if it was a skewer, by which the bunches are afterwards hung up to dry in vast sheds, into which the sun's rays cannot enter, but in which the air circulates freely; they are left to hang there until they become quite dry, and for this, a greater or less time is required, according to the state of the weather. When the drying is effected the leaves are placed, according to their quality, in bales of twenty-five pounds, and in that state they are handed over to the administration of the monopoly.

V.

Abaca, or Vegetable Silk.

The Abaca is exclusively cultivated on the declivities of the mountains; it grows exceedingly well in a volcanic soil, and there shoots up in every direction.

The Abaca produces an abundance of seed, but the seed is not used for reproduction, as its growth would require a long time before the plant could come to maturity fit for a crop. At the foot of the old stock the shoots are found, and are divided into as many seedlings as there are syptoms of germination, and they are set in the earth in such a manner as soon to form new plants.

The ground for the plantation is got ready during the dry season, the brushwood and the young trees are cut down, some of the lofty trees only are preserved to afford shade to the plantation during the first two years. When the soil is well cleared, lines are traced transversely to the mountain, and spaced from three yards, to three yards and a-half, the one from the other, and then holes of from ten to fifteen centimetres, and of about the same diameter, are opened in those lines, and, when the first rains begin, a sprout is laid in the hole, and covered up with earth.

During the two first years frequent weedings are required to remove all the brushwood that grows around the young plants, and at different times during the rainy season, to stir up the earth at their roots with a mattock.

The second year, the long broad leaves rising up from four to five yards, will keep down all weeds and brushwood.

Crops.

The plants in about three years produce from twelve to fifteen shoots each, and yield some fruit, they should then be cut down. The leaves are now severed from the trunks, and taken to the place of manipulation, which is at some little distance from the plantation, where women divide them into thin strips, of from three to four inches in length, and separate the outward from the interior layers. The outer layers furnish the abaca used in making ropes, and the inner ones, being of finer filaments, serve for weaving; the strips are exposed for some hours to the sun, to render them more flexible, and then an Indian places before him a small stool, on which, by the pressure of his foot, he can force down an iron blade; he then places one of the strips on the stool, presses with the sole of his foot on the iron blade, which lies on the strip, and then, with all his strength, draws the strip to him, and by this movement and the pressure the filaments are cleaned from the parenchyme, or soft matter grown with them, and come out quite white, after which it is enough to expose them for some hours to the sun, and they are fit for sale.

Every year, during the dry season, the grower has a fresh crop; for a plantation properly arranged, in a suitable spot, yields indefinitely.

VI.

Coffee.

The cultivation of this shrub is carried on in the same way as in other colonies; it consists in making large seed-beds in places protected from the sun, either naturally by trees, or artificially by little straw huts.

When the coffee plants reach a height of from twelve to eighteen inches they are transplanted in land prepared for that purpose, which is usually selected in large woods exposed to the rising sun, and on a slope, where care has previously been taken to eradicate all the brushwood and small trees, and to preserve those only whose shade may be useful; and then in rows, about three yards distant from each, holes are opened at every two yards, and the young plants are put into them, and the roots are covered up with well-tilled earth.

During the first years it is requisite with the mattock to destroy all the weeds, but when the coffee trees are three years old, and begin to bear, it is enough to give them every year a good weeding, after the crop is taken away: they are topped in the fourth or fifth year, when about ten feet high. If allowed to grow to too great a height, the side branches, which are the best bearers, would be injured in their development, and, in addition, there would be difficulty in gathering the berries.

Crops.

The crop is gathered according as the fruit changes its colour from green to a fine red cherry hue. In our colonies, as soon as the fruits are gathered they are laid in the sun, to dry them in their pulp, and afterwards pounded in a mortar, to separate the dry pulp from the parchment, or second covering of the berry.

In the Philippines, the Indians, after each gathering, bruise the pulp with their hands, and separate the grains by washing them in clean open water, and, after this manipulation, the grains which retain their parchment or second covering are alone dried for some hours in the sun, and then collected in sacks.

By the first method several weeks of drying become necessary before the berries can be separated from the husks; and if the rains occur it will be requisite to turn over the coffee heaps three or four times every day while they are thus drying, or fermentation will inevitably take place, which will prove exceedingly injurious to the quality of the coffee. By the Indian method, one fine day of exposure to the sun will be sufficient to render the berry quite dry, and then the whole crop can be put into the stores.

VII.

Cacao.

The cacao grows with ease in every part of the island of Luzon, but the best quality is produced at Zebou, where, also, the greatest quantity is cultivated.

The spots best suited for the cultivation are alluvial lands, having great depth of soil, and somewhat shaded by trees. The expense of cultivating cacao is, for the first year, greater than that of coffee; for, after removing the weeds, the brushwood, and the trees that give too much shade, a quincunx of ditches is dug, of four or five feet deep, on a square of equal extent; the earth is passed through a hurdle, and in it are mixed pieces of plants which have been broken, and the earth is thrown back into the ditches, and therein are set the young plants, of which such care has been taken as to have them sprouting during the previous three weeks, in a little earth laid in banana leaves.

During two or three years care is taken to dig around the young shrubs, and to eradicate all the weeds likely to prove injurious to them.

Crops.

The crop consists merely in gathering the fruits when ripe, in opening them, in separating the beans from the parchment, and in drying them before the sun.

VIII.

Cotton.

The cultivation of cotton, which is carried on to a great extent, and especially in the province of Ilocos, is, of all the products of the Philippines, that which requires the least labour and expense; it generally follows a crop of mountain rice. As soon as the rice crop is carried off, the ground receives a light ploughing, and in the tracks made afterwards by the plough, at a distance of a yard from each other, some cotton seeds are laid, and covered in the earth. In about two months afterwards the cotton plants begin to flower, and to produce fruit, which is gathered in every day during the hottest hours.

The gathering of this crop lasts until the first rains, which destroy the shrubs, and stain all the cotton that they then produce.

IX.

Pepper.

Formerly the island of Luzon, and particularly the provinces of Laguna and Batay, used to produce a large quantity of pepper, which was exported by the Philippine Company, who had a monopoly of it.

The price was at that time fixed by a measure called *ganta*, which was used both by sellers and buyers. When the growers came to sell their products at Manilla they found that the agents of the company had altered the measure, by making that of the company double the capacity of the one used by the Indians, thereby cheating the sellers. The Indians, furious at this trick, went back to their own country, and in a few days destroyed all the pepper plantations, so that now the island of Luzon scarcely produces pepper sufficient for its own consumption.

The pepper plant is generally cultivated near the mountains, in spots where heavy dews fall and keep up the moisture. This parasite requires but little care; it is propagated by cuttings, and it is enough to take a piece of from twelve to eighteen inches, to bend it together, to cover the middle with earth, and to tie the two points against a prop, of from five to six feet in height, and as far as possible of dead wood, covered with its bark, and capable of absorbing much moisture. The young plant grows up, fastening to the dead wood, and mounts as high as its top; all that is required afterwards is to weed around it, and to dig the earth once a year at its foot.

Crops.

The grains are gathered as fast as they change in colour from green to black. They are collected in heaps, and spread out in the sun for some days, in order to be thoroughly dried.

X.

Wheat.

Wheat produces in the island of Luzon from sixty to eighty-fold, and is grown on the mountains in the different provinces, and in particular that of Batangas. Before sowing it, the Indians prepare the ground altogether in the same manner as for the mountain rice, and their seeding time is at the end of December or the beginning of January. Three or four weeks after the sowing the women give it a good weeding, and in three months and a-half, or four months, the crop is ready for harvesting, and is saved in precisely the same manner as the mountain rice.

XI.

Sugar-Cane.

The cultivation of the sugar-cane takes place according to two methods, which differ from each other:—the one is practised in lands just cleared, and the other in lands that have been already ploughed.

First Method.

The first method affords one of the most effectual means for carrying out a great clearing at a small expense, and is as follows :

Towards the month of October all the trees and brushwood are cut down on the ground which is to be cleared for planting. This work must be done with great care, and it ought not to be neglected, as soon as a tree is cut down, to lop off every one of its branches, and to strip it of the bark; for if any time, even a few days, are allowed to pass, the wood becomes dry, and the barking is not only more difficult but more expensive. Fifteen days after all the trees are cut down, a fine day is chosen, when there is no wind, and when the sun is ardent, to set fire to them. On the following day, when all is burned except the logs of a great thickness, the workmen are employed in forming a fence round the plantation, to prevent it being trespassed on by animals; and to make this fence the trees which have not been burned are used; but the heavy logs, which cannot be removed with ease, are left on the ground, to be burned in the following year. When the fence is completed, or even while it is going forward, some workmen are employed in preparing the soil for receiving the young cane plants; each workman has a line to mark out the rows, at from four to five feet distance from each other, and in each of these rows, at three feet distance from one another, the workmen, with a hoe, open a little hole or furrow, a foot and a-half long, from five to six inches wide, and at least six inches deep, in which the plants are put.

Before the holes are made for receiving the plants, it is indispensable to divide the ground into large squares of from eighty to a hundred square yards, and each of them is separated from the others by alleys of at least three yards in breadth. When all the preparations are ready, the plants are procured. They are the points of the canes which have been already gathered in, and which serve as saplings for the new plantation. They are cut off in lengths of from ten to twelve inches, tied up in large parcels, like asparagus, and laid in water for at least three days, so as to be thoroughly steeped, care being taken that the water is not at all corrupted. After three days' steeping the plants are taken to the new plantation, the bundles are loosened, and the cuttings are given out to the planters, who, stripping off some of the leaves, lay two of them in each hole, in such a manner that each plant lies at length along the furrow or hole; and if the bottom be not quite level, a little earth is added to make it so. The point of a plant rises at each end of the hole, which is then filled up with finely powdered mould. If the plantation has been prepared during great heat, and if the drought be excessive, it is indispensable, before the plants are laid in the furrow, to pour into it from one to two quarts of water.

When the plantation is finished it is not to be touched again until the weeds begin to grow, and great care must then be taken to destroy them as they spring up, otherwise they would soon smother the young canes; but as soon as the latter have grown up, and cover the ground with their large leaves, it is unnecessary to make any further weedings, or to do any other work, up to the time of harvesting the canes.

It is usually from the month of March to the end of May, and even in the beginning of June, that plantations are made according to the method which I have described. Ten or twelve months afterwards the canes are fit for being collected. As the canes are cut down in one of the large squares that form the divisions of the plantation, the alleys round it are cleaned with the greatest care of all the dry weeds, and of all the cane leaves; and at the time of the day when there is least or no wind, that square is surrounded by the work-people, with branches in their hands, and fire is then set to the heaps of leaves covering the ground to the height of from one to two feet, and in a few minutes the whole is consumed. The precautions taken to clean the alleys, and to place the work-people with branches in their hands, arise from the dread of the fires communicating with the other parts of the field from which the cane crop has not been removed.

A few days after the leaves are thus burned, the plough is taken into the ground, and some sods are taken away from near the stumps, so as to strip them, and to throw the earth into the middle between the rows. The first time that the plough is set at work in this ground great obstacles may be met with, which require to be treated with caution; they arise from the great quantity of the roots of the trees, which are not yet rotten, and ploughing there becomes, on that account, a troublesome task. If the difficulties are too great, the pickaxe and mattock must be substituted for the plough, and the foot of each plant must be stripped, by throwing the earth into the middle between the rows. As soon as the first rains begin, and that the weeds shoot up with the canes, a part of them must be destroyed by the plough, if possible, and the rest by the mattock. If the plough cannot be employed, this work of weeding takes place usually three times in the year; at the second time, the lower part of the canes are slightly dug around, and, at the third time, fresh earth is laid to them. But this second digging must be varied according to the fertility of the soil and the age of the canes, for the younger the cane and the more fertile the soil, the less it is useful to put fresh earth to the foot of the plant, and I shall now tell you why.

Inversely to all other plants, the cane tends always to raise itself under the earth; that is to say, if in the first year you plant it six inches under ground, in the second year it will be found at only three inches, in the third year at the surface, and in the fourth year in the earth which has served as the second covering; so that the more you heap earth and the quicker it ascends, the greater the risk you run of losing several crops. In a fertile soil, it is enough to cover lightly with earth the foot of the stock, so that it shall sprout with vigour, and give a large quantity, and then you may augment your second covering, by little and little, to have from the same plantation the largest number possible of new canes.

In the third year, generally, all the stumps of the trees and their roots are destroyed, and almost all the work can then be got through with the plough: the mattock is used only for the second covering, which ought then to be done so as to cover the stock of the cane to the height of from ten to twelve inches.

Such is the course that is to be followed for making a plantation on ground just cleared. One important advice is requisite here, and that is, not to attempt to plant more than can be carefully attended to; for if the mistake is committed, of having too much ground planted, it would be better to abandon altogether a part of the planting, in order to take proper care of the remainder, than to manage the whole badly.

Second Method.

The cultivation of the sugar-cane by the plough costs much less than that by clearing-grounds; but it also gives, in a shorter time two crops, sometimes three, in very good hands.

One of the first conditions is, about the month of November, December, or January, to plough the land three times, and to harrow it twice. When it is will tilled and the earth quite fine, the land is divided into squares of from eighty to a hundred yards, and along each ditch between them alleys are left, of three or four yards in breadth: then divisions are made to facilitate the burning of the leaves after harvest, which is done in the same way as in the cleared lands. When the land is so divided, the third and last ploughing is given, for the purpose of tracing the lines into rows, in which the canes are to be planted. These rows are from four to four and a-half feet asunder, and this last ploughing leaves a furrow, which marks the line for laying down the plants. When the work is finished the plantations are surrounded with palisades, to preserve the canes from animals, which might destroy them; and the plants are got ready in the same manner as for the plantation of cleared lands, and the holes are opened by one set of workmen, while others follow and lay the plants down and cover them with earth.

If the plantations are got ready at the proper season, there is no necessity for watering the plants; but if the season is very dry, care is taken to pour from one to two quarts of water in each hole. The plantations are usually made during the harvest, for it is then that the tops of the plants which are cut down can be easily obtained; but as that occurs at the time of the greatest drought, and water is required, the process becomes tedious and costly, from having to bring to the ground so many thousand quarts of water. To avoid that expense, and also that of weeding, it has been found useful to prepare a field of canes specially designed for plants and for nothing else. The planting is then carried on in the month of December or January—that is, before harvest, when there are no heavy rains, but there is a sufficiency of humidity. The plant then vegetates luxuriously, and is strong and large when the heavy rains begin to fall. But whether the planting be done in times of humidity or of great drought, the process of cultivation is always the same. As soon as the rains begin and the weeds shoot up, it becomes necessary to have recourse to the plough, which is run within the rows, and care is taken to keep the furrow in the middle, and to strip a little the foot of the plants; and, after the ploughing, it is almost indispensable to weed with the mattock and the hand the ground round the plants, in order to thoroughly eradicate the bad herbs which the plough could not reach.

Generally, during the time that the plant requires for growing up to the height at which its leaves are sufficient to keep down the weeds, it is necessary to run the plough three times between the rows, and also to weed them three times. The harvesting is done in the same manner as that of the cleared-ground plantations, and as the plants of one square have been cut down, the leaves should be burned, and as soon as possible the plough is to be run between the rows, and the earth thrown into the middle. I have said that, as soon as possible the plough must be used, because, after the leaves are burned, the ground is moist, and the ploughing is done with great ease; but if any delay is allowed, the glowing sun, at that epoch of the harvest, is so strong that the ground soon becomes parched up, and the ploughing becomes less easy, and more injurious to the next growth.

In good lands the same plant produces two or three crops.

Crops.

The harvesting of the sugar-canes takes place in the Philippines from the month of January to May which is the times of the greatest heats. If this harvesting can be effected within two months, it would be preferable to commence it in the month of March, in order to terminate it about the middle of May; for it is during those months that the sugar-cane produces matter, richer, and better filled with sugar. It is also the time when the rains are not to be found; but when there is a large plantation, and not hands or machines sufficient to finish it in those two months, a beginning is made in January, in order to finish towards the end of May, when the heavy fall of rain commences.

The workmen are divided into four sets: two for the field—one of the cutters, and the other of the carters or carriers of the canes to the manufactory; and two for the manufactory, of whom one is occupied with grinding the canes in a mill, and the others who boil the sugar. To make a good economical harvest of sugar-canes depends upon having a good mill, and upon a proper distribution of the workmen. The mill is the leader of the work; for on its regularity depends the constant, orderly labour of the workmen, with advantage to the grower. When the mill works well, and with good well-directed workmen, they who boil the sugar have not a minute to spare; for they are obliged to boil all the syrup that the mill sends them. If the mill grinds many canes, the cutters are forced to cut an abundance of them, and the men who have the duty of transporting them to the mill cannot be idle while taking them there. It is therefore an essential precaution to have a good mill, and a number of good workmen to keep it properly at work.

Two days before the milling of the canes begins, the practice is to cut as many canes as possible, and they are taken to the mill. This practice has been adopted in order to have beforehand a sufficient quantity, so as to avoid the vexation of seeing the mill stopped from want of a supply, since in that case all the work is stopped, and some of the workmen have to remain idle.

It is always recommended to the cutters to cut the canes as low as possible—that is, on a level with the ground; for every piece left above the ground is so much lost, and becomes an obstacle to the next cultivation.

I shall not enter into the details of sugar boiling, for within some few years the greatest improvements have been introduced into the apparatus used for the purpose, and it would not be possible, in this short sketch, to describe the new machinery, or the methods of making use of the various utensils.

In the Philippines, the last improvement that has been made was to copy that which was done, or perhaps what is now going on, in Bourbon—that is, by working a battery, composed in general of from five to six boilers, gradually diminishing in size; from the first, in which the defecation of the juice takes place, the syrup is successively passed on to the last, in which the boiling of it is effected. Each operation requires forty-five minutes. After the juice has been defecated, and the battery is in full operation, you take of the defecated product from a hundred and thirty to a hundred and fifty pounds of sugar. The chief difficulty in boiling sugar is the defecation, or clarification, by removing extraneous particles, and also the boiling it to the proper point; for practice alone can teach you when one has put a sufficient quantity of lime, in order that the syrup shall be properly clarified, and practice also can alone show when the sugar has been boiled to the proper point.

XII.

Bamboo.

Its Culture, Mode of Planting, Cutting, and Preservation.

The bamboo in the Philippines is a native, plant which grows there almost without any cultivation, on the mountains and in the plains. It presents varieties of fifteen or twenty species, from those of from two to three inches in circumference to others as thick as a man's arm. There are some having in the inside a hollow space, which is sometimes from eighteen to twenty-five inches in diameter. All these various bamboos have their different uses. With the small ones, enclosed fields are fenced in; with the large ones, conduits are made for removing water. When divided into long slight filaments they are made into hats, baskets, ropes of considerable strength, arms and weapons which cut through flesh with as much facility as does steel, and even fleams for bleeding horses and buffaloes; and even kitchen utensils for boiling food, in the same manner as in an iron pot. It is also with the bamboo, that the traveller can in a moment procure fire, as with a tinder-box and a flint.

The cultivation of the bamboo is of the simplest nature; it is transplanted by cuttings and layers. A piece is taken, divided into five or six knots; a hole is made with a mattock, and this piece of bamboo is laid therein with a slight inclination; and is then covered up with earth. The end above ground has two knots, and a split is made in it so as to allow the rain-water to rest there as in a reservoir; if there be a strong drought at the moment of planting, this part is filled with water, and the plant is left to itself. Care is however taken, every three or four months, to remove the brushwood, which might prevent the young plants from springing up to their usual height.

In three years the first cuttings may take place, but to preserve the plant, and to cause it to produce an abundant crop for many years. care must be taken to cut the sprouts which are to be taken at least from four to five yards from the ground. If they are cut on a level with the earth the plant would be entirely ruined; perhaps because the shoots, being entirely stripped, would no longer be preserved from the burning rays of the sun; or because the branches and the leaves, which grow in abundance round the foot of the plant, cannot receive nourishment any longer from the air, and have, therefore, none to furnish to the roots. I state this opinion without confidently asserting it; but it is certain that, in order to preserve a plantation of bamboos, and to have abundant crops of them, the precautions I have pointed out must be adopted.

I shall terminate this sketch by some observations on the Buffalo, which is the faithful companion of the Indian in all his toils.

XIII.

The Buffalo.

The buffalo, when domesticated, is an animal of more docility, and which during its life renders more services to man than does the ox. This benefit depends on its being tamed when young—that is, when only a year old, and then it may be left to the guidance of a child of eight or ten years; but if it is allowed to live untamed until it is three years old, it becomes too restive and wicked. It is quite certain that the tame buffalo will never do the child any injury, for its instinct is such that it knows there is no bad treatment for it to fear from a weak creature. In strength it is superior to the ox; its food is of the coarsest kind, it eats all kinds of herbs, even those that are rejected by the more delicate beasts. The buffalo goes to seek them in the plains, on the mountains, and even at the bottom of every kind of water, where he browses, when the heat forces him to take refuge therein. The Indian associates the buffalo with all his work; with the buffalo he ploughs, and on its back he carries and transports articles across mountains, and by paths that even mules could not travel. The Indian also mounts his buffalo to cross over considerable sheets of water; he places himself, standing, on the animal's broad back, and supports himself by the leather strap. The docile animal swims patiently, and often drags behind it the little cart, then floating on the surface.

The services of the buffalo are so numerous that it would be too long to enumerate them. It is necessary to have lived among the Indians, and to have carried on tillage with them, in order to appreciate, and to know thoroughly, the great difference between the buffalo and the ox.

The female buffalo, being little employed in work, gives a great quantity of milk, which contains a much stronger quantity of butter than that of our cows. Excellent cheese is made from it.

In fine, another eminent service which the buffalo renders is, that he becomes a powerful means of disinfecting the marshy districts. The buffalo is, as it were, amphibious; he spends the night while feeding on the plains, and in the day-time, during the heats, he is in the marshy spots; browsing on the river brinks, and at the bottom of the water; everywhere any plants grow he destroys them, by continually stirring up the muddy bottoms; he causes the noxious animals to perish that are to be found therein, and changes at last the nature of the marsh, which, when frequented by troops of buffaloes, no longer exhales those pestiferous gasses which are the source of the marsh fevers.

P. DE LA GIRONIERE.

AGRICULTURAL IMPLEMENTS

USED IN THE PHILIPPINE ISLANDS.

I.—THE INDIAN PLOUGH.

It is exceedingly simple: it is composed of four pieces of wood (1, 2, 3, 4), which the most unhandy ploughman can put together; the mould board and share, which are of cast iron (5 and 6), are sold in the Philippines for half a dollar.

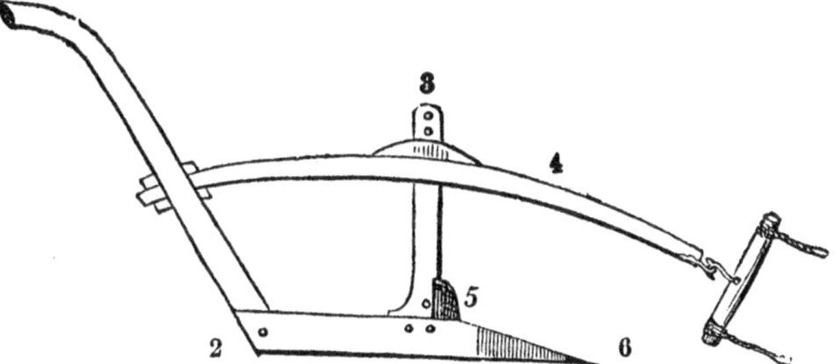

The lightness and simplicity of this plough render it easy to be used in every kind of cultivation, and in the plantations divided into rows, such as those of tobacco, maize, sugar-canes, &c. It is used with great advantage, not only for cutting down weeds, but also for giving to each row a ploughing, which is serviceable to the plantation, and which is less costly and quicker than simple weeding with the mattock.

II.—YOKE FOR THE BUFFALOES.

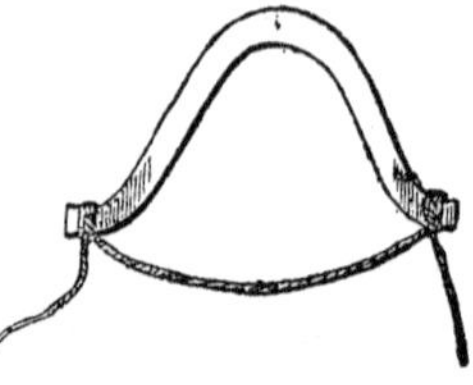

The yoke of the buffalo is of the simplest and most commodious kind. It consists solely of a piece of wood, bent so as to suit in its shape to the withers of the animal; it is worn on its neck, extending to the middle of the shoulder, and is fastened under the neck by a piece of twisted liana- or by a piece of rope; at the two ends of this piece of wood the traces are fastened. Buffaloes are always yoked one after the other, like the horses of the public waggons.

III.—LILIT, OR THE INDIAN SICKLE.

With the crook the rice is caught, which being drawn into the corner makes it easy to take a good handful of it with the left hand; the crook is then moved a little forward, by making a slight movement with the hand, which loosens it; and by the same movement the steel blade comes into contact with the straw, and then by drawing the crook towards you, the handful in the left hand is cut by one stroke.

IV.—THE COMB HARROW.

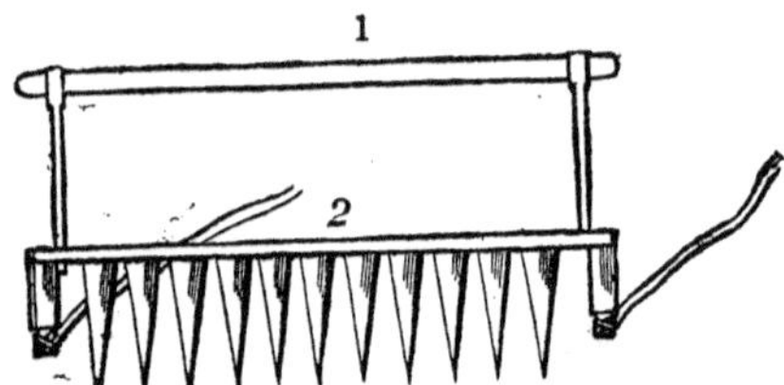

This implement is used exclusively in the cultivation of aquatic rice: for the purpose of reducing the ground to a state of liquid mud. The cross-bar (1) is of wood, and the teeth (2) are of wrought-iron.

V.—A GUILIGEN, OR HAND-MILL.

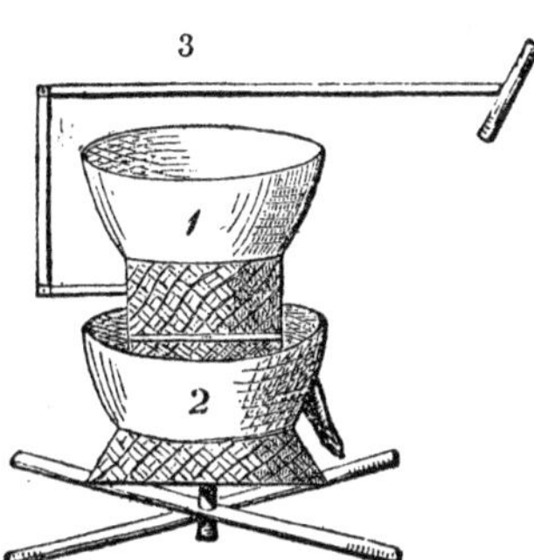

A sort of hand-mortar for separating the rice from its husks (1 and 2); it represents two truncated cones, made of bamboos woven together like a basket. Each cone is separated near the middle by a bamboo division, and the space at the side of the head is filled with well-beaten clay; in this clay are inserted, to a considerable depth, several little boards of palm wood, as broad as the middle finger, one third of an inch in thickness, and four inches in length. They are so placed as almost to touch each other, and in rows, like a mill-stone which has been just picked. These two cones, when so ready, are placed one over the other by the top, and the upper one is turned by means of a wrench (3) on the lower one, and the rice passing between the two grinders is slightly brayed, and nothing is wanted but a few strokes of a pestle, for it to be completely skinned and to show its beautiful white colour.

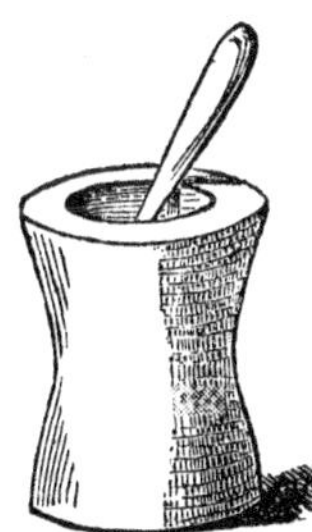

VI.—THE MORTAR.

This form of mortar is found in every Indian cabin, where it is daily in requisition for pounding the rice consumed by the occupants.

Luzon, the name of the principal island of the Philippines, is derived from, or rather is a corruption of, the word *Luçon*, signifying a "mortar."

APPENDIX.

I.

TESTIMONY OF M. GABRIEL LAFOND.

In our own time, a Frenchman, whose name merits an honourable distinction, has rendered an immense service to Manilla, by introducing and perfecting the culture of coffee in the colony. This meritorious individual is M. Paul Proust de La Gironiere, my countryman and my friend.

M. de La Gironiere, born at Nantes, and connected with the principal merchants of that city, left his native place in 1818, as surgeon on board the *Victorine*, fitted out by his uncle for Manilla. Seduced by the natural beauties of the country, he made a second voyage there in the following year; established himself, practised medicine, married the widow of the Marquis de Las Salinas, and eventually, having acquired a considerable estate on the borders of the Laguna, he summoned his elder brother to assist him in working it.

In 1828, the Spanish government, which had lost its American possessions, felt the necessity of taking vigorous measures for the development of its remaining colonies. Cuba was then at the height of its prosperity; and the same agricultural and commercial results were anxiously hoped for the Philippines. A royal decree instituted various prizes for the encouragement of the culture of indigo, cocoa, cinnamon, cloves, tea, and coffee. Amongst these prizes, one of eight thousand piasters,* was promised to any one who would plant and ripen sixty thousand square feet of coffee. M. de La Gironiere entered the field as a competitor, and sent to the Isle of Bourbon for M. Adolphe Delaunay, an experienced colonial agriculturist, to whom he intrusted the direction of the new plantations. In this enterprise he had to surmount obstacles of all kinds: want of hands, want of even pecuniary aid, fruitless experiments, the ravages occasioned by buffaloes, by wild boars, by stags, by monkeys, added to which, the devastation caused by clouds of locusts, similar to those of Egypt. He was likewise subjected to the jealous feelings of other colonists, who constantly endeavored to thwart his efforts; nevertheless, aided by intelligent assistants, his perseverance eventually enabled him to succeed in conquering every obstacle. He drew around him a large population, he built villages, he constructed store-houses, and a beautiful residence: in a word, he changed an unproductive soil into a fertile and magnificent property; and, finally, obtained the prize of eight thousand piasters, which were paid him by Signor Enriquez the representative of the Spanish government. M. de La Gironiere will no doubt find imitators; the prosperity of his wide domain will awaken the apathetic inhabitants of the Philippines; and this example of the power and influence of a single human will, firm and enlightened, cannot fail to effect beneficial results.

Jala-Jala, washed by the limpid waters of the Laguna, is capable of transporting, by means of barges, the produce of its harvests to the warehouses of Manilla, or even on board the vessels destined to convey the same to China, to India, or to Europe Its situation is admirable, and one of the finest of the entire colony. The interest inspired by its creation, the vast labour thereby necessitated and the admirable results which have crowned the same, drew the numerous foreigners, and especially Frenchmen, travelling in these distant parts to Jala-Jala, where they were always received with the noblest and the most generous hospitality.

* The piaster is equal to 3*s.* 7*d.* British currency.

Unfortunately domestic afflictions caused M. de La Gironiere to leave a country where he had lost his wife, his children, and his brother. Arrived in France, the government, upon the proposition of M. Barrot, consul-general at Manilla, and of the brave Marshal Soult, who knew how to reward civic as well as military courage, accorded him the decoration of the Legion of Honour; a recompense deservedly merited. But Spain owes more to Paul de La Gironiere than France. The latter had regarded him as one of her children who has carried civilisation to the other end of the world; will Spain ever recognise the services he has rendered her by the admirable perseverance he displayed with regard to Philippine agriculture?

II.

TESTIMONY OF H. HAMILTON LINDSAY, ESQ.

WESTDEAN HOUSE, CHICHESTER.
August 16th, 1853.

GENTLEMEN,

In reply to your inquiry as to whether I have any notes relative to my visit to the Lake of Socolme, in company with M. de La Gironiere, I am sorry to say that I can find none. I have, however, a vivid recollection of that very curious spot, which is quite at your disposal, should you like to insert it in the translation of La Gironiere's work you are about to publish.

All the natives of the neighbouring villages held this lake in superstitious terror, and declared that any one venturing on it would inevitably be devoured by the hordes of caymans which frequented it, so that when in one of our excursions we proposed to explore it, not one of our boatmen would come with us, we had therefore to go to a village many miles distant to engage a crew. A single canoe certainly might have been exposed to danger; so to obviate any risk, we had two large canoes hauled over the mound —about a quarter of a mile in width, and eighty to a hundred feet high—which separates Socolme from the Laguna; and, having launched our canoes, we made a platform over them, and lashed them strongly together; and then with a party composed of La Gironiere, myself, and a Chinese servant, with eight or ten stout Tagalocs, armed with four double-barrelled guns, pikes, cutlasses, and axes, to repel any attempt at boarding, we proceeded to explore. The number and size of the brutes which we saw certainly in some measure justified the reputation of the lake, though they seemed more afraid of us than we of them. As we proceeded quietly round the banks at least thirty rushed down into the water, we keeping up a constant fire, though without succeeding in killing any.

The lake itself I should say was less than a mile in diameter, nearly a perfect circle, and the sides, excepting towards the Laguna, rising to a considerable height, and covered with trees of a gigantic size. Its depth rapidly shelved from five to forty fathoms about one hundred yards from the shore, the centre having a uniform depth of forty to fifty fathoms. It is evidently the crater of an extinct volcano, the whole adjacent country being volcanic, but its curiosity consists in its bottom being at least twenty fathoms below the level of the sea.

I happen, among some old papers, to find a description of our adventures in the Cave of San-Matteo, which was written the day after our visit, and is therefore more accurate and circumstantial than that of my friend, evidently written from imperfect recollection, many years after the event. I now forward to you the original rough copy, as sent home at the time to my friends in England, and, if you think it worthy of a place in your book, you are quite at liberty to publish it.

La Gironiere's book brings back to my mind many pleasant recollections of early youth, and of two summers spent in rambling over the beautiful island of Manilla; and it gives me great pleasure to have an opportunity of bearing testimony to the kind and generous hospitality I met with at Jala-Jala, which was my head-quarters for many months. There are certainly some strange stories of adventures in my friend's book, to the general accuracy of some—in which I was a participator—I can bear testimony; others, especially those relating to the extraordinary gallantry and daring displayed by him at the time of the cholera, and consequent massacre of Europeans at Manilla, in 1820, were fresh in the recollection of many at the time of my first acquaintance with him. No foreigner enjoyed more completely the esteem and confidence of all classes in Manilla—Spaniards, Mestizos, and Tagals—than "*Don Pablo*," and no man can be better qualified to give authentic and valuable information regarding the resources and agriculture of the island than himself. I therefore look with much interest to the additions promised on these points in the volume you are about to publish.

I have the honour to remain,

Your obedient servant,

H. HAMILTON LINDSAY.

To Messrs. Vizetelly and Co.,
Fleet Street.

ACCOUNT OF A VISIT TO THE CAVE OF SAN-MATTEO, IN THE NEIGHBOURHOOD OF MANILLA.

Manilla, May 26th, 1830.

We have just returned from a visit to the Cave of San-Matteo, which has long been considered as one of the most interesting objects of natural curiosity to be seen in the Philippines; but, as we may consider ourselves as the first discoverers of the wonders to be seen in the innermost recesses of this extraordinary cavern, I will forthwith commit to paper the particulars of our journey while they are yet fresh in my memory.

We left Manilla on the afternoon of the 24th May, and a pleasant drive of an hour and a-half brought us to Mariquines, a pretty village, situated in a fertile valley, which narrows gradually as you continue your journey towards San-Matteo, another large village in the centre of the plain, and which has nothing remarkable to distinguish it. We slept here, and, having made our arrangements for horses, guides, &c., at six the following morning started on our expedition.

As you proceed the valley grows narrower, the mountains on either side increase in height and grandeur, and you enjoy a beautiful view of the mountain Panimitan, in which the cave is situated. On arriving at the village of Balete, we crossed the river, which flows smoothly and silently betwixt high and richly-wooded banks. Our path was in some places barely practicable for horses, winding along the rocky banks of the river, which we had to ford four times before we arrived at the place where we had sent our provisions for breakfast.

The spot where we halted was one which requires the pencil of an artist to give an adequate description of. Directly in front of us were two stupendous mountains, which, from their nearly perpendicular sides, seemed to have been torn asunder by some violent convulsion of nature, and between them flowed the Rio di San-Matteo, no longer calm and placid as before, but foaming and bubbling betwixt huge rocks of white marble. The scene was so striking, that—although to my infinite regret, I have no idea of handling the pencil—I endeavored, by the assistance of a few outlines, and writing down where were to be rocks, wood, and water, to carry away with me what might enable another to delineate the scene.

I must not forget here to make honourable mention of the delicious fish with which we were regaled, as there is something peculiar both in the mode of catching and dressing them. The water of the river is clear as crystal, and in some places very deep, and when the fish are playing on the surface, an Indian dives to the bottom and, rising directly under them, catches the fish in his hand with surprising dexterity; and the mode of dressing them is one certainly deserving the admiration of the whole race of gourmands. A few joints of the green bamboo, about two feet long, are cut, into which the fish is thrust, with some leaves of an herb much resembling sorrel, a few pimentos, and other spices, and a little water is also put in; the mouth of the cane is then stuffed with leaves, and it is put into the middle of a hot fire; as soon as the bamboo begins to burn, the fish is dressed, and I will defy any restorateur of Paris or Amsterdam to produce a better water-souchy than we eat that morning.

All this however caused delay, and it was past ten before we proceeded towards the object of our journey. My only companion was a French gentleman, M. de La Gironiere. We had once more to cross the river at the narrowest part of the gorge betwixt the mountains, of which I despair to give an adequate description—it was nature in its wildest state. The dark mountains frowned perpendicularly over us to the height of near two thousand feet, and the river foamed and rushed in numberless cascades through the enormous masses of white marble, which seemed in vain to endeavour to check its progress. It was a scene which I would gladly have ridden fifty miles to see, even if I had had no other object, and in the time of the rains, the torrent must be awful.

We crossed the river, stepping from rock to rock, and after scrambling about a hundred and fifty feet by the aid of rocks and trees, we found ourselves at the mouth of the cavern, accompanied by about twenty Indians, all provided with long torches made of split bamboos; we also had not forgot to bring wax candles, which afterwards did us good service; a line of twenty yards to measure the cave; flint, steel, and matches, in case of accidents; but, alas! we forgot what was of much importance, and which no traveller who explores mountains ought ever to be unprovided with—a hammer and cold iron chisel.

We entered the cave, and proceeded accurately to measure its depth, of which I had heard such contradictory reports at Manilla. My companion walked twenty yards into the cave, and, as the extremity of the string checked him, stopped and marked on a slip of paper; I then passed him another twenty yards and so on.

For the first two hundred yards the cavern varies from seven to twelve and twenty feet in height, and about twelve in breadth; the roof and sides are composed of a kind of soft calcareous soapstone, with occasional layers of loose stones and sand; at two hundred and fifty yards our way was impeded by large rocks, over which we climbed, and on the right side found a precipice, of which we had been previously warned. We threw in large stones which fell in a pool of water; others which we threw in a slanting direction, and with more violence, escaped the well, and we heard them bounding from rock to rock till the sound was lost; having no ropes we could not descend to examine further, but proceeded on our way.

Here we began to experience the greatest annoyance from the torches of our Indians, which, from the dense smoke they emitted consumed the air, and impeded our respiration. We endeavoured in vain to persuade them to extinguish them, and finding remonstrance useless, I got hold of all I could and threw them into the chasm; upon which many of the fellows got frightened, and left us, and we were thereby quit of two nuisances at once, as the noise they made was intolerable.

The cavern here enlarges, and becomes more irregular; there are huge detached rocks, through which runs a stream of clear water frequently above our knees, in which I observed some crayfish. Occasionally we had to clamber over masses of rock, twenty feet in height, and carefully descend their slippery sides. The scene was truly worthy of Salvator Rosa. The bright glare of the torches which disturbed myriads of large bats or flying foxes from their holes, and illuminated the dusky vault of the cavern, and the dark forms of the half-naked Indians, formed quite a *coup-de-théâtre* of the grandest kind.

At last, after having counted six hundred yards, we reached what had hitherto been considered the end of the cavern. The stream whose course we had followed here formed a kind of basin five or six feet in diameter and issued forth from a hole in the rock, which descended till it touched the water, and formed an insurmountable barrier.

We found, in a cleft in the rock, the broken wine bottles which had been left ten years before by my present companion, and several names cut in the rock. There were here, and in various parts of the cavern, some stalactites, but of a dirty brown colour.

This seemed the termination of our journey, and as we were

nearly stifled by the smoke of the torches, we were thinking of a return, when my companion—who had all through seemed bent upon making some discoveries—descried a small stream of water descending through a narrow aperture in the rock above us, and immediately commenced exploring it. The Indians all declared that it led no further, and that it was impossible to penetrate it; but M. de La Gironiere was already out of sight, and calling on me to follow him, which I readily did. Only one of the Indians would accompany us, and a Chinese boy whom I had brought with me.

I now found myself climbing up a narrow hole, like the funnel of a chimney, composed of irregular rocks, wet with the constant dripping of water; sometimes perpendicular, sometimes slanting or horizontal; at times so narrow that it required the assistance of my feet and arms to force my way through, at others large enough to stand up and barely touch the roof with my hand; but conceive my delight at feeling a fresh and pure air blowing directly in our faces, so strong as to make us fear for our candles. Freshened and revived, and animated by the hope that we were going to penetrate to the other side of the mountain, we sat down a few moments to repose ourselves, and examine the spot we had attained.

The cavern had here enlarged to eight or nine feet in height and more in breadth; it was no longer wet and dirty like the previous part, but the ground and sides were covered with beautiful stalactites of the purest white, forming numerous little pyramids, like loaves of sugar. After a few moments' repose we proceeded exploring, using the precaution always to have three candles lit at once, in case of accidents. On reaching about eighty yards from where we left our Indians, we again thought that we were at the end of the cave. A vault or fissue of the rock rose above us to a height that we could not distinguish the top; most of the rocks were covered with beautiful incrustations and pyramids, of which I broke several to take with me.

On examining this cavern minutely, I discovered to the left a small hole through which I could barely pass my head, which seemed to lead farther, and enlarge as it rose. Here began our difficulties. We longed to get through and pursue our researches, but we had no tools wherewith to enlarge the aperture, perseverance, however, does wonders, and we commenced chipping the rock away as we could with stones. The situation was also awkward as before arriving at the hole; the rocks were so narrow that only one could work at a time, and there was no room for the arm to give force to the blow.

However, it was soon sufficiently enlarged for my Chinese boy to crawl through, and we sent him in with a candle to report; he made good his entrance, ascended a kind of chimney, and we lost sight of him, but in a few moments he returned, shouting with joy that he had found a large room all white. I redoubled my efforts, and, at the expense of numerous scarifications of my knees and shoulders, forced my way, and clambered up through narrow rocks about ten feet, when I found myself suddenly in a large vault which rivalled the famed Grotto of Antiparos.

The ground and a great part of the walls were formed of one mass of pure white or darker stalactites, but all glittering like diamonds, and covered with shining pebbles of every shape and size, with which—like Aladdin in the cave—I instantly commenced filling my pockets. The farther extremity of the grotto was lost in darkness, but the most striking object of all remains to be described.

Exactly over the spot from which I emerged, as from the bowels of the earth, rose a pyramid, white and glittering like the sunbeams on frosted snow, in shape and form like the altar of a church, rising with pillars and branches of stalactites of every imaginable shape to the height of nearly thirty feet. The effect was indescribable. Byron's fabled cave of the Island was realized before my eyes—

Wide it was and high,
And showed a self-born Gothic canopy;
The arch upreared by Nature's architect,
The architrave some earthquake might erect,
The buttress from some mountain's bosom hurled,
When the poles crushed, and water was the world;
Or hardened from some earth-absorbing fire
While yet the globe reeked from its funeral pyre.
The fretted pinnacle, the aisle, the nave,
Were there, all scooped by darkness from her cave.

There with a little tinge of phantasy,
Fantastic faces moped and mowed on high:
And there a mitre or a shrine would fix
The eye upon its seeming crucifix.
Thus Nature played with the stalactites,
And built herself a chapel.

I am far from being a devotee, but I confess that for some moments I felt overpowered by mingled feelings of awe and veneration, which can only be felt, not described. It was not fear! The violent exercise and the situation I had attained in so singular a way had excited my feelings to a high degree, and my reflections were not ill-suited to the place and circumstances.

We had penetrated nearly eight hundred yards into the very entrails of the earth, to a spot now for the first time profaned by human footsteps, where Nature herself seemed to have raised an altar to the honour of the Divinity. The only outlet was a narrow aperture, which a single stone might block up for ever. At that same hour on the very day before, an earthquake had shaken every house in Manilla to its foundations, and the end of the very grotto itself seemed choked by an *écroulement* of stones and earth. evidently of very recent date. I do not believe that any man, even of the strongest nerves, could have prevented some reflections of a serious nature from passing through his mind.

But all this while I have forgotten my poor *compagnon de voyage*, who, being unfortunately an inch or two broader across the shoulders than me, was exhausting himself in vain efforts to force his way through, and almost crying with vexation and disappointment. I went to his aid, and we hammered away alternately till the hole was sufficiently enlarged; but still he did not get through without some severe bruises; and I confess I was not without considerable uneasiness as to how he would get back again on our return, as the difficulty of our exit, feet foremost, would be considerably increased; but reflections were useless, all we had to do was to employ our time to the best advantage, and endeavour to make farther discoveries while our candles lasted.

The grotto might be generally from forty to sixty feet in height, but in the clefts of the rock the summit could not be distinguished;

in breadth about twenty yards, and forty or fifty in length, but at the farther end a great part of the roof and sides had lately fallen in: neither was it covered with stalactites, but consisted of masses of common rock, mixed with earth and sand, of which I brought away specimens. We endeavoured to climb up, but having reached about twenty feet were obliged to relinquish the attempt, from the extreme peril of dislodging the loose pieces of rock, and bringing it all down together. At about thirty yards from the entrance we found a fissure in the rock, from which issued a stream, in appearance like a frozen rivulet covered with snow; the sides of the rock were of the same, and covered with numerous pendent icicles of various size. The want of a hammer and mallet prevented our penetrating farther, but it is highly probable that this leads to other grottoes perhaps more wonderful than the one we were in.

We had now passed nearly four hours in the cave, and, giving up all prospect of getting farther, we began to collect specimens of the various curious objects with which we were surrounded. Here again, for want of proper implements, we were obliged to destroy ten times more than we carried away. The walls were covered with the most beautiful white flakes, jutting out like the drapery of a curtain, from the height of eight or ten feet, which we were obliged to dash to pieces to obtain a specimen, and it was not without a feeling of sacrilege that I broke away a large fragment from the altar. Having loaded ourselves with as much as we could carry, we commenced our return. My friend went first, and, after a struggle of several minutes—of which he felt the effects severely afterwards—he forced his way through, and relieved my mind from considerable anxiety. We followed without much difficulty, and returned to where we had left our Indians, who were in great alarm as to what had become of us, though none ventured to come in search.

We made the best of our way to the mouth of the cave, and, having descended to the river, you may conceive how we enjoyed a bottle of Bordeaux, &c., which we had brought with us, and I quitted the cave of San-Matteo, carrying away with me recollections of its wonders which will not speedily be effaced.

Manilla, June 2nd, 1830.

Our curiosity was so strongly excited by what we had seen that since writing the above we have made another visit to the cavern, in hopes of making further discoveries, and have to thank our good fortune that we have returned in safety.

We this time went provided with pickaxes and hammers, bags to carry away specimens—in short, every implement that we could think of; and three days after our last visit, a party of four—consisting of M. de La Gironiere, two other gentlemen, and myself—returned, resolutely bent on forcing a passage to the other side of the mountain, if possible. We had also profited by our experience, and had an ample supply of wax candles, in lieu of those villanous torches which had so nearly stifled us.

Since our last visit I had also read in a French encyclopedia Tournefort's account of the Grotto of Antiparos, which, although on a larger scale, has much analogy with that of San-Matteo. The most singular coincidence is that the same idea should strike the imagination in the grottoes both of Antiparos and San-Matteo, namely, the extraordinary resemblance of the stalactites to an altar.

M. de Nointet, the French ambassador to the Porte, who visited Antiparos in 1760 (I forget the exact date), went so far as to cause high mass to be celebrated before it, and had a sumptuous entertainment served there to more than a hundred people.

We resolved in some degree to imitate his proceedings, at least as far as carrying with us a cold dinner and a hamper of excellent wine, with which we proposed to regale ourselves in the grotto, and to leave some relics as an encouragement to future visitors, to whom it would be no unwelcome discovery to find a few bottles of Champagne and Chateau-Margaux; but all our projects of amusement ran rather a narrow escape of coming to a fatal termination. We proceeded as before—accompanied by about a dozen Indians—to the basin of water, and commenced, one by one, to ascend the narrow aperture before described.

The Indian who accompanied us on our former visit went first, and I followed immediately after him. On arriving at a very narrow and nearly perpendicular pass, Florentino, after he had ascended, called on me to wait a few moments, and he would enlarge the aperture. Instead of chipping away the corners of the rock, he had the imprudence to strike some violent blows with a pi kaxe at the rocks above him. After a few blows we were startled by hearing him utter a loud shriek, and, at the same instant, we all shuddered to see huge masses of rock come tumbling down through the aperture, nearly immediately over our heads. For a few short moments the feeling of suspense was dreadful: they were moments which none present will soon forget. At length, thank God! the noise ceased, and I called out to Florentino to know what had happened, but received no answer. At the same moment one of our companions below was taken suddenly ill from alarm, or some other cause, and called out for assistance to quit the cave. La Gironiere went to his aid, and I forced my way up through the aperture to assist the Indian, and my alarm was great on seeing him stretched on the ground without any signs of life. I raised him up, and ascertained that no bones were broken, and threw water in his face to revive him, but it was a quarter of an hour before he came to himself sufficiently to explain what had happened.

It appeared that, on dislodging a small rock, several larger ones that were supported by it had fallen in from the roof, giving him some severe bruises, and he, imagining that the whole vault was about to fall in and crush him, had fainted, more from fright than any injury he had received. I was now joined by La Gironiere, and proceeded to examine the state of affairs, the result of which made us doubly thank Providence for our preservation.

We now remarked what had escaped our observation in the ardour of our first discovery, namely, that the watercourse we were in was formed by loose detached rocks, which had fallen in from the roof, which was about six feet high, and, on examination, we found that the whole mass was *freshly* cracked in various parts, and in a most perilous state. A very singular circumstance occurred to the pickaxe which caused the accident. When the Indian in his alarm dropped it, it fell on one side, and I found it supporting a rock of at least four hundred-weight, which had been dislodged, and, by a singular good fortune, had at the moment found a support in the iron of the pickaxe, which was firmly wedged there,—I would not have removed it for much. Feeling convinced that there was considerable danger in proceeding further, we returned to the basin with our wounded Indian to consult.

Having there refreshed ourselves, and recovered from our fright, the idea of coming so far for nothing was not agreeable, and we determined at least to return to the grotto, taking care to try no more experiments of the pickaxe nature. We passed cautiously through the dangerous aperture, carefully avoiding to dislodge any of the loose rocks, nor did we attempt to enlarge the hole at the entrance of the grotto. M. de La Gironiere had suffered so much from his last entrance that he did not again attempt it, and I confess I could not pursue my researches in it with the same pleasure I formerly did. I examined the fissure at the farther end of the cavern, of which I could not see the termination, and which evidently enlarged, but not sufficiently to make it practicable for us to enter; neither did we think it wise, nor had we time enough to try to make it possible for us to force our way through.

The system of the French naturalist, M. de Tournefort, relative to the vegetation of stones or stalactites in the Grotto of Antiparos as far as my humble opinion goes, is not at all borne out by facts here. I possess little or no knowledge of natural history, but the observations I made convinced me that all the stalactites were formed by the droppings of the calcareous water. The extremity of the drapery of stalactite was always moistened, and evidently in the process of formation; and the beautiful pyramids on the ground were found only in places where the roof did not exceed six or eight feet in height, and there was always a corresponding one attached to the roof, from which the water was continually dropping. The ground was also covered with beautiful stones, the nucleus of which was a black pebble, and the incrustation formed round them by the water resembled the crystalised sugar-plums, or *dragées*, so strongly, that a few days afterwards, at a ball in Manilla, I filled a small plate with them, wrapped up in paper, which deceived all the young ladies till they tried to eat them.

We had visited the cave in the dryest time of the year, just before the commencement of the rains, during which the formation of stalactites must be much more active; but still it must have been the work of many ages to form masses of such magnitude as the altar,—the depth of solid alabaster must have been five or six feet.

Having loaded ourselves with specimens of every description as heavily as the very inconvenient road we had to pass through would permit, we once more returned, and on our way stopped and looked into several deep chasms which had never been explored, but which doubtless will merit attention. I descended for about twenty feet into one, by a kind of natural steps cut in the rock, and had we been provided with ropes might have gone further. The air was perfectly pure and free. At a hundred and fifty yards from the entrance there is another branch as long as the principal one, in which we penetrated near two hundred yards. In short, it appears that the whole mountain is intersected and excavated in all directions; hitherto, however, no one has taken the trouble to explore it; indeed, the principal part of the whole island of Manilla is still a *terra incognita*, even to the Spaniards. The Indians are timid and superstitious in the extreme.

They have a curious legend respecting the cavern, which has a singular resemblance to the German tale of the "Three Brothers," in the Hartz Mountains.

An Indian one day entered the cave to catch bats, with the wings of which they compound some sort of medicine. On arriving at the stream of water he saw a venerable old man on the other side, who offered his hand to help him across the stream. The Indian was rather shy of his new acquaintance, and held out the end of his stick, which the old man took, and it instantly turned into charcoal. Upon this the Indian became anxious to return, and thanking the old man for his politeness, told him he did not mean to go any further that day.

The old man then offered him three stones, and, to remove any fear of their burning his fingers, deposited them in the stream. The Indian took them, and retreated as quick as he could, without looking behind him; and, on examining the stones at the mouth of the cave, to his surprise he found them to be three masses of pure gold. The story did not go any further, as to what use he made of his riches. The old Indian who told me this story said it happened long before the arrival of the Spaniards.

H. H. L.

III.

TESTIMONY OF M. DUMONT D'URVILLE.

"The residence of M. de La Gironiere, which we reached in the afternoon, is situated at the extremity of the lake. There, upon a neck of land which overlooks Santa-Cruz, the chief place of the province, is built, in the European style, a commodious dwelling, having two stories. Large warehouses, a sugar factory in full operation, other establishments of lesser importance, and a Tagal village are grouped around the habitation. The whole of this, which is called "Jala-Jala," is the property of a fellow-countryman, M. de La Gironiere. Jala-Jala has been created, organised, watched over, and christened by him. A few years previously this spot consisted of a wild forest and an unwholesome swamp, with here and there the cabins occupied by robbers and pirates. At the present time it is covered with fertile plantations, a profitable manufactory, a tranquil and industrious village. The native population, drawn thither by the existing prosperity, daily increases, while the clearing and cultivating of the surrounding land advances in due proportion. Thus to one of our countrymen is due the merit of having taken the initiative in reclaiming and fertilising this Spanish soil.

"And to accomplish this, how many difficulties, and how much jealousy had to be overcome. An inhabitant of Manilla since 1814, M. de La Gironiere only succeeded in disarming the local antipathies that existed by a long residence in the country, and by a Creole marriage. What had been until then obstinately refused even to a native was accorded to him, a Frenchman, who was confident of his own powers and of the fecundity of the soil.

"We met with the most cordial hospitality at Jala-Jala, from an excellent man possessed of many noble qualities. The supper was gay and abundantly served. We chatted of Favca and of Luzon, and drank in excellent claret to our future voyages, and to the prosperity of the model farm.

"The following day our excursions into the interior re-commenced. Our host gave us jackets and pantaloons of coarse cloth; he caused us to cover our heads with *a salacote*, which served as a protection as well against the rain as the sun. Thus dressed, we went to visit Santa-Cruz, a pretty little town situate on the borders of the lake, in a plain covered with crops. The convent, the church, the white houses, which were detached on the woody hills, soon attracted the eyes of all. Santa-Cruz is the chief market-place for the brisk sale of palm wine, and of cocoa spirits; it is inhabited by Tagals and Chinese; the former being agriculturists, the latter dealers. Unfortunately the site is not healthy, as the inundations in the rainy seasons cause fever and cholera.

"At a further distance, and in a delightful position, is the celebrated little village of Los Banos, which first attracted Europeans to the province of Laguna. As its name indicates, this village possesses baths of mineral water, the virtues of which were formerly held in high repute at Manilla, and cures were quoted, in support of this opinion, of such frequency, and of such an extraordinary nature, as to confound even the medical practitioners. The mountain, on the side of which this village is situate, is evidently the production of a volcano, and the source springing from it is at the temperature of boiling water. Although Sonnerat assures us that he saw fishes alive in it, we must, with other modern observers, place this assertion on the list of travellers' fables. Renouard de Sainte-Croix has proved that no plant could vegetate therein. Every animal plunged into it loses the skin in a moment. An egg becomes quite hard-boiled in four minutes.

"The waters of Los Banos appear to be efficacious principally in diseases of the skin. In former times it was the fashion at Manilla to go and spend a month in the fine season at these hot-baths, where beyond all doubt, as in all other thermal localities, the salubrity of the air, the exercise of the body, the absence of all broils, whether demestic or commercial, a regular and methodical life, and healthy and gentle mode of treatment of diseases, produced on the bathers better effects than did the curative properties of the waters. But during the last fifty years this pilgrimage for health has fallen into disuse. The English invasion in 1762, the appearance of bandits in an island of the lake, the high price of the baths, their being badly kept—all these causes had the effect of keeping the crowd away from the hamlet of Los Banos. Yet there is not to be found in the Pyrenees or in the Alps a site of such an imposing and beautiful kind. Enormous volcanic blocks, with angular and facetted forms, spiral columns, rocky pyramids, bearing on their very topmost crests groups of trees, of which the age and the names are unknown. In the rear of this row of forests and of mountains, arise other mountains and other forests of a different aspect and character, and from a distance exhibit in their great elevation the courses of their torrents into their broad and deep fissures, where range, in untamed freedom, buffaloes, wild boars, stags, and negro tribes, which latter are as savage as stags, wild boars, or buffaloes.

"All these districts appear to have the evident marks of a dilaceration; the sunken peaks show the extinct craters, the blackened stones bear witness to previous eruptions, and to complete those symptoms, Luzon itself at different periods trembles on its basis; the churches, the convents, the houses at Manilla, topple and crumble to the level of the earth. The nearest of those ancient volcanos is a mile from Los Banos. The crater, which formerly emitted fire, is now filled with greenish stagnant water. In this little lake, about a league in circumference, are some gigantic caymans, who there thrive and gambol at their ease. Renouard de Sainte-Croix saw one, the length of which exceeded fifty feet.

"During our excursion to Los Banos, that which struck us most was the prodigious quantity of ducks and ducklings, which were sporting on this part of the lake; the surface was covered with them. The cause of this abundance of one kind of birds was soon understood from knowing the taste of the Tagals, of the Malays, and of the Chinese, who prefer them to other fowl. But we were puzzled to find out how such a wonderful quantity could be hatched; our guide, however, soon solved the difficulty. To serve as substitutes for the ovens that are used in China for artificial incubation, the Tagals have employed the agency of human heat, and they found, among their indolent servants some patient and steady hatchers. A sort of frame is made for that purpose, on which light sticks are laid across, well covered with thick blankets; the eggs are stowed up in the frame in a regular line, being laid close to each other, and kept in their places by ashes which fill up the interstices. The whole is then raised up in a level position a little over the ground, and the sluggish hatcher lays himself at length on this strange kind of sofa; and then he eats, drinks, and smokes, and chews his betel, taking care not to injure the fragile shells he is to fecundate.

"Those hatching men are so clever that they follow day by day the progress of the embryo, and they aid the young bird to quit the shell, when the time for breaking it has arrived. The ducklings are scarce out of the shell when they run to the lake, and dabble in it all the day, and in the evening they hide in the floating cages, which are erected for them on the beach. The rearing of ducks is one of the principal branches of industry in the village of Los Banos and of Santa-Cruz.

"On the following day, which was the last of our pilgrimage, M. de la Gironiere made arrangements for our having a *partie de chasse* according to the strictest rules. At break of day we were awakened by the sounds of the horn, and in a short time dogs and grooms, huntsmen and servants, carriages, horses, palanquins, were all in movement towards the forest. It was almost a royal party.

"The hunt began on the woody sides of a hill, marked by such difficult paths as to be nearly impassable. We had scarcely got into it than the dogs started a stag, an elegant and noble animal, but rather smaller than our fine ones. He came close to Norberg, who took aim, and the stag fell. A mile from thence the pack gave tongue on finding a new prey, which was a wild boar, one of the finest ever seen in the forests of Laguna. On this occasion the honour of the hunt was mine. Shortly afterwards we descended from the crest of the mountains into a plain cut up by copses and marshes, which is the usual haunt of the wild buffaloes, that are the most dangerous animals of these countries, Quiet, obedient, and even enduring when once tamed, the buffalo is terrible in the state of nature. The sight of a man maddens the brute so that its eyes glow, and its nostrils throw out its fiery breath. The unfortunate hunter who misses his aim never escapes: he is lost. No horse in full gallop can reach an adversary sooner; no sanguinary beast maintains such rancour and blood-thirstiness. If he reaches you he pierces you with his sharp horns, he tramples on the earth, he tortures you while you are alive, and he insults you when dead. Even a tree can afford no security against his pursuit, for as he cannot reach his victim on the boughs, the buffalo becomes the jailer before he becomes the executioner; he persists in vengeance, and takes his station as an obstinate sentinel close to the tree of asylum, and never quits his post until exhausted by hunger and thirst. M. Laplace relates that a Tagal of Jala-Jala, while at work in cutting down wood, had the good fortune to escape in a strange manner from a buffalo which had for some time kept him blockaded in a lofty palm tree. Forced by hunger, the woodman had the courage to come down from the tree, and to begin the fight singly with his formidable antagonist. On reaching the ground, the buffalo attacked, but the man avoided the horns by nimbly jumping round the brute, and at length found means with his right hand to seize it by the tail, while with his knife in his left he inflicted many wounds on the sides of the beast. Finding itself thus assailed the buffalo fled like an arrow, but the courageous Tagal kept his hold, and let himself be dragged through the brush-wood, over the rocks, in the marshes, until he at last fell covered with mire and blood in the place where his enemy lay dead.

"To tame the wild buffalo the natives lay traps in ditches covered over with leaves, and when the brute is allowed to quit the inclosure he is so overcome with hunger, that in his weakness and exhaustion he lets himself be led to where the tame animals are feeding, and thus from the example of others he learns the habits of slavery. The buffalo born in a state of domesticity has seldom any desire for independence; the natives even say that it bears on the neck the marks of the yoke of its dam, which forms for the wild buffaloes the degrading brand of exclusion and reprobation.

"Our hunt was accompanied by many incidents too long to be detailed here: at one time it was a re-roused animal, which engaged our attention, at another a picturesque site, then it was a hamlet, then it was a forest. But a cascade near Jala-Jala was one of the things that made a deep impression on us. To reach the spot it was necessary to walk in the bed of the ravine, among sharp and slippery rocks. Notwithstanding the dangers and the unevenness of the way we persisted, and we were fully recompensed by the sight of this immense sheet of water, falling down between walls of a perpendicular rock, and sloped over with trees and lianas, that formed themselves into festoons over the abyss. In this spot there was so much of wild and primitive nature to be observed, the most remarkable silence in the presence of so loud a noise, that our admiration, like our attention, was fully absorbed in the contemplation of the scene. No animals, not even birds, in a spot where water alone seemed to possess life; sometimes, indeed, a bat would dart out from a split in the rock, and hover for a time in the atmosphere, which was impregnated with a thin rain. There was but one way to get out of the bed of the torrent, that of the rock, which appeared to be cut quite perpendicular. The Tagals who accompanied us began the attempt. One of them seizing a long liana which hung from the top to the foot of the granite wall, climbed up, as a mason would do on his knotted rope. Although we had but little practice in this mode of ascent, we made the attempt, and by imitating them, and profiting of the lianas that hung around to aid us, we were successful. The liana which we saw appeared to us to be the same as that which abounds in the virgin forests of America. Its long trunk, which laces itself round the tree and creeps there every way, is covered with a brown, stringy, and coarse skin. When it is cut there flows from its greyish interior a limpid water, without any smell, and not having a disagreeable taste.

"After the great hunt came the little one, which consisted in some small turtles called, "*poniard wounds*," from the small tufts of blood-coloured feathers which they have on their necks. We killed also two monkeys in the thicket, into which they had retreated, and also a gazelle of the kind which La Perouse describes in his voyage.

"Thus in two days, one of promenade and the other of active and fatiguing hunting, we explored the greatest and the richest portion of the district of Laguna; and there we found a country fertile in rice, in pepper, and in indigo; forests which afford the finest wood, as well for drying as for building; and we also learned from the example of a French colonist, the wonderful advantages which can be drawn from such a soil, from such a climate, from such water, and from all such nature.

"Delighted with our trip, we bade adieu to our hosts, and got on board our bark, which speedily took us back to Manilla."

IV.

TESTIMONY OF ADMIRAL LAPLACE.

I GLADLY accepted the pressing invitation of M. de La Gironiere, our fellow-countryman, and proprietor of a handsome residence on the banks of the Laguna, and on the morning of the 17th October, accompanied by Mr. Paris and by Mr. Russell, an American merchant of eminent respectability, and one of my most agreeable acquaintances at Bidondo, I left Manilla in a small boat, manned by Tagals in the service of M. de La Gironiere, whose brother obligingly acted as pilot. To reach our destination we had to ascend the rapid current of the stream. At nine o'clock we halted at Pasig, a Tagal village of some importance, which gives its name to the neighbouring river.

Breakfast was laid out on the grass, and our hunger and good spirits imparted to it a peculiar relish. The lively remarks of the party on the social scene around us made the moments fly rapidly. Before us was a wooden bridge, partly destroyed by time; around its ruins were moored several fishing-boats, with immense nets like an overhanging cloud upon the water. Near the banks innumerable flocks of ducks furrowed the stream in every direction. The number of those domestic birds, all of the same size, excited my curiosity. To my great astonishment, I learned that they were the produce of eggs, hatched by men, who, for a small stipend, have the patience, or rather laziness, to remain constantly lying on the future ducklings. For this purpose the eggs are stowed side by side in a layer of ashes, so as to form an even surface, protected by a trellis frame, and covered thickly with wool or cotton. The whole apparatus is contained in a sort of truckle bed, slightly raised above the floor of the close hut in which it is placed. Such is the sagacity of this novel tribe of duck hatchers that they can tell to a moment when the shells are about to break; then opening them with great great dexterity, they allow the young brood to run to the river, whence they return every evening with a more experienced guide to floating cages, fitted with little drawbridges, which are raised every morning, and let down again at night after the flocks have returned. Indeed, the breeding ducks at Luzon, were they twice as numerous, could never supply the enormous consumption of their offspring by the inhabitants, who have a national relish for that kind of poultry to the exclusion of all others.

After leaving Pasig we continued for some time to coast along grassy banks well shaded by trees. Uneasy glances were cast on us as we passed by buffaloes, lying listlessly on the sod awaiting the hour of labour, while others, wallowing in the slimy water, indicated their presence only by the loud snortings from their nostrils, which alone appeared above the surface of the river.

The increasing rapidity of the current, patches of inundatedland, and the distance of the rice plantations from the houses, soon apprised us that we were approaching the Laguna. We came up with extensive fisheries. A quantity of long bamboos, half buried in the slime, and bound together by ropes of Indian weed, rise above the surface of the water, notwithstanding its great depth, like partitions. These partitions form a narrow laybrinth, in which the fish getting more and more entangled are ultimately taken in nets placed at every outlet. These fisheries bring large revenues to the proprietors who consequently pay a heavy duty, in consideration of which the government overlooks the many injurious effects to navigation, necessarily caused by such establishments. We, too, had to encounter some of these inconveniences, but the magnificent view of the lake extending before us quickly caused us to forget them. The Laguna, of an irregular shape, may, according to the Spanish estimate, be about thirty leagues in circumference, and the general depth varies from twenty-five to thirty feet. This body of fresh water is supplied by a number of streams descending from the higher levels, which are covered with sombre forests, and form, as it were, the first steppe of those different chains of mountains which extend to the interior of the island, and lose their summits in the clouds. The side by which we entered is the only one where the coast is low. It was then completely inundated by the overflow of the lake during the late rains.

The dwelling to which we were directing our course was concealed from view by islands, we were therefore obliged to pass through one of the deep and narrow channels between them; but a strong head wind springing up, our little craft could make no way, and our sailors were completely worn out with fatigue. It was four o'clock: all our efforts to proceed just then would have been vain. We landed accordingly at a point that jutted into the strait, and took refuge in the hut of a poor fisherman, the only inhabitant perhaps of this little desert peninsula. This poor and unfortunate native of Luzon, cut off from all human society, dependant for support only on his own industry, nevertheless knew how to read and write; and this in a country reduced by its masters to the lowest stage of ignorance and degradation. How far does not such a fact as this go to redeem the charges made against the monks of Luzon.

The part of the coast on which we had landed is mountainous, steep, thickly wooded, and impassible, except to wild boars; it presents a reef of rocks extending to the bank, and terminating in a sheer precipice; but all this side of the lake is by no means of such difficult access. Before entering the little strait we had passed a beautiful village, situated on the extremity of a plain bounded by mountains.

Night was approaching, and we had as yet made but half our journey. The breeze, instead of lulling, which is usually the case before sunset, had increased; on the other hand, the chill which we began to feel, together with the clouds of mosquitoes, promised unfavourably for a night of repose; all these powerful considerations, and the rest that our Tagals had enjoyed, decided us to proceed at all hazards. Several times during the remainder of the passage my travelling companions were alarmed by the swell of the lake breaking, from time to time, over our heavily laden boats, by the violence of the wind and the intense darkness. It was eleven o'clock at night before we reached our destination, drenched, benumbed, and starving; but a kind reception, an excellent supper, and the considerate attentions of our hosts, followed by a good night's rest, effectually revived and cheered us.

The proprietor of the residence where I met with such warm hospitality had left France in 1814. The signal services rendered by him to the colony during the terrible ravages of the cholera, his worthy character and amiable disposition, had won him the esteem and goodwill of the principal authorities of Manilla, and the permission, until then steadily refused, even to Spaniards, to possess and cultivate land on the banks of the Laguna. Great energy and perseverance were requisite to carry out, or even to attempt, such a difficult task. These rare qualities were united in our fellow-countryman with varied information and some knowledge of agriculture. He gave up a tranquil and easy life, and with his wife, a pretty Spaniard, belonging to one of the first families of the colony, he came to found, in a wild and almost uninhabited country, an establishment which, by its astonishing progress and the happy effect of example, has taught the Spaniards the value of these hitherto reglected lands, and has thus opened to the colony a new source of prosperity.

I soon rallied my spirits at this delightful spot after the recent depression of Manilla; I even forgot its annoyances, and rejoiced in the freedom which the affectionate attention of my hosts enabled me to indulge. Each day brought some new diversion. Sometimes we set out early in the morning on a sporting excursion, our retinue consisting of nine huntsmen, many of whom, I admit, owed this title chiefly to the fact of their carrying a gun. Our accoutrements were all in keeping with the wild state of the country. They consisted of, for head gear the salacote, equally effective against sun and rain, cloth jackets, ample and stout trousers, and thick-soled shoes. We took with us twenty dogs, in rather poor condition and of different breeds, but staunch veterans, up to any fatigue, and the terror of stags and wild boars; they could scarcely be kept in order by several pikemen acting as whippers-in. Lastly came sundry led horses, a resource in case of need for the laggards, and the whole assemblage, collected by appointment under a huge tree, till then standing in utter solitude, formed a "meet" indescribably novel, animated, and picturesque.

The hunt started in the direction of a lofty hill, covered towards its summit with long grass, and thickly wooded at the sides. We wound slowly up the acclivity by a scarcely preceptible path: the pikemen took the lead. Nets to insnare the game were placed at every pass. Presently the hounds were heard to give tongue in the distance, and the increasing animation of their cry, which every moment became more distinct, proved them to be on the true scent. At length we reached the hunting ground. The post assigned to me was to watch the nets and the pikemen placed at intervals to force the stags to our side. Three of these fine animals had just passed me, so rapidly that I had scarcely time to notice them, and I was in the act of lamenting my want of promptness, when a shot, followed by triumphant shouts, went off at a few paces from me. My host, an expert and indefatigable sportsman, had struck the animal as it was bounding over a marsh, and about to plunge into the thicket. Some of the hounds were already closing round the expiring prey, with flashing eyes and jaws inflamed and distended, as if devouring by anticipation the promised reward of their toil. The entrails of the victim, thrown to them by a pikeman, were demolished in an instant. The body, slung across a horse, was carried home in triumph, to make its appearance at supper.

The concluding part of the sport was not so successful as might have been expected from this brilliant debut. The game took refuge amid the steep acclivities, where the dogs alone could follow it. We continued, however, to ascend by a circuitous path, and at length, after having made our way through a quantity of long, tough, and matted grass, we arrived at the summit of a hill, whence we had a magnificent prospect of the lake. The weather was serene; the water, like a sheet of glass, reflected the mid-day rays of the sun, and threw a gorgeous light upon the distant pile of mountains. This majestic spectacle struck me as contrasting sadly with the insignificant works of man, of which we recognised the feeble effects on the banks of the lake, forming an almost imperceptible speck in the midst of the rich vegetation so lavishly spread around by uncultivated nature. The chain of islands stretching across the Laguna seemed to lie at our feet. My attention was first attracted to the smallest of these islets; it is round, and contains the crater of an extinct volcano, into which the sea has found a passage, and which abounds in fish as well as crocodiles of an enormous size. The curious spot awakens superstitious terror in the minds of the Tagals, who have a strong repugnance to accompany European thither.

Deeply intent upon the magnificent and varied scene before me, I quietly enjoyed the luxury of solitude, the more so that the audible cries of the huntsmen, and the barking of the dogs, secured me from all apprehension of being molested by any of the ferocious animals that infest the country. But when the chase sped down the plains, which all consisted of marsh and jungle, my fears of the wild buffaloes made me anxious to regain the protection of the hunters. This animal, so gentle and tractable when domesticated, is terrible in its untamed state; the sight of man renders it furious, its eyes glare, its nostrils dilate and seem to breathe flame, its unwieldy bulk becomes wonderfully active in the pursuit of its enemy. Nothing can stop its headlong course towards the unlucky sportsman, whose ill-aimed shot has missed or only slightly wounded it. The infuriated beast gores him with long and sharp horns; or should the aggressor seek to escape its vengeance by climbing up a tree, the animal constantly keeps guard below, gloating on the view of its prisoner, until compelled by hunger to depart. A Tagal, from the village of Jala-Jala, engaged in cutting wood, had the good fortune to escape in this manner from an enormous buffalo that attacked him: finding pasturage in the vicinity, the buffalo never for an instant lost sight of the tree in which the woodcutter was concealed; the poor fellow carried no arms except the long knife that the natives always wear in their girdle, and which they handle very expertly. Impelled by hunger he at last descended from the tree, but only to be more vigorously pursued than before. Just, however, as the terrible horns were withdrawn for an instant to gore him, he contrived to seize hold of the buffalo's tail with his left hand, whilst with his right he stabbed him repeatedly with his knife. The astonished animal darted off like an arrow, but being soon exhausted by loss of blood he slackened his pace, and fell dead by the side of the Tagal, who was himself a mass of wounds blood, and mire.

At these hunting parties I was more a spectator than an actor, but exercise restored my health, and when I regaled myself at dinner on the venison or the wild boar, it mattered little to me that they had fallen by a more practised hand.

Shortly before sunset we generally commenced another less fatiguing chase, and one better suited to my sporting talents. It was that of a specious of large, cunning, and mischievous ape, which made great havoc in the sugar cane and rice plantations. These exploits bring it into great odium with the natives, and particularly the children, who are obliged to mount guard day and night to protect the crops from the ravages of the enemy. Guided by these willing auxillaries, and by dogs trained to this novel species of warfare, we easily tracked these apes to their strong holds, then stratagems, and more frequently their nimbleness, baffled our skill; but in the long run, by blockading some isolated tree, where a number of them had taken refuge, they were brought down by a discharge of musketry, and bit the dust with loud cries of rage and despair. Their remains were then ornamentally suspended on the branches of some tree near the scene of their depredations. These animals are amazingly strong, they make enormous springs when pursued, and can be stopped only by a mortal wound; they are no less destructive than fierce, and their teeth are not less formidable than those of beasts of prey.

In the evenings we used to assemble round a table, waiting for supper and listening to the gossip of the village. A little scandal often crept into the conversation, and jokes would pass round at the expense of the Curé, a robust, jovial, and merry Tagal, whose breviary was the sum total of his knowledge, but who, nevertheless, had some natural talent and a great desire for instruction. Not over strict in his own practice, he cordially detested the monks, and had no mercy on his parishoners who were defaulters at the holy table or the confessional, the dues from these sources forming the chief part of his revenues. He was unmercifully rallied on the score of a new niece, who, as well as her intended, was, according to the usual custom, lodged at the presbytery, until such time as her parent should consent to the marriage, which ceremony was to bring a handsome fee to the good Padre Miguel.

The demoralising tendency of this custom in favour of an unscrupulous clergy is obvious; still it goes far to prove their influence over a population whose distrustful and jealous character they have thus been able to mould to their wishes.

Sometimes the conversation took a more serious, though to me a no less interesting turn. Explanations were given of the system adopted to maintain order in the populous districts destitute of regular troops, by means of an organised militia, upon which subject our host, who was captain of the corps stationed at Laguna, gave me detailed information, which led me to conclude that the Spanish, or rather monastic government, warned by past experience had taken due precautions against a new attack of Europeans.

The point where the peninsula of Jala-Jala is connected with the mainland, by mountains rising gradually to a considerable elevation, is remarkable for many picturesque sites. To that quarter therefore, we often directed our morning walks. The coast abounds in rice plantations, through which we were obliged to pass, along embankments constructed for the purpose of irrigation. The ground, moistened by previous rain, gave way beneath our weight, and we sank knee deep in the mud; but our good humour and perseverance were unconquerable, and, indulging at each other's expense the merriment caused by our begrimed condition, we rapidly scaled the mountain.

Our course was guided by the distant roar of the splendid cascade to which we were proceeding. The bed of the torrent, strewn with gigantic rocks, among which the water seethed and bubbled as it dashed towards the lake, was our only path, but of a break-neck character at every step. Nothing however could check us, and the whole party reached the spot without mishap. An admirable scene of savage grandeur then presented itself. From towering rocks, crowned as with a canopy of majestic trees, monster tendrils of the liana hung in immense festoons, forming a vast and gloomy vault, deepened to sepulchral darkness by a cloudy sky. Here the torrent, swollen by long rains, dashed with a stunning noise down the precipitous cliffs, and, bounding over the huge stones piled below, expanded into a beautiful sheet of foam, and sped its impetuous course through the ravines. All animals seemed to have fled this spot, and its gloom and isolation inspired an involuntary emotion of fear. Neither the song of birds, nor the hum of insects was to be heard; our sounds alone mingled with the monotonous sound of the water-fall. Some lugubrious bats, the only tenants of this solitude, emerged from the clefts of the rocks, and wheeled in circles above us, yet the report of a gun seemed to cause them no additional alarm. At length, after much fatigue and some risk, we reached the summit of the cascade, by means of the branches of the liana, one of which, breaking in my hand, left me on a rugged and slippery rock. I was in a great dilemma, and, until rescued by my friends, had horrible misgivings that my untimely fate would add a tragical celebrity to the cascade of Jala-Jala.

After enjoying for a considerable time this new and picturesque scene, we quitted the waterfall and pushed on through the wood to inspect some of the objects of curiosity,—one of them, a brook of singularly limpid water, acrid to the taste, and depositing a slight sediment, resembling in colour oxide of copper. It may, perhaps, have washed in its course some veins of that metal. The natives do not consider it unwholesome, yet they rarely drink it. I thought the taste disagreable, and for some time after drinking it my mouth and throat felt unusually parched. I remarked in these mountains the *liane du voyageur*, so common in the forests of America; its long tendrils, covered with brown fibrous and thick bark, fell in festoons from the apex of a large tree, that seemed bending under their weighty net-work. From the stem that I cut, a few feet above the ground, flowed, through large pores of greyish and well-compacted pulp, a stream of fresh clear water, which had no perceptible odour nor any nauseous taste. Thus has all-provident Nature placed this plant in the burning climate of the New World, and of the Asiatic Archipelago, as an immediate resource to those unfortunate human beings whose lot it is to traverse the vast forests of these regions.

Surrounded by such delightful amusements, and treated with the kindest attention by my host and charming family, I felt the days glide away too rapidly. My health was perfectly restored. The north-east monsoon was about to set in, and the fine season had commenced. I was therefore compelled to resign the delights of so soothing a mode of life, and to return to Manilla, there to make arrangements for quitting Luzon. I took leave with real regret, and the kind concern testified by M. de La Gironiere and his whole family at my departure, increased my earnest desire to meet them again at some future period.

TESTIMONY OF M. MALLAT.

SPEAKING of Jala-Jala, M. Mallat, a French geographer, and author of a work on the Philippines, says:—"The neighbourhood of the lake abounds in every kind of game, and the lake itself is covered with wild-fowl. The property of Jala-Jala, which may be looked upon as a kind of model farm, contains vast woods, where the stag and the wild-boar are hunted. On all sides horses and oxen are met with, which the proprietor sells to the dealers from Manilla.

"The lake abounds with fish, and daily supplies the market of Manilla. Its borders are inhabited by caymans, or crocodiles, amongst which some enormous specimens are to be met with; as, for example, the monster that one day M. de La Gironiere, the intrepid occupant of Jala-Jala, took by nets and killed. It is in the narrows of Quinabutasan that these animals mostly abound, but they are not the only predatory creatures encountered upon the lake, which is infested by pirogues worked by piratical robbers."

THE END.

www.ingramcontent.com/pod-product-compliance
Lightning Source LLC
LaVergne TN
LVHW010130110826
845151LV00002B/316

* 9 7 8 1 4 2 5 5 4 1 8 1 1 *